Little S.

Little Sister

A Second Israel in Seventeenth-Century Scotland

Bob Halliday

WIPF & STOCK · Eugene, Oregon

LITTLE SISTER
A Second Israel in Seventeenth-Century Scotland

Wipf & Stock
An Imprint of Wipf and Stock Publishers
199 W. 8th Ave., Suite 3
Eugene, OR 97401

www.wipfandstock.com

ISBN 13: 978-1-62564-366-7

Manufactured in the U.S.A.

To Claire

"Let us exalt his name together"

Psalm 34:3

Contents

Introduction   1

1   Kingdoms in Conflict   15

2   Blurred Boundaries   31

3   The Great Persecution   40

4   The Coming of Constantine   46

5   The Thirteenth Apostle   54

6   The Gospel Is Law   71

7   The Theodosian Code   75

8   Zeno to Anastasius   80

9   Justin and Justinian   88

10   An Empire Reborn   90

11   The Vicar of God   97

12   Daughter of Rome   106

13   The Stewart Dynasty   112

14   The Reek of Patrick Hamilton   121

15   Mary Queen of Scots   127

16   The Wisest Fool   149

Contents

17   The Road to Revolution   159

18   Covenant Is King   179

19   Bring Back the King   193

20   The Remnant Church   204

21   This Is My Covenant   219

22   The Visible Church   225

23   The Legacy of the Covenant   237

Bibliography   247

Introduction

Scotland, whom our Lord took off the dunghill and out of hell
and made a fair bride to Himself, . . . he will embrace both us,
the little young sister, and the elder sister the church of the Jews.[1]

O N 14 JUNE 1640, the recently appointed covenanting Committee of
Estates, which was assembled in Edinburgh, was working its way
through a fairly lengthy agenda. Technically this body was not the Scottish Parliament which had been dissolved only days earlier. This most
recent Parliament had been unusual to say the least because it had met
without a royal commissioner, and the king had nominated none of its
members. The Committee of Estates was careful at first to avoid calling
itself a rival parliament, but in fact it was the body which had the responsibility of governing Scotland in preparation for the coming conflict with
the king. Both Charles I and the Covenanters were preparing for war
and there was an urgent need to clarify and legitimize the position the
Covenanters had taken in relation to both church and state. Members
were dealing with the eighteenth item, which concerned "the Act anent
the Ratification of the Covenant, and of the Assembly's Supplication, Act
of Council, and Act of Assembly concerning the Covenant."[2] It would be
impossible to exaggerate the importance of this legislation for the Christian church in Scotland and even beyond its borders for many years to
come. However, the content of the Confession of Faith and Covenant,
which was intended to be ratified that day, was far from new. It was a development of previous statements already published, each of which had
themselves incorporated material from earlier documents. Behind the
covenant lay the King's Confession of 1581, and behind that was the Scots

1. Rutherford, *Letters*, no. 28, 87–88.
2. Thomson and Innes, *Acts of the Parliament of Scotland*, 270.

Confession produced by John Knox and his colleagues and accepted by the Scottish Parliament in 1560.

One of the many obstacles to the Scottish Reformation was that it took place when Mary, daughter of James V, and her French husband, Francis, occupied the thrones of both France and Scotland. The Roman Catholic queen was supported by the political and military power of France, and therefore it was a matter of concern to a Protestant England that the Scottish Reformation should succeed. It was with English encouragement and support that "the six Johns" drew up the Scots Confession within a fairly short space of time. The six compilers were, first, John Knox, who, at the request of Scottish Protestant lords, had returned from Geneva in May 1559. Second was John Willock, a Reformed minister who later became superintendent of Glasgow and moderator of the General Assembly. Third was John Winram, a minister and scholar who was to become superintendent of Fife and Strathearn. A fourth compiler was John Spottiswoode, who was made superintendent of Lothian and officiated some years later at the coronation of James VI. Fifth was John Row, who had recently returned from Rome to support the Reformation and ministered in Perth. The sixth John was John Douglas, rector of the University of St. Andrews. The confession these six men drew up was accepted in 1560 by the Reformation Parliament and was subsequently established in law in 1567. The first ten articles were an expression of the doctrinal tradition of the early church, but the remaining fifteen dealt with those issues which were at the heart of the Reformation. These were matters like justification, sanctification, faith, scriptural authority, Christ's offices, the civil power, the authority of the church, and the sacraments. Hazlett writes,

> Comparatively unusual are the combination of systematic and biblical theology, the stress placed on ecclesiology and the sacramental eating of Christ's flesh and blood, and the explicit treatment of Christian ethics. Though the "Papistical Church" is denounced, the Papacy is not mentioned. While the most discernible theological influence on the Confession is Calvin's Institutes, his voice in it is less exclusive than many maintain. Theologically the document is relatively syncretistic.[3]

---

3. Hazlett, *Dictionary of Scottish Church History*, 752.

This was a reaffirmation of the doctrines in the Scots Confession, although these are not set out in detail. The document begins with the confirmation that

> the only true Christian faith and religion . . . received, believed, and defended by many and sundry notable Kirks and realms; but chiefly by the Kirk of Scotland, the King's majesty, and three estates of this realm . . . is expressed in the confession of our faith, established and publicly confirmed by sundry Acts of Parliaments, and now of a long time hath been openly professed by the King's Majesty, and the whole body of this realm both in burgh and land."[4]

There followed a firm rejection of papal authority and a fairly detailed list of Roman Catholic doctrines and practices which the Kirk condemned as being contrary to the Scriptures. It was also felt necessary to include in the King's Confession an oath professing the complete sincerity of the subscribers and a declaration of their intent to defend the person and authority of King James I, their country and Christ's evangel. These political elements in the confession and its enforced subscription were designed to root out any secret Roman Catholics. It was believed by some that the pope had given permission for Catholics to sign the Scots Confession and thereby retain positions in government while remaining loyal to Rome. These anxieties were hardly discouraged by Queen Elizabeth I of England, whose advisers were equally suspicious of "popish plots" which might be hatched by European Roman Catholic powers. However, the political aims of the confession were not entirely successful. Lumsden writes,

> This Covenant or "Confession" was largely signed. Among others who subscribed it were the Duke of Lennox and Lord Seaton who remained Papists at heart. One wonders if this was a case of wilful deception, to promote the Roman cause and allay all Protestant suspicions, or whether it was but a part of the policy the Jesuits were promoting in the country. Whatever their real intentions were, they acted a deceitful part in these transactions.[5]

Presbyterians certainly interpreted the King's Confession with its oath as a binding promise upon the Kirk and people of Scotland for all time to come and a barrier to episcopacy or any changes in form of

4. Lumsden, *Covenants of Scotland*, 108.
5. Ibid., 111.

worship. Their intentions, however, could not prevent James from rein-troducing bishops to the Kirk by 1610 and forcing through a number of liturgical changes known as "the Five Articles" at a General Assembly held in Perth in 1618 to be ratified by Parliament in 1621. As monarch of England, Ireland, and Scotland since the death of Elizabeth in 1603, the changes were part of a series of measures designed to bring the Kirk into conformity with the churches of England and Ireland.

The death of James in 1625 brought his son Charles I to the throne. However, any degree of political skill his father had possessed seemed to be absent in the character of the new king. His determination to Angli-canize the Scottish church focussed on a Scottish version of an Anglican prayer book which was intended to be used compulsorily under pain of excommunication. It was seen by the Scots as "popish" and became the trigger which set off, in 1637, a flood of petitions to the Scottish privy council and rioting in Edinburgh. The following year, the National Cov-enant was drawn up as an appeal to the whole of Scotland to resist the ecclesiastical policy of the king and his Anglican advisers. It was an ex-pression of revolution. Donaldson, commenting on the significance of the Covenant, writes,

> The Covenant was not the work of hysterical ultra-protestants; the hand of shrewd lawyers is plain in it. It was an ingenious stroke to begin with a recital of the old anti-popish covenant of 1581 which King James had signed, for this might deceive the uncritical into believing that nothing new was involved. A large part of the Covenant consisted in nothing more than a long list of statutes, favourable to the reformed religion which the king was held to have violated, and a reminder of his coronation oath. Here was something more than anti-popery for this was an appeal to the rule of law, against the royal prerogative and the king's arbitrary courses, an appeal to history and precedent. Here too was an assertion of parliamentary authority, for the list of statutes implied that parliament made the laws, and that only parliament could change the laws. This was something new in Scottish history.[6]

The signing of the National Covenant began in Greyfriars Kirk, Edin-burgh, on 28 February 1638. The assembled company was addressed by two men. One of them was Lord Loudon, representing the nobility, and the other, Alexander Henderson, the minister of the parish of Leuchars

6. Donaldson, *Scotland*, 313.

and one of the architects of the Covenant. After the speeches, Archibald Johnston of Wariston, Henderson's partner in drafting the Covenant, read out the document and the signing began. The nobles signed first, then the lairds. The following day hundreds of ministers and burgh commissioners added their names. Copies were sent to every part of Scotland and even to supporters at the court in London. It is perhaps not insignificant that lists were kept of those who signed and those who did not.

It was established in law by the Act anent the Ratification of the Covenant that it was to be applied to "all his Majesty's subjects of what rank and quality soever under all civil pains." Specific mention was made of those holding public office and both masters and graduates of universities "and finally all members of this kirk and kingdom subscribe the same with their words prefixed to their subscription." All that the covenant implied was not immediately clear to all those who signed it, but the intention that it bound the whole nation together was unmistakable. The "members of this kirk" and of "this kingdom" were the same people and the notion of being a member of one but not the other was not to be considered. A variety of measures were used to ensure acceptance of the Covenant. Ministers had to become Covenanters or be ejected from their parishes. Bribery was attempted in the case of the Marquis of Huntly, whose financial affairs were in a perilous state. It proved an unsuccessful attempt to secure his support.[7] Local committees were set up by the Covenanters to ensure the conformity of ordinary people by threat of excommunication or other means.

Support for the covenant rolled along on a swelling tide of enthusiasm, and opposition was limited. One of the more notable attempts at resistance was in the northeast. In Aberdeen the city magistrates decided to refuse to sign, and a group of six theologians who came to be known as "the Aberdeen Doctors" prepared a document consisting of fourteen demands which they required the Covenanters to answer. A Covenanter deputation composed of politicians and ministers travelled north to the city to demand acceptance of the Covenant. The covenanting ministers were refused an opportunity to preach in the city pulpits but did succeed in addressing large crowds from the balcony of the Earl Marischal's house. It had little effect and resistance remained fairly solid. The visiting ministers provided the required answers for the Doctors, who replied to the answers, and in turn received answers to the replies. It was clear that

---

7. Donaldson, *Scotland*, 319.

neither side would be convinced by the other, and the matter was only solved to the satisfaction of the Covenanters when the Earl of Montrose marched north with an army. Military threat broke the opposition, and the Aberdonians signed the Covenant. Of the six doctors who had provided theological justification for the resistance in Aberdeen, two died of natural causes fairly quickly. The remaining four were removed from the offices they held in church or college. John Forbes, professor of divinity at King's College, spoke of "daily threatenings" but appears not to have been seriously harmed. The Covenanting Synod of Aberdeen which deposed him in 1641 seemed, in fact, to do so with reluctance.[8]

The Act of 1640, which gave the covenant legal force, was only one element in a revolutionary movement which brought profound political and religious change to Scotland. The decades which followed saw a period of civil war between people and king. Covenanters themselves became divided into moderates and extremists. Support by a Scots army for English parliamentarians against Charles I brought the opportunity for an unsuccessful attempt by the Covenanters to "presbyterianize" England. The execution of the king by Cromwell, the Scottish coronation of his successor Charles II, and his speedy exile, followed by the subsequent occupation of Scotland by English Commonwealth forces, left the divided Covenanters unsure about the degree of cooperation they ought to offer to the occupying government. When the exiled Charles II was eventually restored in 1660, the event brought, at first, hopes of royal favour to both moderate and extreme Covenanters. Charles had already signed the covenant in 1650 as one of the humiliating conditions imposed on him by the Scots to gain their support for his succession to the throne. Within two years of the restoration, however, the Church of Scotland was again governed by crown-appointed bishops and archbishops who also sat in Parliament and exercised all the traditional privileges and responsibilities of episcopal government. The National Covenant was outlawed in 1662, and it became clear that Charles was determined to exercise absolute control of the Kirk. The carrot and stick policies adopted to deal with the resistance of the Covenanters brought about, in the following decades, some extremely harsh periods of persecution, some intervals of tolerance and conciliation designed to coax the covenanting moderate dissenters back into an Episcopal church, and more than one armed conflict with militant extremists in the covenanting ranks. In time, the Covenanters as

8. Henderson, "Aberdeen Doctors," 10.

a national resistance movement dwindled into a few groups of protesters quarrelling with one another, as well as with king and government, each group claiming to be the only genuine Christian church in Scotland.

In 1689, to prevent the succession of a Roman Catholic monarch, the Scottish crown was offered to William, Prince of Orange, whose government abolished episcopacy in the Kirk, and restored presbyterianism the following year, although the religious settlement was not based on the National Covenant. William refused to be as much of a persecutor as the more extreme Covenanters would have wished and Episcopal ministers who acknowledged him as monarch were permitted to continue in their ministry. The few remaining covenanting groups gradually diminished in numbers, some becoming praying societies, and at least one group, known as the Gibbites, retreating to form a community in the Pentland hills and recognising no other Christians in Scotland.[9]

Although defeated politically, and crushed by military force in their own day, there can be no doubt that the main principle for which the Covenanters were striving, that of the church's freedom from state control, became so much part of Scottish Presbyterianism that its eventual triumph was inevitable. The struggle against an Erastian system of church government had been a major factor in a long and bitter conflict in which the warring factions were prepared to use every available means to gain a victory over their opponents. The freedom for which the Covenanters fought by no means brought the fulfilment of all their hopes, and what they did achieve was not won without bloodshed, imprisonment, and a variety of economic hardships accepted by those who suffered these things as the price necessary to be paid if they were to be loyal to the kingdom of God. It is the simple truth that within the covenanting ranks there were Christian men and women whose courage and endurance was exceptional. There were faithful disciples of Christ whose faith was tested and refined to a degree unknown in quieter easier days. There were saints whose lives spread the fragrance of the presence of Christ wherever they went. There were spiritual giants in the land who would make men of another age say, like the spies who returned from Canaan, "We seemed like grasshoppers in our own eyes."[10]

9. Cowan, in *Scottish Covenanters*, 106, provides a description of the Gibbites who were bizarre by any standards.

10. Num 13:33.

However, the vision of Scotland as a covenanted nation, while demanding the freedom of the church to live without interference from kings or politicians, most certainly did not carry with it the personal freedom of each and every man to worship as he chose, nor did it imply the freedom of any church to exist apart from the Presbyterian Church, which fulfilled the terms of the Covenant. Both the Covenanters and the Stuart kings had this, at least, in common. Scotland was a kingdom and in a kingdom, the subjects were not left to choose whether they would obey or not. Whether the will of God for his church was to be interpreted by a general assembly or by a divinely appointed monarch, when that interpretation had been accepted by political rulers, it had to be established by the civil authority as the law of the land. It was to be enforced on every subject, and disobedience to it was to be punished. In 1669, Lauderdale, the Scottish secretary of state to Charles II, bullied the Scottish Parliament into passing the Act of Supremacy. He boasted to Charles about how he had frightened the opposition into agreement, and described the act as that "which makes you sovereign in the Church; you may now dispose of bishops and ministers and remove and transplant them as you please. . . . This church or no meeting nor ecclesiastical persons in it can ever trouble you more."[11] These circumstances certainly came to represent for the Covenanters the worst conditions under which the people of Scotland might be compelled to live and worship, but the perceived solution to the problem was not to allow men to believe and worship as they chose but to impose with equal severity the faith and order expressed in the National Covenant in place of that which had been imposed by the king. To permit the continuation in Scotland of people who refused to live and worship, as Covenanters believed God required, was not to be tolerated. The civil authority, even if it could no longer legitimately control the kirk, was nevertheless duty bound to take heed to the guidance and instruction which the kirk provided and to ensure that every subject in the kingdom conformed, at least outwardly, to the required standards. Describing the period immediately after the signing of the covenant, Lynch writes, "The identities of Church and state were merged into a covenanted nation. Even if the ministers did not find office in the covenanting state, they were secure in their position as its conscience."[12]

11. Airy, *Lauderdale Papers*, 138.
12. Lynch, *Scotland*, 256.

It has to be recognised that the Covenanters were no different in this respect to much of the rest of Christendom, and the necessity to impose, by law, a profession of the Christian faith and what was believed to be an appropriate lifestyle was unquestioned. In this the Covenanters were no less enthusiastic than their worst enemies. On 4 June 1640, it became an offence to go fishing instead of being at worship on the Sabbath day. This law like many others was enacted by Parliament at the request of the General Assembly, and those who failed to keep it were punished.[13] On 4 January 1644, Parliament passed an act confiscating the income and the estates of any who had been sentenced for failing to sign the covenant. Provision was made for the maintenance of their wives and children, but their funds were otherwise seized for public use.[14] After the restoration of Charles II in 1660, the policy of enforcing what was believed to be a Christian profession and lifestyle on the nation remained in place. The Parliament of 1662 compelled all ministers to offer praise and prayers of thanksgiving for the birth and restoration of the king. Any who refused were removed from their churches. Over the following decade, dissidents could face prison for praying or teaching, even in a private house. They might be fined if their children were not baptised within thirty days or baptised in circumstances which did not meet with government approval. "Anabaptists" and Quakers were forbidden to gather for worship. Throughout a stormy and bewildering period of Scottish history, all kinds of changes took place. Forms of worship and ministry, representation in Parliament, church government, and finance all changed. The factor that remained unaltered and unchallenged by the national church, in whatever form it appeared, was the use of state machinery to enforce Christian profession and lifestyle on the whole nation.

The period of covenanting rule lasted almost fifteen years, and while one of its spiritual foundations might have been built on the principle expressed so forcibly and clearly to James VI at Falkland by Andrew Melville,[15] that there were two kingdoms in Scotland, it was virtually impossible to lay down a clear line of demarcation between them which could have been recognised in practical daily living. Given the age in

13. Thomson and Innes, *Acts of the Parliament of Scotland*, 268.

14. Thomson and Innes, *Acts of the Parliament of Scotland*, V.I, 61.

15. In September 1596, Melville, as a commissioner of the General Assembly, met with James VI at Falkland and in the course of the interview reminded the king that while he was sovereign in the kingdom of Scotland, he was a subject in the kingdom of Christ.

which the covenant flourished, it was no surprise that its supporters did not limit its authority to those who bound themselves to it willingly. To simply offer the Covenant as a matter of free choice to the people of Scotland would have seemed like a betrayal of the grace of God given at the Reformation and the abandonment of their most solemn responsibilities. It seemed there was an inescapable obligation of a Christian monarch and a Christian parliament to enforce the covenant on a Christian people in obedience to the will of God.

The political factors in the Covenant were the most immediately understandable as a simple declaration to be loyal to king, country, and kirk. There was a genuine fear that Scotland might be absorbed by its more powerful southern neighbor, and this was not entirely without foundation. Robert Baillie, who became principal of Glasgow University and was one of the Scots commissioners to the Westminster Assembly, feared that Scotland "might become an English Province to be imposed upon forever hereafter at the will of the Bishop of Canterbury."[16] The Covenant, therefore, had to express the unity of the Scots as an independent nation, with its own Parliament and its own Kirk, and at the same time to assert the loyalty of the Scots to the crown. One of the reasons for the Covenant was declared to be

> for maintaining the King's Majesty, his person and estate; the true worship of God and the King's authority being so straitly joined, as that they had the same friends and common enemies, and did stand and fall together. . . . And in like manner with the same heart, we declare before God and men, that we have no intention nor desire to attempt anything that may turn to the dishonour of God, or to the diminution of the King's greatness and authority; but, on the contrary, we promise and swear, that we shall, to the uttermost of our power, with our means and lives, stand to the defence of our dread sovereign the King's Majesty, his person and authority.[17]

It is generally agreed that the Covenant promised what was impossible to deliver. There was a commitment to freedom from the authority of the king in religious matters, and at the same time a commitment to uphold that same authority. Yet however much it lacked in logical consistency, it did make clear the intention of creating a single independent

16. Baillie, *Letters*, 66.
17. Lumsden, *Covenants of Scotland*, 238.

church which was at the same time a nation loyal to its sovereign. There were to be no rival churches or rulers permitted in Scotland, and monarchy as a system of government was unchallenged.

The articles expressing the doctrinal content of the covenant were less easy to justify in their compulsory acceptance. The National Covenant of 1638 began by affirming that it was built on the already established foundation of the Confession of Faith, "subscribed at first by the King's Majesty and his household in the year 1580; thereafter by persons of all ranks in the year 1581, by Ordinance of the Lords of Secret Council and Acts of General Assembly." This was "the King's Confession" which opened with a reaffirmation of the Scots Confession, described as

> the confession of our faith, established and publicly confirmed by sundry Acts of Parliament, and now of a long time hath been publicly confessed by the King's Majesty, and the whole body of this realm both in burgh and land; To which confession and form of Religion we willingly agree in our consciences, in all points, as unto God's undoubted truth and verity, grounded only upon His written Word."[18]

To the writers of the National Covenant, it was important to emphasize that it was not an alternative to the statement of the faith that had been established at the Reformation. It was the same doctrines, "in all points," grounded in Scripture alone. Those who signed it were professing to believe every one of the doctrines which had been set out by Knox and his colleagues in the twenty-five articles of the Scots Confession. Moreover the subscribers were determined to assert their complete sincerity: "We call the living God the searcher of our hearts to witness, who knoweth this to be our sincere desire and unfeigned resolution, as we shall answer to Jesus Christ in the great day, and under the pain of God's everlasting wrath, and of infamy and loss of all honour and respect in this world, most humbly beseeching the Lord to strengthen us by his Holy Spirit for this end."[19] It was not only the political demands but the doctrines of the National Covenant that were forced, sometimes at the point of a sword, on those who could not subscribe it with a good conscience. Lynch comments,

> It is difficult to imagine that many of the nobles, lairds, ministers and burgesses who signed the Covenant in Greyfriars Church in

18. Ibid., 108.
19. Lumsden, *Covenants of Scotland*, 240.

the capital on 28 February and 1 March 1638, and still less those who had it read out to them over the course of half an hour in churches in all parts of the country in the next few weeks, would have understood what it really meant.[20]

The perception of themselves as a body of people within national boundaries to be, at the same time, both a nation and a church was not peculiar to the Covenanters. In this they simply conformed to the thinking of their day. Perhaps what they did have was an opportunity to be even more radical in working out the implications of the separation of church and state. For the first time in centuries, clergymen had no place in Parliament. The king's control of that body was broken when the crown-appointed bishops were rejected and Parliament could meet and disband without royal permission. The privy council was replaced by committees. The minor aristocracy had a much greater representation in the ruling body when the voting power of the lairds was virtually doubled. Parliament was no longer a rubber stamp to give authority to the business that the Lords of the Articles had effected. Every matter now had to come before the full voting body. Within a relatively short time the king was forced to agree that officers of state should have parliamentary approval. Covenanters were in control of both executive and judiciary, local committees dealt with minor issues like debt or breach of the peace, and the church was thoroughly Presbyterian with the right to free assembly. If ever there was a time to consider the inevitable consequences of attempting to enforce by law, on a whole nation, what were essentially matters of faith, it was the age when the Covenanters ruled Scotland. When the link between church and state had been examined and debated and shaken to its foundations, the responsibility of the civil authority to control both behaviour and doctrine in the church remained unchallenged among Scottish Presbyterians. They were almost unanimous in the certainty that it was the duty of the civil magistrate

> to take order that unity and peace be preserved in the church, that the truth of God be kept pure and entire, that all blasphemies and heresies be suppressed, all corruptions in worship and in discipline be prevented or reformed, and all the ordinances of God duly settled, administered and observed. For the better effecting whereof, he hath power to call synods, to be present at

20. Lynch, *Scotland*, 264.

them and to provide that whatsoever is transacted in them be according to the mind of God.[21]

The place of the civil magistrate in society was seen in a different light by other groups of Christians, e.g., the English Independents. The Congregational Savoy Declaration of 1658 and the Baptist Confession of Faith of 1677, both of which repeated most of the Westminster Confession word for word, stressed the respect and obedience due to the civil magistrate but left it in no doubt that his authority did not stretch to interference in the doctrinal issues of the church. The only body with a responsibility to ensure that "the truth of God be kept pure and entire" was the church herself. The Presbyterian churches in America, while holding to the Westminster Confession as their statement of faith, altered the chapter which dealt with the civil magistrate for that very reason.[22] It seemed to the independent churches that the attempt to compel the profession of spiritual convictions by force of law, with penalties for the disobedient, must inevitably lead either to hypocrisy or martyrdom. The irony in the situation created by the covenanting revolution in Scotland was that in a day when freedom of faith and worship were essential elements in the conflict, the lessons of history should be forgotten, and a principle that had to be considered most carefully in the early days of the relationship between church and state was rejected by the defenders of Christian liberty, to the damage of the church in Scotland for generations to come.

Thirteen centuries before the Covenanters appeared, the church had grown from a little band of fearful disciples to an international and organised body which made up approximately 10 percent of the entire population of the Roman Empire.[23] It was the conversion of the emperor Constantine to the Christian faith that changed the shape of the church irrevocably. Up till that point, the Christian church, in legal terms, had neither rights nor recognition within the state, and yet it was this Roman monarch who remained outside of the church until his baptism shortly before his death who considered the lesson the Covenanters refused to recognise. The Holy Spirit alone can bring men to faith in the Son of God, and he does it not by overruling or damaging their power to make decisions, but by persuading and convincing their hearts and minds to

21. *Westminster Confession*, ch. 23, art. 3.
22. Schaff, *Creeds of Christendom*, 720.
23. Baynes, *Constantine the Great*, 12.

willingly trust and follow Christ. A church which required professions of faith made under threat was sowing the seeds of its own destruction. By failing to work out in practical terms a real separation between church and state, the Covenanters repeated the errors of the later church in the Roman Empire, but with far less excuse. By clinging to a church-state relationship inherited from pagan Rome, which seemed to give the church immediate political and social advantage, the ground was prepared for the germination and growth of the very factors which would bring the outward structure, so carefully built by the Covenanters, to an end. For the men of the Covenant, state and church were not two separate bodies but two aspects of a single entity. Nothing else could be considered no matter how far away that concept was from the church of Christ and his apostles. So why did an idea that would never come close to acceptance by modern Christians seem so obviously practical to the Christians of seventeenth-century Scotland.

To trace the development of those factors which moulded Scotland into a covenanted nation-church, it is necessary to begin with the "household of God that was built on the foundation of the apostles and prophets, with Jesus Christ himself as the chief cornerstone."[24]

---

24. Eph 2:19–20.

1

Kingdoms in Conflict

A class hated for their abominations who are commonly called Christians.[1]

IF THERE WAS ONE thing Jesus Christ made clear in all that he said and did, it was that his kingdom was spiritual and his rule was not to be established by political or military force. He was neither a revolutionary nor a political reformer. He posed no obvious threat to the Roman emperor nor to the Jewish authorities. Yet he was tried as a criminal before two courts of law, one religious and the other a civil court. The religious court was the Jewish Sanhedrin, a body of considerable authority in the time of Christ. It dealt with much of the internal government of Judea and even exercised a measure of control over the Jews of the Diaspora. It operated through its own administration, had its own police force and was responsible for the arrest and trial of Christ.

Superficially, at least, the court procedure seemed to be weighted on the side of the prisoner. There was a quorum of twenty-three judges who could, by a simple majority of one, acquit the accused, whereas a "guilty" verdict needed a two-thirds majority. Acquittal could be pronounced on the day of the trial but if the prisoner was to be condemned, this had to be withheld for consideration for a period of twenty-four hours. Where there was doubt about a conviction, the accused would be given the benefit of that doubt and set free.[2] In spite of all this apparent advantage to the prisoner, it was clear that when Christ stood before the Sanhedrin,

1. Bettenson, *Documents*, 2.
2. Douglas, *New Bible Dictionary*, 1144.

his conviction was a foregone conclusion. The trial was simply a legal procedure arranged to bring about his death and the purpose of the court was to authorise his execution for the crime of blasphemy. The verdict was agreed before the evidence had been heard.

However, it was precisely in the execution of a death sentence that the Jewish court met with a legal obstacle. Although the power of life or death was given to the Sanhedrin by Jewish law, this was not recognised in Roman law and the reality was that in a case which involved capital punishment, the law of Rome overruled Jewish law, and a verdict by the procurator representing the Roman Empire was required. The death sentence passed on Christ by the high priest Caiaphas and his fellow judges for the crime of blasphemy could not be carried out by that court. Neither was it a simple matter of the procurator, Pontius Pilate, rubber stamping the decree of the Sanhedrin. For the death of Christ to take place, a second trial was necessary under Roman law and a second accusation had to be leveled against the prisoner for which the appropriate penalty would be death. Furthermore, for the accusation of a crime against Roman law to be successful, that crime had to be political and not religious. There was indeed a state church in the Roman empire, and the emperor himself was its chief priest, but Christ was not accused of any crime relating to Roman religion A charge of blasphemy against the God of Israel would not be considered in a Roman court, therefore the solution was to accuse Christ of rebelling against the political authority of the emperor by proclaiming himself to be a king in Judea.

Apart from the complete lack of any evidence to substantiate such a charge, it was never the policy of Rome to permit its legal machinery to function as the political arm of the Sanhedrin, and this is confirmed by the immediate reaction of Pilate to the charges brought against Christ. The gospel writers indicate a genuine reluctance on his part to be used to bring about Christ's death. He attempted to have the charges against Christ dismissed as inconclusive. When this failed, he tried to have him freed under a traditional amnesty, since whatever else Christ was, he was no threat at all to Roman authority in Judea. Failure to achieve his acquittal was not due to the inadequacy of Roman law but to the lack of integrity in the governor charged with its administration. There can be little doubt that the law of Rome was, in broad terms, a benefit within the empire, however in local situations where the rule of law was in the hands of a provincial governor, it was far from impossible that a threat of mob violence or a manipulation of the legal machinery might lead to a miscarriage of justice, and Pilate was an unstable man under a considerable degree of political pressure.

Appointed by the emperor Tiberius in AD 26 as governor of Judea, Pilate found Jewish political forces both complex and difficult to contain. The appointment of the Jewish high priest was by Pilate's authority. He controlled high priestly vestments and temple funds. He had hundreds of cavalry soldiers and thousands of infantrymen to reinforce his decisions, but what he lacked was the political skill to keep the Jews under control. He had, early in his government, antagonised the Jews by setting up in Jerusalem standards which bore an image of the emperor. Only when it became clear that the worshippers of the God of Israel were prepared to sacrifice their lives to resist such an offence was he persuaded to remove the images from the holy city. His dedication of a set of golden shields bearing his own name and that of Tiberius within his quarters at Jerusalem,brought another protest to the emperor, who decided in favour of the Jews and ordered the removal of the shields. On more than one occasion Pilate attempted to solve local problems by the use of military force to massacre rioters and execute political leaders. His career ended in disgrace when he was summoned back to Rome to answer to the emperor for his brutality. However, in spite of his flawed character, this was the man charged with the administration of Roman justice before whom Christ was on trial for a political crime. Even a ruler as harsh and insensitive as Pilate knew exactly why Christ had been accused by the Sanhedrin and what justice demanded, but what he feared more than anything else was yet another complaint by the Jews to the emperor. The threat by Jewish leaders to report him to Tiberius for political disloyalty forced him to agree to the execution of the prisoner. The now-famous gesture of washing his hands to indicate that he rejected responsibility was indeed no more than a gesture. The fact was that Christ could not be crucified except for a political crime against Roman law, and the only authority permitted to pass sentence was represented by Pilate. The sign fixed to the cross which read "This is the King of the Jews"[3] was intended to be an indication of a capital crime for which the appropriate punishment was carried out.

This encounter of Christ, the head of the church, with the law of the state in which that church grew and flourished was certainly not the

3. Douglas, *New Bible Dictionary*, 996.

beginning of a legal or formal relationship, but it was the first step in a growing interaction between the church and imperial Rome which developed in the following centuries to an extent that must have been unimaginable to the Christian apostles who first set off to evangelise their pagan world. The insignificant band of disciples grew to become one of the most powerful forces in Roman life and culture. Beyond all doubt the empire was brought under the influence of the Christian church in almost every aspect of its existence. However, if it was true that the empire was shaped by the church, it was equally true that the church gained the dubious advantage of being moulded by the empire. In the relationship between church and state, pagan Rome stamped a pattern on the church's life and thinking, traces of which are still discernible in the twenty-first century. Within a comparatively short space of time, in historical terms at least, the little flock of Jesus had grown into an ecclesiastical organisation modelled on the Roman administration. In the future it would claim to have the right to exercise not merely spiritual authority over all who professed faith in Christ, but political and temporal authority over Rome, the Western Empire, and later the world.

By the earlier part of the fourth century, without the use of military weapons or political influence, the church had conquered prejudice, misrepresentation, the harshest persecution both physical and psychological, and more than one attempt at the complete destruction of the entire Christian community. It was when all this had been accomplished that the dangerous concept of a Christian state became firmly established and the church began to lose the distinction between the things that belonged to Caesar and the things that belonged to God.

When Christ stood before Pilate, it was the confrontation of two radically different kingdoms. The attempt to forge them into one changed the shape of the church from the fourth century onwards. Three centuries later, the so-called "Donation of Constantine" appeared. This document, by which the emperor Constantine was held to have given to the current bishop of Rome the imperial palace, the diadem and crown, and the tiara and purple mantle, as a symbol of all the power which was to be transferred from state to church, is now universally recognised as a forgery. It was probably written sometime in the eighth century and as a record of historic fact it has no worth at all. The value of the document lies in the reason it was considered necessary. It was needed to provide historical and theological justification for the structure and authority which the church sought to possess and exercise at the time when it was written. It was accepted as genuine from the ninth to the fifteenth century and has been cited by at least ten popes and other writers. A work of fiction, its composition was nevertheless important to be able to explain the transfer of the entire imperial political structure from emperor to pope.[4] The church which Christ built upon the foundation of faith had travelled a very long way from Jerusalem to Rome.

Evidence for the expansion of the church immediately after Pentecost is recorded to some extent in the book of Acts and the Letters of the apostles. When Paul met with James, the leader of the Christian community in Jerusalem, the church in that city was already numbered in "many thousands."[5] By the time the apostle arrived in Rome as a prisoner, about the year AD 60, there were Christian communities around the eastern coast of the Mediterranean, across Asia minor, and into Europe and Rome itself. The next two-and-a-half centuries provided a record of continuous expansion for the Christian church. By the early years of the fourth century there were disciples of Christ in almost every part of the empire and even beyond its borders. From the northwest, there were strong Christian communities in Gaul, and the British church could send three bishops to the Council of Arles in AD 314. In the southwest there were churches along the African coast and across the narrow western end of the Mediterranean into Spain. In the east the followers of Christ were to be found from Egypt and as far north as Georgia, northeast of the Black Sea. Armenia had become a Christian kingdom, King Tiridates and the royal family being baptised about AD 300, and while the claim that the church in India was founded by the Apostle Thomas is probably legend, the early spread of the gospel from Syria into India is probably not.[6]

Neither was the growth of the church merely numerical and territorial. It grew socially and intellectually. It spread to every level in Roman society. There were slaves, craftsmen, and merchants. There were soldiers and civil servants. There were lawyers and politicians. There were knights and senators. There were even members of the imperial family who followed Christ. The Christian gospel was preached and defended against its critics. The church produced scholars, teachers, and apologists equal to

4. Coleman, introduction to *Treatise*.
5. Acts 21:20.
6. Bruce, *Spreading Flame*, 291.

any of their pagan rivals, and who proved to be more than able to relate Christian truth to Roman culture, philosophy, and the political thinking of their time. There were famous theological schools in cities like Antioch, Caesarea, and Alexandria. The very need to clarify and explain the Christian message developed the theological acumen of its teachers.

There was another area of growth in the life of the church which was of no little importance and that was the development of ecclesiastical organisation. A wide variety of religions had always been an aspect of Roman life that was wholly familiar, but in the world of imperial Rome, religion tended to be inherited from family, and any different system of belief was generally local in a tribe or people and confined to the territory they occupied. The Christian church on the other hand was everywhere. It was flexible enough to allow for local variation in practice but united through the organisation of its bishops. There was a means of intercommunication and strong links between believers in one part of the empire with those in another. Outside of the imperial government itself there was nothing else in the empire with the same organisational skills as the church of Christ.[7] It has been estimated that by the middle of the fourth century, the church had something in the region of six million members, which represented about 10 percent of the entire population of the empire.[8] To achieve so much in less than three centuries, the expansion of the church was somewhere between a flow and a deluge. It was impossible for a change of such magnitude not to provoke strong reaction.

In the beginning, opposition to Christians stemmed mainly from their Jewish neighbours, and Roman authorities tended to resist attempts to be manipulated into the persecution of the church. Acts 18 describes an occasion when the Apostle Paul was dragged before the Roman proconsul, Gallio, but when that magistrate realised that the law Paul was accused of breaking was in fact a Jewish religious regulation, he threw the accusers out of court. There is good reason to believe that the Roman government saw the first Christians as a branch of Judaism and therefore legally permitted. The collection of documents attributed to the Christian apologist Tertullian, writing about AD 200, includes a statement that

> Tiberius in whose time the Christian faith came into the world,
> having received information from Palestine of the events there
> which had revealed the truth of Christ's divinity, brought the

7. Drake, *Constantine and the Bishops*, 103.
8. Ibid., 175.

matter before the Senate and gave his vote in favour of setting Christ among the gods. The Senate rejected the proposal
because it had not given its approval of its own initiative. Caesar maintained his opinion and threatened the accusers of the
Christians that they acted at their peril.[9]

The incident is most probably without historical foundation, since only
Tertullian mentions it and although Eusebius repeats it in his account
of the early church,[10] he is simply citing Tertullian's work. It would be
hard to find a modern historian who would take it seriously, however
the story does reflect certain aspects of Roman rule which are not too
far from the truth. It is true that Tiberius preferred diplomacy to force in
dealing with what he would see at the time as a Judean religious problem.
It is also true that Roman religion in the first century would have little
difficulty in adding another local god to the accredited list. Whenever
outbreaks of persecution occurred in the early days of the church, these
tended to be the result of the spontaneous eruption of an angry mob and
took place usually where the Roman presence was weak or even absent.
Christ and Caesar were still far enough apart to preclude any organised
state oppression of the church. Throughout the lifetime of the Apostle
Paul, the impression is given that he continued to see the Roman Empire as a largely benign source of order and discipline within which the
church could flourish. At his trial before Festus, Paul declares, "I am now
standing before Caesar's court where I ought to be tried," and when he
exercises his right as a Roman citizen and appeals to Caesar, we have
no reason to doubt that he expected to be acquitted, since he had not
transgressed the law of Rome.[11]

In his letter to the church at Rome, Paul portrays the government of
his day as worthy of respect and obedience. Christians must not consider
rebellion nor even resentment against political authority. They are to be
law-abiding tax payers, not simply because they risk punishment otherwise, but because behind the civil authority stands the authority of God.
Their sense of right and wrong should compel them to be good citizens.[12]
It must be remembered, however, that when Paul wrote these instructions to the church at the heart of the empire, he was writing to Christian

9. Bettenson, *Early Christian Fathers*, 165.
10. Eusebius, *History of the Church*, 39.
11. See Acts 25.
12. See Rom 13:1–7.

disciples whose faith and worship was completely separate from that of a pagan state ruled by a pagan emperor. The same section of Scripture would be used many times in future centuries to justify state control of a national church. While Paul wanted the church to be composed of citizens obedient to the secular ruler, it would be a complete distortion of his teaching to imagine it could be applied to a situation where a monarch or government, professing faith in Christ, could thereby claim the authority to control the doctrine and worship of the church.

As the church continued to grow it became clear to an increasingly hostile Roman society that Christians were not like other citizens. They did not adopt the "live and let live" approach to other religions which was part of Roman culture. They claimed the God they worshipped was in fact the only true God, and that his incarnate Son, Jesus Christ, was the only Saviour of mankind. Their refusal to observe the normal social and religious conventions of the day could only lead to further hostility. The moral and ethical qualities engendered by Christian faith were neither recognised nor understood, and the initial local and unofficial persecution of the church was perceived to be opposition against a corrupt religious sect. It sounds perhaps incredible to modern ears that the Christians should be accused of offences like cannibalism, infanticide, incest, misanthropy, and atheism,[13] but these views, held by pagans about Christians, helped to create an atmosphere that allowed persecution to shift steadily from mob violence to governmental decree.

In AD 64, in the reign of the emperor Nero, the city of Rome was engulfed in flames. The cause of the fire cannot be traced with any certainty, but the Roman historian Tacitus mentions the rumour that it had been started deliberately on the orders of Nero. He writes,

> All the endeavours of men, all the emperor's largesse and the propitiations of the gods, did not suffice to allay the scandal or banish the belief that the fire had been ordered. And so, to get rid of this rumour, Nero set up as the culprits, and punished with the utmost refinement of cruelty, a class hated for their abominations, who are commonly called Christians. Christus, from whom their name is derived, was executed at the hands of the procurator Pontius Pilate in the reign of Tiberius. Checked for the moment, this pernicious superstition again broke out, not only in Judea, the source of the evil, but even in Rome, that receptacle for everything that is sordid and degrading from

13. Sordi, *Christians and the Roman Empire*, 37.

every corner of the globe, which there finds a following. Accordingly, arrest was first made of those who confessed [sc. *to being Christians*]; then, on their evidence, an immense multitude was convicted, not so much on the charge of arson as because of hatred of the human race. Besides being put to death they were made to serve as objects of amusement; they were clad in the hides of beasts and torn to death by dogs; others were crucified, others set on fire to serve to illuminate the night when daylight failed. Nero had thrown open his grounds for the display, and was putting on a show in the circus, where he mingled with the people in the dress of a charioteer or drove about in his chariot. All this gave rise to a feeling of pity, even towards men whose guilt merited the most exemplary punishment; for it was felt they were being destroyed, not for the public good but to gratify the cruelty of an individual.[14]

It is clear from the record of Tacitus that he believes the Christians to have been innocent of the charge of being incendiaries. He indicates that he is repelled by the sheer cruelty of the means by which they were executed. There is also a hint of insanity in the emperor's behaviour which grew more bizarre until his suicide four years after the fire. However, in spite of all this, Tacitus has no doubt that although they are not to blame for burning Rome, the Christians are guilty of so many other crimes that they deserve to be punished as an example of Roman justice, and that the punishment would be "for the public good." It was this general condemnation which made it expedient for Nero to select the church as a scapegoat. It was surely an irony of history that the emperor Nero, to whom the Apostle Paul confidently appealed for justice, and who was on the throne when he wrote his letter to the Romans, was the ruler who set a precedent for the state persecution of Christian disciples. At this point in the development of the church, it was plain that it was not a branch of Judaism. The separation of the two faiths had long been clear, and so the Christian community was no longer seen as a Messianic group coming under the umbrella of a permitted religion, and yet it was not for that reason the persecution took place. It was justified in Roman eyes because of the corrupt and wicked practices in which the Christians were believed to be engaged. The state might have viewed the church as illegal and immoral, but it was not yet seen as a threat in any way. Christians were simply bad subjects who had to be dealt with firmly. The following

14. Bettenson, *Documents*, 2.

decades brought continued church expansion, with periods of persecution moderated by a more tolerant attitude from some of the emperors. However, the element of plotting and treachery that was never far below the surface of Roman political life tended to breed suspicion of anything unorthodox. Domitian, who reigned from AD 81 until his assassination in AD 96, was suspicious by nature and executed a number of people for a variety of crimes, including those accused of "atheism," which almost certainly meant Christians who would not engage in the acts of worship demanded by state religion. It is possible that the severe conditions described in the book of the Revelation are a reflection of his reign. The death of Domitian was followed by the brief reign of the emperor Nerva, whose relaxation of the pressure on Christians brought the release of John from the isle of Patmos.

Trajan, who reigned from AD 98 to 117, was less tolerant. He had to rule over a growing empire and tended to see organisations of any kind as having a potential for subversion. It is recorded that he refused to permit the formation of a fire service in one of the provinces because he suspected that it might turn into a political organisation. One of the few groups to be permitted was a burial club and even Christians were allowed to form these.[15] Trajan did not wish to see Christians being hunted down, but their following of an illegal religion and their refusal to recognise state worship meant that those accused of being Christians had to be tried and punished if found guilty. In AD 112, a governor called Pliny was sent by the emperor to the province of Bithynia. He was a man trying to work out a policy for dealing with people he did not understand, and a letter he wrote to Trajan shows him to be concerned that Christian influence had led to the desertion of temples and the neglect of Roman worship in his province. He clearly believed that he had to take some kind of firm action to counteract this alarming trend, yet he was reluctant to engage in a ruthless destruction of the church. He wrote to the emperor,

> It is my rule sire to refer to you in matters where I am uncertain. . . . I was never present at any trial of Christians; therefore I do not know what are the customary penalties or investigations, and what limits are observed.[16]

Pliny wants to know whether he should be more lenient towards the elderly or those who are obviously frail. Should those willing to give up

15. Bruce, *Spreading Flame*, 169.
16. Bettenson, *Documents*, 3.

the Christian faith be pardoned or should there be nothing to gain by recanting. He also raises the most important legal question in a developing situation; should he punish Christians simply for being Christians, or do they need to have committed a specific crime against the state before being liable to punishment. He reports on his present course of action,

> This is the course I have adopted in the case of those brought before me as Christians. I ask them if they are Christians. If they admit it I repeat the question a second and a third time, threatening capital punishment; if they persist I sentence them to death. For I do not doubt that whatever kind of crime it may be to which they have confessed, their pertinacity and inflexible obstinacy should certainly be punished. There were others who displayed a like madness, and whom I reserved to be sent to Rome since they were Roman citizens.[17]

Pliny goes on to inform the emperor of the practical outcome of his policy. When local pagans got to know he was willing to execute Christians for the mere profession of their faith, it encouraged a flood of accusations against the church. Many Christians were denounced anonymously and responded in a number of different ways when questioned. Some denied they had ever been Christians, and to prove it they willingly offered worship to the Roman gods and cursed Christ. These were immediately discharged. Others admitted they had been Christians at one time but were no longer followers of Christ. These also demonstrated their loyalty to Roman religion in the same way. There were also some who were anxious to convince the governor that being a Christian was no threat at all to Roman life and culture and so they described what happened at a typical church service and testified to the way in which their faith bound them to observe the appropriate moral and ethical standards in social, commercial, and domestic activity. They had also ceased meeting together for a common meal in order to avoid the least suspicion that they were ignoring the government edict forbidding the gathering of secret societies. Pliny seemed to have considered this picture far too wholesome to be true of a depraved sect like the Christians and so he ordered the torture of two deaconesses to find out the truth. His letter to Trajan reveals a man looking for a pat on the back when he reports the success of his policy. Temples are frequented again. Sacred rites are renewed and the business of selling offerings for sacrifice is thriving once more. The emperor in his

17. Ibid.

reply commends Pliny for the way he has handled the Christian problem. He confirms leniency is to be shown to those who recant and warns against accepting any accusations which are anonymous. Roman justice cannot be administered on the basis of spiteful anonymous accusations.[18]

The correspondence between Pliny and the emperor Trajan might, at first glance, seem to provide a tidy solution to a relatively minor problem. It does, however, offer a glimpse of a much greater problem that was not going to disappear. Although Pliny claims that he is capable of dealing with the matter, he is forced to admit that "the contagion of this superstition has spread not only in the cities but in the villages and rural districts as well." For the church, the initial shock of state persecution has been absorbed and assessed. The relationship between state and church is not hard to define. The state is an enemy which has to be conquered or endured. Trajan and his administrators are not madmen blindly lashing out at the church in irrational fury. They are politicians responsible for the stability of the empire, looking for the most practical means of dealing with a problem which they are beginning to suspect might not be solved by force alone. The threat of martyrdom was not an effective deterrent for everyone. More than a few were willing to pay exactly that price. Some indeed, like Ignatius, bishop of Antioch in Syria during Trajan's rule, seemed not only willing but eager to offer his life. After his arrest, on the way to Rome, where he expected to die in the arena, Ignatius wrote a number of letters to advise and encourage Christian churches. To the Christians at Rome he wrote,

> I die for Christ by my own choice unless you hinder me. I beseech you not to show inopportune kindness to me. Let me be given to the wild beasts, for by their means I can attain to God. I am God's wheat and I am being ground by the teeth of the beasts so that I may appear as pure bread. Rather coax the beasts that they may become my tomb, and leave no part of my body behind, that I may not be a nuisance to anyone when I have fallen asleep. Then shall I be truly a disciple of Jesus Christ when the world shall not even see my body. . . . Let all come, fire and cross and conflicts with beasts, hacking, cutting, wrenching of bones, chopping of limbs, the crushing of my body, cruel chastisements of the devil laid upon me. Only let me attain to Jesus Christ.[19]

18. Bettenson, *Documents*, 6.
19. Bettenson, *Early Christian Fathers*, 45.

Far from discouraging Christians by the graphic description of what he expected to happen to him, Ignatius found that delegates from many churches gathered together to meet him along his route between Antioch and Rome. They were there to encourage him, to express their love and admiration for his faithfulness and to learn from his example. The day would come when other concerned bishops would be at pains to prevent their flock from openly and deliberately provoking the officers of the state religion in the hope that it would ensure their place in the roll of martyrs. Meantime, although Pliny was confident that he could deal with the situation in his province, had he listened carefully enough he might have heard the distant sound of a warning bell.

State policy towards the church remained largely unchanged in the reign of Hadrian, who became emperor in AD 117, and Antonine, in AD 138. Subjects reported to be Christians must still be punished if found guilty, but there was no sympathy at all for those who reported Christians out of malice. In a letter to one of his proconsuls in Asia, Hadrian warns that official to be vigilant, "lest the inoffensive should be disturbed, while slanderous informers are afforded an opportunity of practicing their vile trade." The emperor would not allow his authority to be the instrument of mob rule. Whatever measures were taken against Christians, the procedure must be legal and the proconsul must be as ready to punish those bringing false accusations against harmless citizens, as he is to punish real lawbreakers. Hadrian writes,

> If our subjects of the provinces are able to sustain by evidence, their charges against the Christians, so as to answer before a court of justice, I have no objection to their taking this course. But I do not allow them to have recourse to mere clamorous demands and outcries to this end. . . . If anyone accuses and proves that the aforesaid men do anything contrary to the laws, you will pass sentences corresponding to their offences. On the other hand I emphatically insist on this, that if anyone demand a writ of summons against these Christians, merely as a slanderous accusation, you proceed against that man with heavier penalties, in proportion to the gravity of the offence.[20]

The emperor Antonine continued the policy of his predecessor. Those proved to be Christians continued to be punished, but there is an impression that he had no great enthusiasm for the task. Eusebius records that

---

20. Bettenson, *Documents*, 10.

the Christians of Asia petitioned the emperor to intervene on their behalf and that their petition, while it did not result in a change in the law, did gain an imperial response. Antonine wrote to his local administrators, telling them to beware of an excess of zeal in prosecuting Christians for being atheists. He wrote,

> I know that the gods also take care that such persons should not go undetected: they are far more likely to punish those who do not worship them than you are. You get them into serious trouble by your accusations of atheism and thereby strengthen their determination: and if accused they would choose apparent death rather than life for the sake of their own god. And so they are the real winners when they agree to part with their lives rather than to carry out your commands.[21]

The emperor also mentions that it has not escaped his notice that in a recent series of earthquakes, the Christians have exhibited a far higher degree of calmness and courage than their persecutors. The result has been a greater confidence in the god they worship while official state religion has been neglected.[22] It was also during this period that the famous martyrdom of Polycarp, the Bishop of Smyrna, took place. The church historian Eusebius reproduces a letter which describes his arrest and death. We are told that the police who came to arrest him were surprised at his age and gave him an hour to pray and compose himself before taking him to his execution. He presented a calm and dignified appearance as he walked into the stadium to the roar of a huge crowd. At first, magistrates urged him to deny the charge.

> The governor pressed him further: "Swear and I will set you free: execrate Christ." Polycarp replied, "For eighty six years I have been His servant and He has never done me wrong: how can I blaspheme my King who has saved me?" When the other persisted, "Swear by Caesar's fortune," Polycarp retorted, "If you imagine that I will swear by Caesar's fortune, as you put it, pretending not to know who I am, I will tell you plainly I am a Christian." . . . "I have wild beasts," said the proconsul, "I shall throw you to them if you don't change your attitude." "Call them," replied the old man. . . . "If you make light of the beasts," retorted the governor, "I will have you destroyed by fire unless you change your attitude." Polycarp answered, "The fire you

21. Emperor Antoninus, cited in Eusebius, *History of the Church,* 115.
22. Eusebius, *History,* 115.

threaten burns for a time and is soon extinguished: there is a fire you know nothing about, the fire of judgement to come and of eternal punishment, the fire reserved for the ungodly. But why do you hesitate? Do what you want." ... Such was the story of blessed Polycarp.[23]

The arrest and execution of Polycarp by being burned alive was in fact illegal, since he had been hunted down contrary to imperial policy and had at first tried to evade capture. He only accepted martyrdom when it was plainly inevitable. His death is an example of an imperial policy that was not working. Recognition of the gods of Rome was the required evidence of political loyalty, and considerable numbers of Christians refused to compromise on this issue.

Marcus Aurelius succeeded Antonine in AD 161. He was a stoic philosopher with an intellectual recognition of responsibility towards his fellow men, and at first there seemed to be hope that he might be more tolerant towards the church. This was not, however, the outcome of his reign. Christians continued to be executed as lawbreakers, or sent to work in the mines. The awareness that the Christian faith was still regarded in court circles as a dangerous and obstinate force made it easier for local outbreaks of persecution to take place. It was about this time that the spread of Montanism further damaged the Christian cause. Montanus was the leader of a revivalist movement which reacted against the developing formality of the church. There developed a tendency to withdraw from the world and await the imminent return of Christ. For this reason Montanists rejected public office and military service at the very time when barbarians were pressing strongly against the boundaries of the empire. The Roman state, which was beginning to grasp the growing size and structure of the church, was not yet able to distinguish the difference between politically dangerous groups like Montanists and the more orthodox Christian community.[24] Governors who, by law, were obliged to resist mob rule felt safe to indulge it. In Gaul, in AD 177, the attack on the church was particularly fierce. In the cities of Lyons and Vienne many Christians died not so much as the result of a legal process but at the demands of a bloodthirsty and maddened crowd. The fury of the mob spared neither old nor young. Servants and members of Christian families, in fear for their own lives, brought accusations against

23. Ibid., 122.
24. Sordi, *Christian and the Roman Empire*, 73.

harmless disciples. Slaves died alongside their masters. Some died in the prisons before they were brought out for execution. Others were tortured to death. Some were beheaded and others torn to pieces by animals in the arena. Christians were not even permitted to bury their dead. The bodies of those who had been martyred were burned and the ashes swept into the River Rhone to mock the Christian hope of the resurrection.[25]

The sheer ferocity of the opposition to the church at this time is attributable to a number of factors. In a society where a rational explanation of events was lacking, men were turning more and more to magic and astrology to give them confidence for the future, and the Christian faith was implacably opposed to these practices. In the same period of time there seemed to be an unusually large number of natural disasters, like plague, flood, and famine. It was considered that these were a judgement sent by the Roman gods as a punishment for the neglect of official worship and the tolerance of a rival faith. There was also a growing military threat from the barbarian tribes outside the borders of the empire which required greater resources in terms of finance and troops if it were to be controlled. The church was seen as a corrosive influence on the unity and loyalty necessary to meet such demands.[26] At the same time, there was no weapon in the Roman armoury powerful enough to withstand the growing influence of the Christian gospel. The usual weapons of force and repression resulted only in repeated failure.

There had certainly been minor variations in the conditions under which Christians struggled to live during the past century, but the church continued to be something alien to the accepted life and culture of the Roman state, and each was the enemy of the other. Whatever views Christians were beginning to develop about the Roman empire, official government policy was to see the church as a disease that threatened Roman society and had therefore to be eradicated. Christ and Caesar remained in a conflict, which seemed to be a war to the death.

25. Eusebius, *History*, 147.
26. Bruce, *Spreading Flame*, 177.

2

Blurred Boundaries

There is reason to believe that Philip was a Christian
and on the day of the last Easter vigil he wished to share
in the prayers of the church along with the people.[1]

COMMODUS, WHO FOLLOWED MARCUS Aurelius in AD 180, seems
to have been regarded as more sympathetic towards the church,
perhaps through the influence of his wife Marcia. Certainly a number
of Christian prisoners were released from the mines during his reign.[2]
Eusebius claims that the church grew in a period of relative peace and
that Christians began to appear in the families of Roman aristocracy.[3]
However, in the following years, while there was an ebb and flow in the
tide of church-state relations, the overall trend was towards greater state
opposition.

Septimus Severus became emperor in AD 193, and nine years later,
a decree was issued forbidding the conversion of anyone to the Jewish
or Christian faith. This was the first specific law against conversion to
Christ. Persecution broke out across the empire and was especially fierce
in the African churches. Alexander Severus, whose reign began in AD
222, would appear to have been more sympathetic towards Christians.
He is reputed to have wanted to find a place for Christ in the pantheon of
Roman gods. Christians began to appear in the ranks of the Senate and

1. Eusebius, *History*, 206.
2. Ibid.
3. Ibid., 169.

in court circles. The church gained the right to hold corporate property, and Eusebius records the interest of Mamaea, the emperor's mother, in the faith. The historian wrote,

> The emperor's mother Mamaea was one of the most religious and high principled of women, and when the fame of Origen spread so far that it came to her ears, she set her heart on securing an interview with him and testing his universally admired skill as a theologian. By good luck she was staying in Antioch, so she sent a bodyguard of soldiers to fetch him. He stayed with her for some time, revealing to her many things to the glory and the virtue of the divine message.[4]

In AD 235, the tide of tolerance towards the church turned when Alexander Severus and Mamaea were assassinated by the troops of Maximin the Thracian who then elected their commander as emperor. Eusebius blames the political rivalry between Maximin and his predecessor for the new emperor's antagonism towards the church, and this was expressed in his order that Christian leaders who were active in the spread of the gospel were to be executed.[5] The trend was, however, reversed yet again when Maximin was succeeded by Gordian in AD 238, who in turn gave way to Philip the Arabian in AD 244. Eusebius writes,

> There is reason to believe that Philip was a Christian, and on the day of the last Easter vigil he wished to share in the prayers of the Church along with the people; but the prelate of the time would not let him come in until he made open confession and attached himself to those who were held to be in a state of sin and were occupying the place for penitents. Otherwise, had he not done so he would never have been received by him in view of the many accusations brought against him. It is said that he obeyed gladly showing by his actions the genuine piety of his attitude towards the fear of God.[6]

Eusebius was writing roughly a century after the event, and it is not easy to gauge the accuracy of his assessment regarding the spiritual condition of Philip. His penance before participating in Christian worship was necessary because it was believed he had connived at the death of Gordian,

---

4. Ibid., 198. Origen was a theologian, an apologist, and the head of the catechetical school at Alexandria.

5. Sordi, *Christian and the Roman Empire*, 95.

6. Eusebius, *History*, 206.

but there is no reason to doubt the reality of his sympathy towards the church and the resulting growth of the Christian faith in his day. The record certainly demonstrates that there were no special conditions for entry to the church to permit emperors to avoid recognition of their sin. In spiritual matters, the authority of the church superseded the political authority of the emperor

It has been suggested that Philip could see the possibility of the Christian faith becoming the religion of the whole empire where the political ideas of Rome could be combined with the gospel. There were also some in the church who were open to the view that it was the Roman Empire that protected the world from the coming antichrist, and would last until the end of the age.[7] The reality was quite different. There were many Romans in the middle of the third century who believed that the reign of Philip had to be brought to an end. The empire was facing increased military threat from the Goths in the north and from the Persians in the east. Not all Christians were willing to defend the empire by force of arms and this brought about a suspicion of Christian disloyalty. There was even a section of the church outside the eastern border of the empire, which was suspected of supporting the Persians. Something had to be done, and in AD 248 the Senate united with the masses in arranging the death of Philip and the son who might have succeeded him. The fear that Philip's tolerance of the church had angered the gods of Rome and the unpopularity of his fiscal policy opened the way for Decius to take power the following year.

The edict of Decius in 250 was wide ranging. It commanded

> provincial governors and magistrates, assisted where necessary by local notables, to superintend the sacrifices to the gods and to the genius of the Emperor, to be performed by all on a fixed day. Many recanted; others bought certificates or had them procured by pagan friends. There seems to have been wholesale connivance by the officials.[8]

This legislation was not aimed specifically at Christians. It was a requirement for every citizen, but in the course of events Christians were caught in the wider net. Persecution began in Rome and spread to the provinces. The first executions, including that of the bishops, were in the city. Other presbyters were imprisoned. As the circle of oppression widened,

7. Sordi. *Christian and the Roman Empire*, 98.
8. Bettenson, *Documents*, 18.

conditions in the provinces became worse than those in the capital, so that some of the victims found their way to the city of Rome, where the situation was marginally better.

There were a number of factors in the relationship between the church and the Roman state which began to be visible in this period of time. It was plain that the policy for dealing with the church was not working. The old laws which were used against individual Christians were not adequate to deal with the church as a whole. Followers of the Christ had been punished not so much for what they did as for what they refused to do, i.e., to practice the official Roman religion. It was seen to be necessary to recognise, in a legal sense, that the Christians were not simply a multitude of individual and disloyal subjects, but part of a single body which must be attacked and destroyed as a whole. The purpose of Decius was to achieve one empire and one religion. At the same time, the popular antagonism towards the church was not as intense as it had been, and it was not impossible to find examples of Christians who had been helped by pagan neighbours. The ambitions of Decius were not fulfilled in his own lifetime, since he died within two years of becoming emperor. Eusebius reports that he and his sons were murdered, but it is widely accepted that he was killed in battle against the Goths.

After Decius came Gallus in AD 251, then Valerian in AD 253, during whose reign the pressure on the church was intensified. An edict of AD 257 denied Christians the right to meet together or to have access to their cemeteries. The following year another edict brought a death sentence for Christian clergy, while Roman senators or knights who were found to be Christians were deprived of their rank. Christian noblewomen were exiled and suffered the confiscation of their property. Government employees who followed Christ were sent to labour camps and the current bishops of Rome and Carthage were both martyred.

Valerian seemed to have a real fear of the state becoming "Christianised," and yet his attempt to destroy the church had the curious effect of giving the church a corporate existence in legal terms. When Gallienus, the son of Valerian, chose to show imperial favour by restoring Christian property, he could not do this by merely curtailing current persecution. He was forced to revoke the edicts his father had issued. In doing so he had to deal with the church as a legally recognizable body with certain rights, and moreover, a body which might appeal to the law to have those rights enforced.

There was another factor in favour of the church at this time. It was the policy of Gallienus to diminish the power of the Senate. It was becoming clear that imperial control had to be built, not on a strong Senate but a strong army, and Gallienus therefore was able to bestow some kind of recognition on the church without the need for Senate approval. Christian leaders were tempted to hope that the worst days of persecution were over. The state had come to respect the legal rights of the church but made no attempt to influence her doctrine or worship.

Over the next quarter of a century there seemed to be relative peace for the church. And it was perhaps the new sense of security that led to an extraordinary event in the year AD 268. The church at Antioch in Syria had as its bishop a man called Paul of Samosata. He was not only an ecclesiastical leader but a political figure. He was in charge of the collection of taxes and also functioned as a magistrate in the region. A considerable degree of opposition arose to his ministry, and his critics formed the firm intention to depose him in order to elect a new bishop. The excommunication of Paul was officially on the grounds of his heresy concerning the incarnation. It seems likely, however, that there was as much complaint about his lifestyle as his doctrine. Eusebius reproduces the document which lists the charges against Paul, and which represented the view of the whole synod. It was addressed to Bishop Dionysius of Rome and Maximus of Alexandria, but copies were also sent to all the provinces of the empire. Paul of Samosata was described as

> a man who was once nearly penniless having neither inherited a competence from his forebears, nor acquired one by the labour of hand nor brain, but who now has amassed immense wealth by committing illegalities, robbing churches and blackmailing his fellow-Christians. He deprives the injured of their rights, promising them help if they will pay for it but breaking his word to them, and makes easy money out of the readiness of those entangled in court proceedings to buy relief from their persecutors. In fact he regards religion as a way of making money . . . he is ambitious and arrogant decking himself out with worldly honours and anxious to be called ducenarius rather than bishop, and swaggers in city squares reading letters aloud or dictating them as he walks in public, surrounded by a numerous bodyguard, some in front and some behind.[9]

9. Eusebius, *History*, 248.

The document goes on to describe how Paul has turned the place of worship into a theatre, sitting on a throne of his own design and encouraging the congregation to leap to their feet applauding him and waving handkerchiefs. He has formed a ladies choir to sing hymns addressed to himself at the Easter festival and while there is no specific accusation of immorality, the reference to his "spiritual brides" certainly raises the possibility.

Even if allowance is made for a degree of exaggeration by those who want to build a watertight case against Paul, it is clear that the bishop they seek to depose is not a simple pastor whose life is taken up with the spiritual concerns of the flock. Paul is a man who has moved with the times. He has taken every social, political, and commercial advantage afforded by his office in the new atmosphere of state toleration. It is not easy to get rid of such a man, and Paul refused to relinquish the position or the property he regarded as his own. Three separate synods since AD 264 had condemned him, but he would not give way to his appointed successor. It was at this point that a course of action was adopted by both parties in the dispute, which indicates a profound change in the way the church looked upon the state. An appeal was made to the emperor Aurelian to give his decision on the matter. Not surprisingly he consulted with the bishop of Rome and accepted that bishop's view as the catholic orthodox position, and so Paul was forced to yield his bishopric to his successor Domnus. Bearing in mind that the official reason for the dismissal of Paul was his doctrinal error, the appeal by the church to a pagan emperor to enforce the decision of the synod was an extremely significant first step along what proved to be a very long and dangerous road. The end might have seemed to justify the means, but the appeal to state authority became an established factor in church affairs from this point onwards. The Christian leaders who appealed to the emperor to settle a matter of faith and discipline were already beginning to see the church not as a theocratic community separate from every other political or religious body, but as one of the many religious components within the Roman Empire over which Aurelian ruled by right. In many of the future battles which troubled the church, doctrine was used as the hook on which could be hung the real conflict between national, political, or even military rivals.

It would be no surprise at all to Roman citizens that Paul of Samosata behaved like the Christian version of a pagan Roman pontiff and tried to combine the role of priest and politician. This was exactly the tradition with which they were familiar in pagan Rome. Priests of the Roman state religion were not "clergy" in the later Christian sense. They were often men of high rank who saw in the priesthood a position of political influence. Cicero was one of the college of augurs, responsible for the interpretation of auguries taken by magistrates. Julius Caesar himself was a pontiff in his boyhood, and later "Pontifex Maximus." Roman religion was not concerned with inward spiritual experience but with outward religious observance, and a separation between religion and politics was not practical.[10] The decision of the emperor to have Paul removed from office would almost certainly be based on political expediency and have very little to do with a search for truth. The appeal by the church to a pagan emperor must surely also raise the question of what kind of church would see this as a wise course of action. In a sense it was a church that was the victim of its own success. The multitudes of pagans coming into the church meant that a great deal of Roman religion was given Christian garb until its devotees learned to work out the social and moral implications of the new faith. The language was Christian but the mindset was pagan. Only four decades later, a council of bishops at Elvira produced a set of rules for clergy and laity which had to censure, among other things, laymen who combined their Christian profession of faith with a pagan priesthood, wealthy Christian ladies who provided garments for pagan festivities, members of the Christian community who might have beaten their slaves to death, gamblers, clergy with adulterous wives, and those who combined their ministry with usury and an immoral lifestyle. There was also a warning for clergy whose business interests kept them from fulfilling pastoral duties.[11]

In spite of the optimism at the end of the third century, the golden age for the church had not yet arrived. There were three ingredients coming together which would eventually prove to be explosive. First, the sheer size of the Roman empire made it difficult to govern and defend. Administrative difficulties were a challenge even to Roman skills. Resources in terms of manpower and money were not limitless, and the pressure of barbarian forces on the boundaries of the Rhine and Danube were getting stronger every year. The political and military machinery of Rome was becoming overheated and in danger of breaking down.

10. Bailey et al., *History of Christianity*, 30.
11. Chadwick, *Church in Ancient Society*, 184.

Second, Roman religion, the great unifying force in the empire, was inadequate for the task. The traditional Roman gods to which appeal was so often made as a rallying cry did not preside over a faith that remained static. The primitive agricultural animism which had developed through the centuries into polytheistic religion had been transformed from state-controlled worship into worship of the state. But even in pagan Rome there was a growing movement in religious thought towards the worship of one God. In parallel to the trend towards monotheism was the movement to centralise religion in the worship of the state, then the person of the emperor as symbolic of the state and then in the emperor himself as a divine being. It had a value in maintaining political unity through the official enforced practice of state religion, but by the end of the third century it was more political than religious, and its effect was wearing thin.

Third, the growth of the Christian church was unstoppable. What could imperial government do against people who counted it an honour to be allowed to suffer for Christ. The church certainly had its problems, but these were like the waves which seemed to advance and retreat. The tide however was moving in only one direction and threatening to sweep over the empire. Tertullian, the great African apologist and teacher, writing about the beginning of the third century, gives the impression that he is challenging the Roman empire to do its worst. He wrote,

> We are but of yesterday and today are grown up, and overspread your empire; your cities, your islands, your forts, towns, assemblies and your very camps, wards, companies, palace, senate, forum, all swarm with Christians. Your temples indeed we leave to yourselves, and they are the only places you can name without Christians. What war can we be now unprepared for? . . . We could also make a terrible war upon you without arms, or fighting a stroke, by being so passively revengeful as only to leave you; for if such a numerous host of Christians should but retire from the empire into some remote region of the world, the loss of so many men of all ranks and degrees would leave a hideous gap and a shameful scar upon the government; and the very evacuation would be abundant revenge. You would stand aghast at your desolation, and be struck dumb at the general silence and horror of nature, as if the whole world was departed. You would be at a loss for men to govern and in the pitiful remains you would find more enemies than citizens; but now you exceed in friends because you exceed in Christians.[12]

12. Tertullian, *Apology*, 104.

The state religion of Rome was threatened by an enemy against which it had no defence. After Gallienus, over the next sixteen years, a series of emperors brought about no major changes in the relationship between church and state, but the inevitable final conflict could not be postponed for much longer as political and military pressure within the empire increased. In AD 284, the emperor Diocletian came to power.

3

The Great Persecution

An imperial decree was published everywhere ordering the churches to be
razed to the ground and the Scriptures to be destroyed by fire.[1]

DIOCLETIAN WAS A MAN with a vision. He saw a state strong and secure from external military threat and internal political unrest. He
saw a united community built on Roman religion and Roman law. He
saw an empire where, in an atmosphere of a traditional Roman tolerance,
each nation might worship its own gods but would, in addition, willingly
and publicly acknowledge the gods of Rome in a way that demonstrated
the political loyalty implied by such acknowledgement. However, what
he could also see with equal clarity as a major obstacle to the fulfillment
of such a vision was an extensive multicultural and multiethnic Christian church which crossed national and linguistic boundaries, but which
was united in its determined refusal to pay homage to any God except
the "God and Father of the Lord Jesus Christ." It seemed to the emperor
Diocletian that the policy of his immediate predecessors in permitting
the church to grow in numbers and in material and political influence
could not be continued. Christians were a threat which he could not ignore. Diocletian was not a man who had come to empirical power by the
privilege of birth or by the purchase of political support. He was a soldier
whose battle experience had taught him that compromise and toleration
were not effective weapons in a conflict, and there seemed to be no way
to avoid a war to the death with the Christian church.

1. Eusebius, *History of the Church*, 258.

Diocletian was born into poverty in Dalmatia about AD 240. Like many another poor young man of determination and ability, he found that a military career offered the most promising future, and his qualities were recognised as he climbed the ladder of promotion. While still a young man, he was appointed to the imperial bodyguard. He became a consul in AD 283. In the same year the emperor Carus died in suspicious circumstances and was succeeded by his sons, Numerian and Carinus, both of whom died by the hand of an assassin. It was in these days of political instability and violence that Diocletian was chosen as emperor, and it is significant that his elevation was initiated by his own troops. The Senate was no longer the powerful king maker it once had been and it had lost whatever control over events it might have possessed in earlier times. The only power which could enforce political change in the days of Diocletian was military strength, and it was this which brought him to the throne in 284.

It was the policy of Diocletian to defend rather than to enlarge his empire. His goal was to have strong defences against the barbarians who were a continual source of trouble on the very extended borders of his realm, and also to be safe from political intrigue at home. His solution was a power-sharing scheme with fellow-rulers who were chosen not because of their lineage but because of their ability. In 285, he appointed Maximian as a second "Augustus," or emperor. Maximian, unlike Diocletian, came from a branch of the Roman nobility, but had also pursued a military career. Based in Trier, he had responsibility for control of the Gauls and the western part of the empire, while Diocletian, in Nicomedia, intended to deal with the Persians and rule in the east. In 293, the diarchy became a tetrarchy. Each of the Augusti received a deputy in the appointment of two "Caesars." In the west, Constantius was appointed Caesar under Maximian, and in the east, Galerius was the Caesar supporting Diocletian.

The two new Caesars clearly felt the need to establish their authority by the appropriate political alliances, and so Constantius divorced his wife Helen in order to marry Theodora, the stepdaughter of his Augustus, Maximian, while Galerius married Valeria the daughter of Diocletian. The four rulers were established in different parts of the empire and in fact seldom met together, but each one was a seasoned military commander chosen because Diocletian believed the security he sought depended on military units that were efficient, disciplined, mobile, and flexible. By the end of his reign, new arms factories were built to supply a combined force of at least fifty legions.[2]

Although Diocletian was first and foremost a soldier, he was enough of a politician to see that sheer military strength was not capable of solving every problem he had to deal with. He divided his empire into different sections. He made the provinces much smaller in size but greater in number. Of course the new arrangement required many more administrators. There was also a new layer of government, the diocese, between the imperial court and the provinces. The new provinces were covered by twelve dioceses and where the old provinces of the second century had required about one hundred and fifty administrators, the number in the fourth century grew to three thousand in the eastern empire alone.[3] The size of the army necessary to maintain secure borders brought pressure to bear on the economy, and since the empire was no longer absorbing the wealth of newly conquered territories, the growing costs of administration and maintenance had to be met by higher taxation. Diocletian used poll tax and property tax to provide funding for his ambitions. This was certainly a more stable and predictable means of finding the necessary finance, but it was far from popular. The unpopularity was especially true of Rome, because since none of the four rulers was based in that city, its tax privileges were lost. Diocletian also had to find some way to deal with inflation, and an edict of AD 301 fixed the maximum prices of a list of standard commodities and wages as one means of control. Another attempt to control inflation was the regulating of the purchasing power of silver. If this remained stable, other coins might vary in relation to the silver coinage.[4] There was a deliberate separation of military and financial administration to minimise any internal challenge to the regime.

In all of the political and economic reforms introduced by Diocletian, the Christian church was virtually unaffected for almost two decades. It was not political reformation but his religious policies that brought the church into the worst persecution it had known for centuries which became known as the "Great Persecution." The emperor's vision included a renewal of traditional Roman religion, with himself as spiritual leader. The historian Westbury-Jones writes,

2. Rees, *Diocletian and the Tetrarchy*, 24.
3. Drake, *Constantine and the Bishops*, 118.
4. Rees, *Diocletian and the Tetrarchy*, 44.

> We must always bear in mind that the ancient state of Rome was
> also a Church. The city had its State religion, of which the civic
> magistrates were priests. The empire was a politico-ecclesiastical
> institution. It was a Church as well as a State. A city-state entailed
> civic worship, and an empire-state meant emperor worship.[5]

Diocletian appears to have deliberately adopted a court style which would
distance himself from all but a few of his subjects. Only those above a certain rank could be admitted to the imperial palace and the emperor had to
be treated with the greatest reverence. On visits to major cities, cheering
crowds were organised, speeches made, statues erected, and panegyrists
would address the head of state in the most flattering language. Diocletian would be described in divine terms, although it is hard to be certain
whether this, for him, was simply an accepted element of Roman culture
or whether he was honestly convinced of his own divinity. Since the days
of Octavius in 27 BC, the emperor had been given the title of "Augustus"
and this was originally a title given to a god.[6] In 287, Diocletian took the
term "Jovius," recalling Jupiter, and Maximian took "Herculius," linking
himself with Hercules. It was not too great a step to move from praising
the emperor for his godlike virtues, to praising him as an incarnation
of one of the gods. What seems to be clear is that Diocletian was determined to hold together the many different groups within his empire by
the glue of ancient Roman religion, and at the heart of this was sacrifice.
Even if this was not sacrifice to the emperor, it was certainly sacrifice on
behalf of the emperor. Inward spiritual or moral transformation was not
the central object of the Roman sacrificial system. Rather the purpose
was the gaining of divine approval necessary for the welfare of the state.
There was no clear division between political and religious loyalty. They
were simply different aspects of the same relationship of each individual
citizen to one society.

Since the conflict with Persia was an ongoing problem, Diocletian
was concerned about the danger of any foreign religion. Manichaeism
was an eastern religion that had spread from Persia throughout the Roman empire. The followers of Manichaeism were suspected of disloyalty
because of its Persian origins, and the persecution of the Manichaeans
prepared the ground for persecution of the Christians. There was also
evidence of Christians in the army refusing to offer sacrifice for the

5. Westbury-Jones, *Roman and Christian Imperialism*, 34.
6. Bailey et al., *History of Christianity*, 34.

well-being of the emperor and having to renounce army service on those grounds. This kind of rebellion brought the penalty of execution, although the sentence was carried out for the breach of army regulations and not for the profession of a Christian faith. Up to this point, whatever persecution was suffered by the church in the reign of Diocletian had been sporadic and local, but the emperor reached a decision that the eradication of the church would become the official policy of the whole empire. In February 303, the first edict of persecution was issued.

Christian places of worship were destroyed and Scriptures burned. Those who would not offer sacrifice lost their judicial rights, Christians in high office were removed and those in imperial service became slaves. It took some time before the edict was put into practice in all the provinces and the enactment of it and the resistance to it tended to be absorbed into existing local political disputes.[7] Later the same year, a second edict condemned to imprisonment clergy who would not conform, with a further ruling that those who were willing to sacrifice might be released. Some of the clergy did conform to the imperial command, but many endured long prison sentences. The effect on the church was to face the alternative of losing their leadership or losing confidence in the loyalty of those leaders to Christ.

The following year, 304, a fourth edict was issued which applied the rule requiring sacrifice to entire communities. Since there were many parts of the empire, especially in the east, where entire towns or cities were Christian, this had a devastating effect on parts of the church. Many Christians suffered death by the most cruel means, however, the need for so many edicts within such a short time span suggests a policy which did not produce the results for which it was designed. Neither was it popular throughout the whole empire. The days had long gone when Christians were seen as depraved troublemakers. Far too many of them were useful and responsible citizens. Neither could it be ignored that when plagues of one kind or another came into a community, the Christians looked after their people who were sick while the pagans tended to desert them. Pagans were too pragmatic to ignore the truth that anyone who became infected stood a better chance of survival if he was a Christian. It was not impossible for local magistrates to ignore the rules in order to protect Christian citizens, and for pagans to help Christian neighbors.

7. Rees, *Diocletian and the Tetrarchy*, 63.

The religious policy of Diocletian was not the only aspect of his vision for unity that was not fulfilled. His political unity disintegrated fairly quickly into a scramble for supreme power. In 305, Diocletian chose to resign, and perhaps reluctantly, his co-emperor Maximian had to resign at the same time. Each of the two Caesars received the title of "Augustus" and was promoted to one of the two vacant places to become the new co-emperors. Each new emperor then required a deputy, and so, the emperor Galerius in the east was supported by Maximinus Daia, while Constantius in the west had Severus as his Caesar. These men were both protégés of Galerius, and their appointment was making an important statement. While Diocletian had no sons, Constantius had a son called Constantine, and Maximian's son, Maxentius, would also, in a different era, have been in line to succeed his father. In passing over both children, the point was made that the office of emperor was one to be gained not by lineage but by merit, which, in the early part of the fourth century might be interpreted as military competence. This principle, however, proved to be something of a two-edged sword.

4

The Coming of Constantine

Everyone who has the same desire to observe the religion
of the Christians may do so without molestation.[1]

CONSTANTIUS, THE WESTERN EMPEROR, did not live long, but shortly
before his death, his son Constantine joined him in Britain, and
when the death of Constantius occurred in July 306 in York, his troops
proclaimed Constantine as their new Augustus. In fact, the right to make
such an appointment belonged to Galerius, as the senior emperor. He was
willing to recognise Constantine by the title of "Caesar," and Constantine
was wise enough and patient enough not to argue about it. Maxentius,
however, made a bid for similar power, and in October of the same year,
with the support of the Praetorian Guard in Rome, he declared himself
to be the "Prince." The senior emperor, Galerius, had no option but to
meet the challenge of the self-styled prince, and sent the western Caesar, Severus, to march on Rome and crush Maxentius. Maxentius clearly
felt the need of political support and persuaded his father, Maximian, to
come out of retirement and join his cause. The father-son alliance proved
to be too strong for Severus, who was defeated and died soon after in
captivity. The eastern emperor, Galerius, now realised that he must himself deal with the usurper, and so he also set out for Rome at the head of
an army to remove Maxentius from power. As the confrontation with
Rome developed, Galerius was no more successful than Severus had been
and, after the defeat of Galerius, Maxentius was left with an empire that

1. Eusebius, *Church History*, 379.

comprised Italy, Sicily, Corsica, Sardinia, and part of North Africa. Further west, Constantine for the moment awaited developments, neither supporting nor attacking Maxentius.

Galerius, in spite of his defeat, was still officially emperor in the east and called an imperial conference at Carnuntum in 308 to appoint Licinius, another protégé and career soldier, as the replacement for the dead Severus, but having the rank of Augustus. This was approved but left a most confused situation in which seven men, including the retired Diocletian, claimed imperial power. Maximian, in a last desperate bid to control the situation, tried to have Constantine poisoned but failed, and as a result, committed suicide in 310.

Galerius at this point was a dying man, and before his death in 311 he issued an edict relaxing some of the severe conditions that were in force, giving the church a measure of freedom to worship and seeking the prayers of the Christians for his own desperate condition. The historian Eusebius, who described in graphic terms the appalling conditions of his death, asserted that it was the judgment of God for the cruelty with which he had persecuted the church. He also records a translation of the edict.

> In view of our benevolence and the established custom by which we invariably grant pardon to all men, we have thought proper in this matter also to extend our clemency most gladly, so that Christians may again exist and rebuild the houses in which they used to meet, on condition that they do nothing contrary to public order. In a further letter we shall explain to the justices what principles they are to follow. Therefore in view of this our clemency, they are in duty bound to beseech their own God for our security, and that of the state and of themselves, in order that in every way the state may be preserved in health and they may be able to live free from anxiety in their own homes.[2]

It is hardly surprising if the Christians were cynical about this reversal of the policy of Galerius. Eusebius asserts that it was due completely to the providence of God since Galerius was devoid of pity or humanity of any kind towards the church. He was seen as being even more hostile than Diocletian and had tried to destroy the church not only by open persecution but by propaganda like the forgery called the "Acts of Pilate" which was an attack on the Christian gospel and was for a time taught

---

2. Eusebius, *History of the Church*, 280.

in schools.[3] His edict of toleration certainly gives no hint of a Christian faith but stresses his own clemency towards stubborn subjects. However, this is no more than could be expected in an official edict from the ruler of a pagan empire. It also reflects perhaps the political reality of the day. Persecution might be able to control the external machinery of religion. What it could not do was remove the convictions and ideas from the hearts and minds of men which they sincerely believed to be the God-given truth. Maxentius in Rome, viewed as a usurper, was no lover of the Christian gospel, but nevertheless restored Christian property and freedom of worship to the subjects under his command. It is more than likely that his motives were governed by the need for political support to establish his recent military successes, rather than any genuine concern for the welfare of the church, but there can be no doubt that the church was helped during his reign, since the number of Christians and clergy increased, and a North African bishopric was restored.[4]

The death of Galerius left four main contestants. Maximinus Daia laid claim to the territory which had been under the rule of Galerius. Maxentius was still in control of Rome, Italy, and North Africa. Licinius was the second Augustus in the eastern empire with no intention of being the subordinate to Maximinus Daia, while Constantine remained in power in the northwestern section of the empire, controlling Britain and the Gauls. It was clear that the vision of Diocletian to achieve political and religious unity was in pieces. By autumn 312, Constantine had invaded Italy and was marching towards Rome at the head of his army. An attack on Maxentius was by no means an easy task, but a number of factors had weakened his position. In Africa, another military claimant to the imperial throne had appeared, and for a time the grain ships supplying Italy had been prevented from sailing. This brought a food shortage and higher taxes, which damaged the popularity of Maxentius in Rome. It had also proved to be too restrictive to have two emperors in the same city. The father-son alliance which had defeated both Severus and Galerius had been broken, and the older Maximian had to flee from his son in 310. He sought the protection of Constantine in Gaul for a time, as a private citizen who had given up all political ambitions, but when Constantine was campaigning against the Franks, Maximian made his last bid for power, and seizing Constantine's treasury, tried to use it

3. Bruce, *Spreading Flame*, 185.
4. Drake, *Constantine and the Bishops*, 122.

to buy the support of a part of the army. On Constantine's speedy return, Maximian was captured and permitted to commit suicide.

The forces of Constantine and Maxentius eventually fought a decisive battle at the Milvian Bridge over the river Tiber in Rome, and on 12 October 312, Maxentius was dead, and his part of the empire belonged to Constantine. Eusebius gives a fairly detailed account of the battle, describing how Maxentius constructed a pontoon bridge across the river which collapsed, sending himself and his troops into the water in a manner comparable to the defeat of Pharaoh's army as they attempted to pursue the Israelites through the Red Sea.[5]

> The wretch himself, then his armed attendants and guards, . . . "sank as lead in the mighty waters." So that they who thus obtained victory from God might well, if not in the same words, yet in fact in the same spirit as the people of his great servant Moses, sing and speak as they did concerning the impious tyrant of old: "Let us sing unto the Lord for he hath been glorified exceedingly: the horse and his rider he hath thrown into the sea. He is become my helper and my shield unto salvation." And again, "Who is like unto thee O Lord among the gods? Who is like thee, glorious in holiness, marvelous in praises, doing wonders?"[6]

Constantine's victory at Rome was itself significant enough for the Christians in the western part of the empire, since he was known to be sympathetic to their faith. Of far greater significance was the conviction of Constantine about the reason for his victory. Eusebius records that before his troops were engaged in the battle for Rome, Constantine had determined to seek the help of the "One Supreme God." It was while he was in prayer to this God whom, as yet he did not know, he received a vision. Eusebius is careful to cite the emperor himself as his source for the record of what occurred and to say that he personally witnessed the oath taken by Constantine to confirm the truth of the account. Reporting what he heard from Constantine, he writes,

> About noon, when the day was already beginning to decline, he saw with his own eyes the trophy of a cross of light in the heavens, above the sun, and bearing the inscription, "conquer by this." At this sight he himself was struck with amazement and

---

5. Schaff, *Nicene and Post-Nicene Fathers*, 493.
6. Schaff, *Nicene and Post-Nicene Fathers*, 493.

his whole army also, which followed him on this expedition, and witnessed the miracle. He said moreover that he doubted within himself what the import of this apparition could be. And while he continued to ponder and reason on its meaning, night suddenly came on; then in his sleep the Christ of God appeared to him with the same sign which he had seen in the heavens, and commanded him to make a likeness of that sign which he had seen in the heavens, and to use it as a safeguard in all engagements with his enemies. At dawn of day he arose and communicated the marvel to his friends: and then, calling together the workers in gold and precious stones, he sat in the midst of them and described to them the figure of the sign he had seen bidding them represent it in gold and precious stones. And this representation I myself have had an opportunity of seeing.[7]

The description given is of a golden cross surmounted by a wreath containing the first two letters of the name "Christ." From the crossbar was suspended a richly embroidered banner, and above it, a portrait of the emperor and his children. Constantine is said also to have had the same two initial letters of the name "Christ" displayed on the shields of his soldiers.

All kinds of theories have been offered to explain what happened to Constantine before his battle for Rome. They vary from the unquestioned acceptance of a God-given supernatural revelation, to the denial of any supernatural element at all. It can also be debated whether or not the faith Constantine professed was Christian in any real sense. What seems to be beyond dispute is that Constantine himself was convinced that he had been visited by God, since he entered the battle as a declared believer in the God worshipped by the Christians. The outcome of his conflict with Maxentius was in a sense a very public test of whether or not his faith was justified. It is equally clear that Constantine attributed his victory to the power of God, and the effects of his new faith were almost immediate. Persecution in the western empire was over.

Within a matter of months, Licinius and Constantine met at Milan. The occasion was the marriage of Licinius to Constantia, the half sister of Constantine. On this occasion, a joint edict was issued in January 313, by the emperors, which granted liberty to all to worship as they chose. Eusebius records the text of the edict.

---

7. Eusebius, *Life Constantine*, 490.

When I, Constantine Augustus, and I, Licinius Augustus, came under favourable auspices to Milan, and took under consideration everything that pertained to the common weal and prosperity, we resolved among other things, or rather first of all . . . to grant both to the Christians and to all men freedom to follow the religion which they choose, that whatever heavenly divinity exists may be propitious to us and to all that live under our government. We have therefore determined with sound and upright purpose that liberty is to be denied to no one to choose and to follow the religious observance of the Christians, but that to each one freedom is to be given to devote his mind to that religion which he may think adapted to himself, in order that the Deity may exhibit to us in all things his accustomed care and favour . . . now everyone who has the same desire to observe the religion of the Christians may do so without molestation. . . . Liberty is granted to others also who wish to follow their own religious observances; it being clearly in accordance with the tranquillity of our times, that each one should have the liberty of choosing and worshipping whatever deity he pleases. This has been done by us in order that we might not seem in any way to discriminate against any rank or religion.[8]

The edict was vitally important for the Christian church. It guaranteed their freedom to worship and protected new converts from abuse. It meant that the Roman state church, which had imposed a form of worship on all its subjects, was for all practical purposes a thing of the past, and there was no intention by the state to interfere in the faith or worship of the Christians The special mention of the Christian faith leaves little doubt of the favour in which it was held by Constantine; however, the document was a fairly good example of political discretion. The army was far from Christian and it was still the force on which the emperor had to depend for his authority. Many citizens of the empire remained convinced of the need to recognise the old Roman gods, therefore the edict carefully stopped short of any specific reference to the "God and Father of our Lord Jesus Christ." For many years, in fact, Constantine kept the title of "Pontifex Maximus," which he held as head of the Roman state church, and his successors used it for decades after him. Neither was there any implication that the gods worshipped by citizens who were not Christian were in fact lifeless idols, although this was certainly the Christian belief. It was also clear that while the emperor may have favoured the Christian

8. Eusebius, *Church History*, 379.

faith, he was not going to actively oppose other religions. This new state policy of toleration did not give any legal advantage to the church, but it did give equality with every other religion.

There may have been a certain degree of reluctance on the part of Licinius to be as tolerant as his brother-in-law and co-emperor, but their alliance was politically necessary, and Christians in the section of the empire over which he ruled were given, initially at least, the same liberty as those governed by Constantine. A copy of the edict of Milan was sent to the third emperor, Maximinus Daia, who saw in it evidence of a plot against his own position. Persecution to some extent continued where he reigned in the east, and eventually the tension between himself and Licinius erupted into open warfare. He invaded Asia Minor and his army moved into Europe. He appears to have survived the first phase of the war and, aware of the success of the policy of Constantine and Licinius, an edict of toleration appeared in his name in a hopeless attempt to rally the support of those he had formerly persecuted. This, however, could not prevent a final defeat by Licinius, and he died at Tarsus a few weeks later. In June 313, the day after his victory over Maximinus Daia, Licinius issued an edict granting the same terms to the Christian subjects of Maximinus as had been expressed in the Edict of Milan. The whole empire was now under the authority of two Augusti committed to the protection of the Christian church. From border to border, Christians could worship as they pleased without fear.

The two emperors, however, although establishing the same policy of toleration, were not of the same faith. Although Licinius had restored the property and recognised the funds which belonged to the church, Constantine demonstrated a genuine belief in the Christian God, while Licinius remained a pagan. It was perhaps because of this difference that the Christian subjects of Licinius tended to look to Constantine as their "Christian" emperor, although Licinius was their legitimate ruler. The alliance between the two emperors was under pressure and did not last. The difference in the approach of Constantine and Licinius towards the Edict of Milan was the difference between enthusiasm and reluctance. Licinius maintained pagan worship and tended to weed out Christians in the court and the army, suspecting them of loyalty to Constantine. He remained convinced that the key to political power was the favour of the gods, and therefore subjects who prayed to the Christian God on behalf of a rival emperor were a threat. Persecution on a minor scale began to take place, and when Constantine, in a campaign against the Goths in 324, moved an army into the territory of Licinius, he called it invasion and went to war. The first battle was won by Constantine at Adrianople and the second at Byzantium. Licinius escaped but surrendered at Nicomedia and as a continuing threat, was executed by Constantine in the spring of 325.

Many Christians interpreted these events as unassailable evidence that the emperor Constantine was the gift of God to his church. The empire was at peace and under the control of a Christian monarch There was nothing to prevent the unhindered expansion of the church of Christ throughout the world. Days of persecution were over. The need for martyrdom was gone. By the power of God, the church had triumphed over every enemy, and there was nothing on the horizon except greater glory.

5

The Thirteenth Apostle

I myself, then, was the instrument He chose, and esteemed suited for the
accomplishment of his will. Accordingly, beginning at the remote Brittanic
ocean, and the regions where, according to the law of nature, the sun sinks
beneath the horizon, through the aid of divine power I banished and utterly
removed every form of evil which prevailed, in the hope that the human race,
enlightened through my instrumentality, might be called to a due observance
of the holy laws of God, and at the same time our most blessed faith might
prosper under the guidance of his almighty hand.[1]

CONSTANTINE RULED AS SOLE emperor from 324 until 337, and during these thirteen years it is beyond doubt that many aspects of Roman society improved socially, morally, and spiritually. For the first time
in its short history, the Christian church was the object of state approval
and the effect was virtually immediate.

Sunday became a public holiday to mark the day of the resurrection. Christian places of worship began to multiply. Within a short space
of time there were more than forty in the city of Rome, and many of
them could only be described as magnificent. The design was based
on the traditional Roman basilica, and since in many cases they were
financed by the generosity of the imperial family and dedicated to the
Christian apostles, their decoration and adornment was to the highest
standard that could be achieved. The same pattern was followed in other

1. Eusebius, *Life of Constantine*, 507.

leading cities of the empire, like Jerusalem, and later in the new capital of Constantinople,[2] where the emperor prepared his own tomb. Money flooded into the ecclesiastical coffers and grants of land were made to the officers of the church. Copies of Scripture were financed. The clergy were excused from public duties, and labour and materials for the construction of church buildings were supplied from provincial resources. Property or funds which had been taken from Christians were restored. Christian prisoners were released and exiles came home.

In public life, it became clear that to be a Christian brought great advantages. In the eastern part of the empire, now under Constantine's control, where Christians were more numerous than in the west, provincial governors who were Christian were preferred, and where a governor maintained the traditional Roman religion he could only practice it in private, since public sacrifices were forbidden to civic leaders.[3] The effect of this kind of legislation was to divorce government office from what had been the official state religion. The practice of slavery continued, but Jewish masters were forbidden to own Christian slaves, and those found to be ignoring this ruling were fined and their slaves liberated. When estates were sold or divided, the families of slaves were not to be separated.

There was a change also in the means of punishing convicted criminals. Crucifixion was abolished. Branding on the face was prohibited. The period of time between arrest and trial was reduced. Regulations were applied to ensure that prisoners had sufficient light and air, and where possible, chains were removed. The custom of exposing unwanted children did not become illegal immediately, but the emperor did introduce a type of family allowance to help the poorest families provide for all their children. By this means, the death rate of unwanted children was greatly reduced. There was a new approach to the care of the most vulnerable members of society in general.

One of the major changes was in the way the bishops of the church were viewed by the emperor. They became his advisors and instructors. They also gained a new legal status. A bishop could release slaves on his deathbed without written documentation. Slaves belonging to other Christians could be lawfully emancipated in the presence of the bishop or congregation. Church courts were permitted to rule on civil matters, and the judgement of a bishop became acceptable for civil authorities.

2. Daniélou and Marrou, *Christian Centuries*, Vol I., 236.
3. Huttman, *Establishment of Christianity*, 72.

Inevitably there were many who crowded into the Christian church and who sought appointment to its ministry who had a very superficial conviction about the truth of the gospel. There was a noticeable increase in numbers of those seeking ordination which could not be separated from the tax benefits of their office. Legislation had to be devised to prevent wealthier citizens from entering the ranks of the clergy and steps were taken to curb the habit of appointing several clergymen to replace one who had died.[4] The highest honours in Roman society were now open to the officers of the church, and it was not unknown for bishops to be appointed for their political, legal, or administrative skills rather than a pastoral concern for the flock of Christ. The church historian Eusebius spoke in glowing terms of Constantine being appointed by God himself to bless the church and bring the knowledge of Christ to the whole world. The reality, however, was that the faith of Constantine was not at all easy to assess in simple Christian terms.

At one extreme there are historians like the nineteenth-century Jacob Burckhardt, who considered the continued support of Constantine for pagan rites, his recognition of officials, his continued headship of Roman religion as pontifex maximus, and his postponement of baptism almost until his deathbed as evidence that the emperor was nothing more than a power-hungry dictator who had enough political skill to see that the church, which possessed an organisation second to none and was spread throughout the empire, should be enrolled as an ally and not confronted as an enemy. Burckhardt wrote,

> Attempts have often been made to penetrate into the religious consciousness of Constantine and to construct a hypothetical picture of changes in his religious convictions. Such efforts are futile. In a genius driven without surcease by ambition and lust for power there can be no question of Christianity and paganism, of conscious religiosity or irreligiosity; such a man is essentially unreligious, even if he pictures himself standing in the midst of a churchly community.[5]

Eusebius, as a contemporary church historian, took a different view and presents a picture of Constantine as the God-appointed deliverer of the church. His account of the life of Constantine ends with the following words:

4. Westbury-Jones, *Roman and Christian Imperialism*, 206.
5. Burckhardt, *Age of Constantine the Great*, 262.

> Standing as he did alone and pre-eminent among the Roman emperors as a worshipper of God; alone as the bold proclaimer to all men of the doctrine of Christ; having alone rendered honour as none before him had ever done, to his church; having alone abolished utterly the error of polytheism, and discountenanced idolatry in every form: so, alone among them both during life and after death, was he accounted worthy of such honours as none can say have been attained to by any other; so that no one, whether Greek or Barbarian, nay, of the ancient Romans themselves, has ever been presented to us as worthy of comparison with him.[6]

It is not impossible that both versions of the emperor have some truth in them. There is nothing at all surprising in finding new converts to the Christian faith whose view of the doctrines and practices they must adopt is seen, initially at least, through unsanctified eyes. When Constantine came to power, Roman religion headed by the emperor had already begun to move in the direction of monotheism. Keresztes writes that when Constantine set out to capture Rome, he had already considered the example of his father, who had begun to pray to the one true god and was himself convinced that divine help was necessary if he was to be victorious in the forthcoming battle. The famous vision of the cross in the sky, the command "By this conquer," and the appearance of Christ in a dream were, he believed, given in response to his own prayer.[7] Theologians and historians have argued over the origin and reality of the experience, but it is generally accepted that Constantine himself believed it was from heaven. His troops certainly marched into battle under the sign of the cross before any victory was assured, and Constantine and the whole Christian world attributed his subsequent military success to the favour of Christ. There was much in the reign of Constantine as a professedly Christian monarch which gave cause for concern, but it need not be explained in terms of his deliberate hypocrisy.

That the emperor's search for God was not motivated by the need to save his soul should not surprise us. It was not Constantine's first priority. He was a military emperor and what he needed was divine power to enable him to conquer and rule. The first impression made upon his mind by the Christian faith was not written on a blank page. When he committed his future to the God and Father of the Lord Jesus Christ he already

6. Eusebius, *Life of Constantine*, 559.
7. Keresztes, *Constantine*, 16.

had a fairly firm idea of the role he expected to play. He was convinced that the revelation he received had not been given to a humble seeker of truth who just happened to be monarch of the Roman Empire. Christ had appeared to him precisely because he held imperial power and authority. Even if, as Eusebius claims, Constantine did seek the guidance of Christian teachers and devote himself to the study of Scripture,[8] he did so as "Pontifex Maximus." He was the bridge between God and the people, responsible for the maintenance of divine favour towards the state. The only assurance he had that the welfare and prosperity of the empire could be made secure was based on the assumption that the one true God, whom he had recently discovered, should receive the worship required from his subjects. In the mind of an emperor of Rome there could be no division between religious and political activity. Fortunes of war, natural disasters, economic changes had all been the results of the relationship between Rome and her gods. Now that the emperor was convinced of the error and folly of polytheism, the one true God must take the place of the former pagan deities, but the outworking of the relationship was largely unaltered in the mind of Constantine. The New Testament picture of a church completely separate from any state machinery or state control had no place in the religious thought of the Roman world of the day, and there is abundant evidence that Constantine never ever considered such a church, even after his conversion. The church was part of his empire, and he saw it as his divinely appointed mission to promote the spread of the truth to the farthest boundaries. Roman emperors had been traditionally responsible for maintaining the "pax deorum," the peace of the gods. As emperor, Constantine expected not simply to participate in the affairs of the church but to supervise them. This might have been anathema to the apostolic community of the first century, fighting for survival against persecution, but to the millions of Roman citizens now flooding into the church, there was nothing unacceptable about it. The great majority of them expected nothing less from a Christian emperor.

An early indication of the religious policy Constantine intended to adopt was given when he was still allied to Licinius his co-Augustus. When they met in Milan to celebrate the marriage of Licinius to the half sister of Constantine, a joint edict was issued early in 313. This so-called "Edict of Milan" is important in that it is probably one of earliest legally enforceable policies of religious toleration. It did not make the empire

---

8. Eusebius, *Life of Constantine*, 491.

Christian to the exclusion of all other religions, but it did mean the end of the Roman state church and priesthood. From Milan onwards, citizenship did not carry with it the obligation to fulfill any specific religious worship under threat of punishment. While Christians are the only religious community mentioned by name in the edict, and the right to convert to the Christian faith is asserted unambiguously, the edict makes it equally clear that the new conditions are for the benefit of all men. The two emperors declare:

> It ought to be granted to the judgement and desire of each individual to perform his religious duties according to his own choice . . . liberty is to be denied to no one . . . to each one freedom is to be given to devote his mind to that religion which he may think adapted to himself. . . . Liberty is granted to others also who may wish to follow their own religious observances; it being clearly in accordance with the tranquillity of our times, that each one should have liberty of choosing and worshiping whatever deity he pleases. This has been done by us in order that we might not seem in any way to discriminate against any rank or religion.[9]

The enthusiasm of Licinius for the policy is not as certain as it might be, but Constantine was the driving force. His motives are plainly stated: "That whatever heavenly divinity exists, may be propitious to us and to all that live under our government," and the earthly reflection of that divine favour that would follow "the tranquillity of our times." The edict gave the Christians all the freedom they could wish for as a minority in the empire, but it took some time before they realised the importance of state toleration for those Romans who remained worshippers of the old gods. In fact the day would come when Constantine had to remind Christians who sought revenge on former persecutors, or who were aggressive in their zeal to gain converts, that God had used him, as emperor, to punish persecutors. His reminder also sent out a signal that he intended to police Christian aggression against the worshippers of rival gods.[10]

The policy of toleration was not in fact something that Constantine had suddenly adopted upon conversion. Very shortly after joining his father Constantius in Britain, his father died, and Constantine was proclaimed emperor by his army at York in 306. It was about this time,

9. Eusebius, *Church History*, 379.

10. Digeser, *Making of a Christian Empire*, 137.

the Christian theologian called Lactantius was writing the Divine Institutes, which were an attempt to persuade his contemporaries by rational
and philosophical argument that Christians worshipped the one true
God and that the polytheism of the official Roman religion was illogi-
cal. Lactantius argued that the Christian faith, far from being a threat to
the empire, was in line with all that was best in Roman history, culture,
and philosophy. He taught that God's law, natural law, and Roman law
had a common basis. Lactantius tended to see his fellow citizens not as
pagan enemies of the gospel but as potential Christians on the road to a
true faith.[11] One of the principles dealt with at some length in the Divine
Institutes is that the practice of religion imposed by force is worthless. In
chapter 54, entitled "Of the Freedom of Religion in the Worship of God,"
he writes,

> Who will hear when men of furious and unbridled spirit think
> that their authority is diminished if there is any freedom in the
> affairs of men? But it is religion alone in which freedom has
> placed its dwelling. For it is a matter which is voluntary above all
> others, nor can necessity be imposed upon any, so as to worship
> that which he does not wish to worship.[12]

Before his conversion to Christ, Lactantius had been appointed by the
emperor Diocletian as a teacher of Latin Rhetoric at Nicomedia. His
newly found Christian faith compelled him to resign when persecution
began in 303, but when Constantine came to power, the new emperor
saw in Lactantius a teacher whose learning and ability attracted his admiration. This led to the appointment of Lactantius as tutor to Constantine's
son, and by 310 he was installed at the imperial court at Trier. From this
time onwards, the correspondence of Constantine shows a familiarity
with the Divine Institutes, sometimes using the phrases of Lactantius to
express the same arguments.[13] The policy of toleration was one to which
the emperor held throughout his reign. For all the favour and encouragement given to the Christians and the witness of Constantine that he
was one of their number, his new understanding of a right relationship
between the Christian church and the state would not allow him to turn
the church into a Christian version of Roman state religion. He continue
to express his conviction that genuine piety was the result of an inward

11. Ibid., 142.
12. Lactantius, *Epitome of the Divine Institutes*, 44.
13. Digeser, *Making of a Christian Empire*, 135.

spiritual relationship to God and could not be created by coerced acts of outward ceremony. The punishment of those who would not obey the gospel must be left to God alone and the only force exerted by Christians on their fellow citizens must be the moral force of verbal persuasion. Constantine was virtually obsessed with the need for unity in the empire but believed that a policy of tolerance and forbearance would unify more of his subjects under the Christian banner than any other means.

The church, however, which Constantine took under his wing was far from pure and not itself free from division. About the end of the first decade of the fourth century, a council of nineteen bishops took place at Elvira in Spain. The rules for Christian behaviour enacted by the council show that church discipline was an ongoing problem. Christians who were absent from worship on three consecutive Sundays were excommunicated, while those who lapsed for longer periods could be treated as apostates and only readmitted after ten years' penance. Some prominent Christian citizens had accepted appointment as magistrates and even some as pagan priests. There were clergy who tolerated their wives' adulterous behaviour and others who combined ecclesiastical duties with money lending. There were some who lived with women to whom they were related neither by marriage nor blood. There were others who neglected the church because of their business interests. Christian women who beat their slave girls to death would be excommunicated for seven years if the death was intentional, five if it was not. Rich Christian women were providing robes for their pagan neighbours to wear on the occasions of pagan worship.[14] The church in Constantine's reign was clearly a mixed multitude, and it was in fact a major issue of discipline which brought the emperor to exercise imperial authority over a divided Christian community.

A problem which dogged the church for generations was concerned with the validity of the ministry practiced by clergy who had compromised in some way during a period of persecution. In 312, Caecilian, a deacon in Carthage, was ordained as bishop of that city, thereby making him one of the major figures in the African church. This posed a problem for some of his fellow bishops, since he was a man under suspicion. During the "Great Persecution," Caecilian, then an archdeacon, and his bishop Mensurius, had followed a policy of keeping their heads below the parapet. Caecilian actively discouraged would-be martyrs by picketing

14. Chadwick, *Church in Ancient Society*, 182.

the prison in Carthage to prevent food supplies reaching imprisoned Christians, who were in his judgement far too ready to defy the authorities.[15] When Mensurius died, Caecilian became bishop in his place. The ordination was rather hurried because opposition was expected. The bishops of Numidia, many of whom were not present at the event, were largely supportive of the martyrs and opposed to any kind of compromise with Roman government. Bishop Felix of Apthugni, who ordained Caecilian, however, was one of those accused of having surrendered copies of the Scriptures to the persecutors of the church during the reign of Diocletian. Since the African church had some difficulty in controlling an excessive zeal for martyrdom rather than compromise, the surrender of Scriptures was seen by many as the kind of disloyalty which would invalidate any future ministry by the compromiser. By this standard, the ordination of Caecilian, who had himself a tarnished reputation, at the hands of a man like Felix was therefore invalid and without legitimate authority. The fact that Caecilian was supported by the bishop of Rome only added to the opposition, since bishop Marcellinus of Rome was himself accused of compromising in a similar way.

Those who objected to Caecilian were powerful enough to depose him and to appoint Majorinus in his place as bishop of Carthage. They then took the significant step of sending a report to Constantine and petitioned for his confirmation of their action. This appeal might appear surprising to Christians of the present age since it was addressed to the emperor, not as a Christian leader but as the political head of state, and sought the authority of a non-Christian government to enforce what they believed to be a matter of Christian discipline. There were however social and financial factors behind the request. Church property confiscated during the recent persecution was being restored. State funds were reaching the African churches, and it was important that the Numidian bishops and their supporters should not exclude themselves from imperial favour.

The great desire for unity and Constantine's perception of the church as a major influence in sustaining it meant that he took seriously any signs of division in that body. Advised by bishop Ossius of Corduba about the political ramifications of a split in the church, the emperor arranged a council. Although Constantine was not himself present, he appointed Miltiades, current bishop of Rome, and three other bishops from Gaul

15. Ibid., 184.

to judge the matter. The appointment of the Gallic bishops was deliberate because there had been no official persecution in Gaul as there had been in Africa, and their views would be less prejudiced. Caecilian and ten supporting bishops, attended together with ten bishops from the opposition group, then called Donatists after the charismatic and energetic leader, Donatus, who had succeeded Majorinus at Carthage. The Donatists expected to be involved in arbitration, but Miltiades, who had no intention of leaving the outcome either to chance or providence, drafted in another fifteen Italian bishops whom he chose personally. Furthermore he conducted the proceedings in strict accordance with Roman civil law.[16] The Donatists, expecting ecclesiastical arbitration, found themselves the defendants in a court case and walked out. Caecilian was the winner by default, and the Donatists appealed to Constantine for justice.

The emperor, in an attempt to defuse the situation, agreed, and ignoring the verdict which had been reached at Rome, called a new council of bishops from all his provinces. This was held at Arles in Gaul in August 314, and significantly neither Ossius nor Miltiades were present. The importance of this council was threefold. It was the first church council in the western empire. It was called not by any leaders of the church but by the head of state, and it simply overruled the previous decision. The result, however, confirmed the legitimacy of Caecilian's ordination and ministry, upholding the Roman verdict, so the Donatists played their last card. They appealed to Constantine for an imperial judgement. He again accepted their plea, dismissed the Council of Arles, and brought Caecilian and his accusers to appear in person before him at his court. The process took about a year, but in the meantime it was discovered that one of the documents incriminating Caecilian was a forgery. The imperial patience was at an end. The victorious Caecilian and the disappointed Donatists returned to Africa.

It is sometimes pointed out that it was the schismatics who appealed to the head of state to overrule a decision of the church,[17] but their view of Constantine's role in church affairs was not so different from that of their opponents. It was accepted by both sides in the dispute that the emperor could call and dismiss church councils as he chose. Predictably, the conflict did not end with the decision of Constantine. Upon the return of the disputants to Africa there were riots, and separate Donatist churches

16. Drake, *Constantine and the Bishops*, 218.
17. Keresztes, *Constantine*, 61.

led by rival bishops continued to multiply until the number of Donatist bishops rose to perhaps two hundred and seventy[18] It is not hard to see that there were other serious theological issues hanging on the Donatist hook. What was the essential nature of the church? Was it to be limited to those whose faith and piety had been tested and proved in the furnace of affliction, or was it to be, as Constantine wished, a church for the masses of the empire? The question of the failure of the church's ministers in a time of trial also raised the issue of what made their ministry valid or invalid. If an unworthy bishop administered baptism or ordination to a candidate, should the ceremony be repeated at the hands of one whose faithfulness was beyond reproach? These questions were not solved overnight, but Constantine had made his decision. In his eyes, the supporters of Caecilian represented the view of the catholic church. The Donatists were labelled as dangerous schismatics. Their growth was a severe test of the emperor's policy of tolerance for all, and in fact for a brief period there were attempts to force the Donatists to abandon their separate existence. However, in May 321, Constantine decided they should be left to the judgement of God. After Constantine's death they suffered periods of repression and revival, even becoming for a short time the majority group in the African church. Donatus himself died in exile about 355, but the churches which were identified by his name lasted until the seventh century. In 324, the new capital city of Constantinople was founded. This was to be Constantine's "New Rome." The old city of Rome was the centre of the empire's pagan origins, but the new city was a creation inspired by a vision of Christ[19] There was a new Senate which included a number of prominent Christians. The greatest difference to the church was that a new centre of authority in the east had been established. While respect was given to the Roman bishop, the transference of the imperial court to Constantinople reflected on the city as a new centre of ecclesiastical power. Coins of the period bore the image of the new Rome and the old Rome sharing a throne.[20]

If Constantine hoped to find the church at peace in the east he was to be sorely disappointed. He found himself embroiled in a dispute which concerned not only the discipline of the church but the heart of the Christian faith itself, namely, the person of Christ and the nature of

18. Latourette, *History of Christianity*, 139.
19. Chadwick, *Church in Ancient Society*, 188.
20. Ibid., 189.

his relationship to the God the Father. In the early years of the fourth century, the spiritual leadership of the eastern churches was in the city of Alexandria in Egypt, where Alexander was bishop. One of Alexander's presbyters, Arius, was expressing the view that if the terms "Father" and "Son" were meaningful at all they carried the implication that the Father must have existed before the Son, and therefore the Son was created out of nothing and not eternal like the Father. Alexander, opposed to anything that might seem to undermine the deity of Christ, condemned these views, and his dispute with Arius became serious enough to lead to the presbyter's excommunication. The disciplinary action of Alexander was supported by Sylvester the bishop of Rome, but Arius also had a powerful ally in bishop Eusebius of Nicomedia, who was not only close to the imperial palace in a geographical sense but was related to Constantine and had the privilege of being the first bishop to serve him as an ambassador. Other bishops were gathering on either side of the theological divide and the unity of the church was under threat.

Bishop Ossius of Corduba, whose advice Constantine had sought in the Donatist schism, had moved east with the emperor and was now sent to preside over a council at Antioch in 325 to settle the matter. The bishops at Antioch produced a statement in strong condemnation of Arius, although a few supported him, including Eusebius of Caesarea, who was provisionally excommunicated for his support of such a heresy. The excommunication and ongoing dispute were to be reconsidered at a synod due to be held at Ancyra later in the year, but Constantine, knowing that bishop Marcellus of Ancyra was a fierce opponent of Arius, and anxious to avoid further division, changed the location to Nicea because it was closer to the western bishops and his palace there gave him opportunity to personally supervise the proceedings.

The council opened in June 325. Constantine made a dramatic entrance and a speech which, if theologically vague, left no doubt about what he wanted the outcome to be. He condemned dissention as the work of Satan and urged peaceful agreement as the only thing pleasing to God.[21] Eusebius of Caesarea offered his own baptismal creed to the council, and since it had the approval of Constantine, he was reinstated as bishop, and the emperor urged everyone to agree that his creed represented the faith of the church. A crucial term which appeared in the creedal statement was the word homoousios. It signified that Christ was

21. Drake, *Constantine and the Bishops*, 254.

"of one substance" with the Father, and its inclusion was almost certainly arranged by a number of the opponents of Arius before the council took place. This was confirmed at the insistence of Constantine and the advantage of using this term was that it was not free from ambiguity. The motive for its use was not that it was the most accurate expression of the truth but that its lack of precision might attract the greatest measure of support. The emperor had, in fact, written to Alexander and Arius informing them in clear terms that agreement was required and the creed did in fact gain the support of the great majority of bishops. Whatever reservations they might have had were set aside and all but two signed it. The two dissenters were exiled by Constantine, who would tolerate no threats to the unity of church and empire. Pressure to conform was such that in time even Arius himself signed the creed, and Athanasius, who succeeded Alexander to the see of Alexandria in 328, was required to receive Arius back into the communion of the church. He refused, and a few years later Arius appealed to the emperor for reinstatement. In time, an arrangement was made for Arius to be received back into communion by the bishop of Constantinople, but he died before his return to the fold could take place.

The council of Nicea became known as an ecumenical council and its findings were certainly assumed to be authoritative for the whole Christian church, worldwide. The source of that authority was, however, to become a matter of debate. Three explanations were offered. Some of the Greeks believed it was the imperial presence which gave authority to Nicea. Other bishops held it to be the attendance of councillors from every part of the empire which bound churches to obedience. Some others from the western churches claimed it to be the ratification by the bishop of Rome, which gave final authority to the Nicene decisions.[22] Whatever might have been the correct theological foundation for the Council of Nicea, in practical terms the strongest factor in bringing about the required agreement was the determination of Constantine. Defiance of the emperor was simply not an option, as those who attempted it found to their cost.

In May 337, Constantine became unwell and moved to his palace in Nicomedia. He became a catechumen, was baptised by Eusebius of Nicomedia, and died the same month. Although for his baptism the emperor had set aside his imperial robes, his funeral was a state occasion arranged

22. Chadwick, *Church in Ancient Society*, 205.

by the army which had raised him to imperial rank in earlier days. The procedure was dominated by senior army officers, and bishops were only permitted to be present after the pagan ceremony of consecration had taken place to signify that the emperor had become a god.[23] Although it was beyond doubt that Constantine had died as a professing Christian, his church was not yet the church of the Roman state. Even the design of the mausoleum which was prepared for him was capable of more than one interpretation. The imperial remains were in the middle sarcophagus in a row of thirteen, each of the six on either side being dedicated to one of the twelve apostles. The symbolism was clear to the Christian church. Constantine had referred to himself as a bishop appointed by God for those who were outside the church, and in the following century hymns were written which hailed him as equal to the apostles. Those of his subjects who were not Christian might, however, have interpreted the symbolism in a different way. Previous emperors had been buried in the midst of statues representing the twelve gods of Olympus, and in coins imprinted with the image of Constantine rising to heaven, he is riding a chariot drawn by four horses, which was an image traditionally associated with the worship of the sun god.

The life and witness of Constantine had enough integrity to convince his Christian subjects that his faith was real but he also possessed enough political skill to convince those who remained outside the church that he had not abandoned the traditions and values of the Roman empire. His reasons for turning to the God and Father of the Lord Jesus Christ were certainly not those of the first disciples who heard the call to repentance and faith by the shores of Galilee, but it was impossible for Constantine, on a human level, to think of any kind of relationship with God which would not be reflected in the political, economic, and military success of the Roman Empire. He ruled both church and state as aspects of the same divinely appointed mission and when he died he left a church where the major decisions affecting the life of that body were taken by a ruler who had not even yet been baptised into the body of Christ. As emperor, Constantine appointed, deposed, exiled, and restored the church's leaders. He decided matters of discipline and doctrine even when he did not have a clear understanding of the issues involved. He might indeed have been sincere in trying to solve problems which were specifically Christian, but he did so with the mind and heart of a traditional Roman emperor. The

23. Ibid., 211.

result was that a pattern was set in the relationship between church and state which has never fully disappeared, even up to the present day. It was not a marriage made in heaven and it produced centuries of struggle for the control of what came to be called Christendom.

The death of Constantine left a number of possible heirs to his throne, but the army effectively established the claims of his three sons by the assassination of their rivals. Constantine II ruled the western empire. Constans controlled Italy and Africa, while the third son, Constantius II, was emperor in the East. Each one professed to be Christian but shared their father's view that church and state were best ruled by a single monarch. Over the following decades a complex power struggle took place in which political and religious rivalries became inextricably linked. Emperors used the missionary activities of the church to extend the rule of the state so that to accept the Christian faith was to accept the rule of the emperor also. They allied themselves with bishops whose supporters would confirm their political and military base, and the bishops eagerly gave political support to whichever emperor would enforce their own doctrinal position or ecclesiastical authority.

The tension between eastern and western churches grew worse with genuine doctrinal differences being complicated and obscured because of the alignment and realignment of groups of bishops with one leader then another, while conflict among the emperors led, in August 353, to the triumph of Constantius as the sole surviving son of Constantine.

At this period, the most influential theologian in the eastern church was Athanasius, bishop of Alexandria. Constantius, however, believed him to be disloyal, and the hostility between the emperor and the bishop was lifelong. Athanasius, who was a powerful figure by any standards and as politically astute as any churchman of his day, was the recognised champion of Nicene orthodoxy. He held strictly to the Nicene Creed and the "homoousios" formula, expressing the nature of Christ, and tended to lump together all opposition to himself under the heading of "Arianism." He had already demonstrated his readiness to resist the emperor when he had refused to receive Arius back into the church in defiance of an imperial command, and now Constantius saw him as a continuing threat because, among other factors, he had a considerable number of supporters among the bishops of the Latin west, as well as his many followers in the Greek church of the east.

Constantius continually sought to base the security of the empire on ecclesiastical and political unity in church and state, but conflict was inevitable. Church councils could not agree on doctrinal formulae. Supporters of rival claimants to the papal office fought each other in the streets of Rome. Eastern and western bishops struggled for supremacy. A creed produced at the council of Constantinople in 359, and forced on the delegates by the emperor, disintegrated on his death in November 361. Julian, who followed Constantius as emperor in the west, abandoned any profession of the Christian faith and did all he could to restore and promote the traditional state religion of pagan Rome. A small number of bishops attempted to combine pagan and Christian worship, but in general the church stood firm, and when Julian was succeeded by Jovian, the political skill and personal authority of Athanasius helped to restore past losses and even to achieve a measure of freedom from imperial control. The basic problems, however, which divided the church were as troublesome as ever. Then an event which took place in 370 resulted in the bishop of Rome establishing his claim to leadership of the western church.

In 366, Pope Liberius had died. His two rival successors, Ursinus and Damasus, had groups of supporters which fought a three-day pitched battle in the streets in which 137 combatants were killed.[24] Damasus was eventually successful in his claim, but in 370 he had to face the accusation of being responsible for the crime of murder. The charge was brought by a Jewish Christian but was unsuccessful. However, Damasus had learned a lesson from the experience. At a synod held in Rome in 378 there were three matters high on the agenda. First, the acquittal of Damasus was formally recognised and registered. Second, since the emperor Valentinian had died in November 375 and his son Gratian ruled in his place, it was to this young man that Damasus appealed for a decision that in future any charge against the bishop of Rome should be dealt with either by the emperor himself or by a council of bishops, but not by the civil court. Third, he asked that the bishop of Rome be recognised to have authority over other bishops and represent the superior before whom accused bishops should be brought and to whom they should appeal. This plea for imperial confirmation of papal authority was based on the belief that such authority descended from the Apostle Peter himself through episcopal succession. Gratian gave general agreement to these requests

24. Chadwick, *Church in Ancient Society*, 315.

but assumed that the existing canon laws dealt with the matter. In fact, they were interpreted differently by the eastern and western church. The Greek version of church law was not clear about Roman supremacy over the worldwide church, but the Latin version was amended to make it plain, and Damasus began to take steps to reinforce this interpretation.

Latin, which was the language of the majority of Romans, became standard for worship. He sought the suppression of other religions like the Manichees, and those Christians he considered to be heretical were dealt with by violence. He tried to get the emperor to remove bishops who did not hold to the Nicene Creed and claimed it had universal authority because it had been ratified by Pope Sylvester at the Council of Nicea. The implication of this was, of course, that Sylvester, as bishop of Rome, possessed the authority to give such ratification. Damasus now began to use Roman records to confirm papal power and argued that the orthodoxy of other churches could be tested by their communion with Rome. It is hardly surprising that this view was unacceptable in the east. While theologically orthodox himself, Damasus, for a time, supported the ministry of a man like Maximus, a bishop of Constantinople whose ordination was considered invalid by a large number of his fellow bishops. At this same period, there was a small but troublesome congregation at Antioch led by a presbyter called Paulinus, later to be consecrated as bishop. This group was separated from the other Antiochene Christians by their extreme view of the unity of the Father and the Son as a single "hypostasis," but enjoyed the support of Damasus and the west. Tension between east and west, however, was to be affected by military and political events more than current theological divisions.

The eastern emperor Valens, in attempting to resist the growing military power of the Goths, had been defeated and killed in battle in August 378. Such a victory for barbarian forces sent a shockwave throughout the Roman empire, and the western emperor Gratian hurriedly sent for Theodosius, a trusted and experienced soldier from Spain, to reorganise and encourage the defeated Roman army. In 381, Theodosius was proclaimed the new emperor in the east and came to exercise a greater imperial influence over the church than any ruler since Constantine.

6

The Gospel Is Law

Those persons who follow this rule shall embrace the name of Catholic Christians. The rest however whom We adjudge demented and insane, shall sustain the infamy of heretical dogmas, their meeting places shall not receive the name of churches, and they shall be smitten first by divine vengeance and secondly by the retribution of Our own initiative, which We shall assume in accordance with the divine judgement.[1]

WHEN THEODOSIUS SUCCEEDED VALENS as ruler of the eastern empire, changes were inevitable. Although he was emperor in the east, he was a Spaniard and had, therefore, been nourished on western traditions and culture. He was also, unlike Valens, completely convinced that the faith of Nicea was the only genuine expression of Christian truth. In military and political activity Theodosius showed a pragmatic willingness to compromise and negotiate. He accepted huge numbers of men into military service who had previously been disqualified because they were not sufficiently "Roman." He allocated land to Gothic invaders within the boundaries of the empire when it became clear they could not be kept out. Later in his reign he was able by skilled negotiation to achieve a fairly long period of peace with the traditional Persian enemies. It was in the matter of Christian doctrine that the emperor was inflexible and Theodosius, unlike his predecessor, was more than willing to become involved in the affairs of the church. In February 380, he issued

1. Pharr, *Theodosian Code*, 440.

an imperial decree which was to be binding on all his subjects. Orthodoxy was defined in terms of the Nicene formula, and those who rejected the Christian faith virtually set themselves outside of the empire and its citizenship. The following year he called a council at Constantinople, in May 381, which would provide ecclesiastical confirmation of the imperial decree. In the sixty-eight years since Constantine and Licinius issued the decree of Milan, the policy of the Roman empire had changed from freedom of worship for all, to the enforcement of the Christian faith on every citizen, whether those citizens believed it or not. It need not be assumed that the determination of Theodosius to achieve religious uniformity was simply his understanding of the powerful support this would provide for the political unity of the empire. The emperor genuinely believed he was responsible to God to do all in his power to ensure the appropriate worship and the personal salvation of his subjects, and personal salvation was a matter about which Theodosius was in deadly earnest. In many ways Theodosius, because of his energetic search for unity in the church, was far from unwelcome to western churchmen. He encouraged church councils and sought answers to problems which commanded a broad measure of agreement. At the same time, he was prepared to purify the empire from everything he believed was unacceptable to God. He held that the Christian faith was a God-given revelation and that his duty as God's servant was to impose that faith on his subjects. He was prepared to execute some followers of a rival religion like the Manicheans and was just as severe on heretics. He used informers and inquisitors in church affairs. The choice for not a few of his subjects was a profession of the Christian faith or the death penalty, but within a decade the sincerity of the emperor's own faith was to be tested to the uttermost.

The religious zeal of the emperor created space for the church to increase in political power, and Ambrose, the current bishop of Milan, was not a man to waste what he saw as a God-given opportunity. The bishop Ambrose was the son of a prefect of Gaul. He grew up in Rome surrounded by clergy and under the guidance of a pious mother and an elder sister, Marcellina, who became a nun. Clearly a gifted administrator, he entered the civil service and became the governor of Liguria in 370, based in Milan. In 374, Auxentius, the bishop of Milan, died and left two candidates to compete for the post. Rival groups of supporters threatened to riot, and Ambrose, as civil governor, was called in to establish the peace. However, his standing in the whole community led to a popular demand that he should himself be elected as the new bishop. Although not even baptised at the time, he was consecrated to the office within eight days, and in time became one of the most powerful men in the church. His influence over the emperor Theodosius was almost without limit, and Ambrose would not give an inch to anything that was not the orthodox Christian faith.

A measure of the power Ambrose had over the emperor Theodosius can be gauged by his readiness to publicly discipline and humiliate him if he believed it necessary. In 390, in the city of Salonica, a star charioteer was arrested for homosexual rape. His fans rioted in protest, murdering the commander of the city and a number of other officers. To punish such a violent disturbance, Theodosius, on a day when the hippodrome was packed with spectators, dispatched his troops, and seven thousand citizens died in the slaughter. Since the troops were Gothic soldiers, the massacre was depicted as a pagan attack on Roman Christians. Ambrose wrote a letter to the emperor which, although written in courteous and respectful terms, gripped him as if in a vice. Ambrose offered him the stark choice of repentance or excommunication from the church.

> Ambrose had a shrewd psychological knowledge of Theodosius and his performance was subtle and masterly. . . . Theodosius was tormented not just by moral guilt but by a very real fear of eternal damnation. Thus it was that an astonished people beheld an extraordinary spectacle as the Ever-Victorious, Sacred Eternal Augustus, Lord of the World put aside his gorgeous imperial regalia, and for several months wept and groaned as a humble prostrate penitent in the Cathedral of Milan. It was all the more extraordinary in its stark public contrast between the despotic and universal power of the emperor and the grovelling abasement of that same power before the priests.[2]

The relationship between church and empire had changed a great deal since the conversion of Constantine. Constantine was ruler of an empire of which the church was only one part, and like all the other parts it was subject to imperial authority. Ambrose, however, saw Theodosius as a member of the church and therefore subject to the authority of its bishops. This was a major modification in the way the church viewed the empire, and it was another significant step along the road to what the medieval church would become. Constantine sought to bring his citizens to

2. Williams and Friell, *Theodosius*, 122.

believe the gospel by persuasion, being convinced that genuine converts could be gained in no other way. Theodosius, as a faithful servant of God, intended to impose the gospel on the empire, and those who did not obey its demands must suffer the consequences. The result was a united church in a united empire, but the unity rested on a foundation that was weak militarily, politically, and spiritually.

In 393, Theodosius raised his sons, Honorius and Arcadius, to imperial rank, but when he died in 395 at the age of forty-eight, the real power behind the throne was in the hands of Stilicho, a Vandal army officer and the emperor's adoptive son-in-law. Conflicts military, political, and religious in both east and west continued to make genuine unity a vision that could not be realised, and as the empire began to show signs of disintegration, especially in the west, one of the main factors in this process was the growing military power of the barbarian forces. The borders of the empire became harder to defend, and tribes which had moved into Roman territory as allies became enemies. Some barbarian leaders were bought off with gold. Some were given titles and positions of authority in the Roman army. Others were baptised into the church. The tide, however, was unstoppable. By 408, the city of Rome was blockaded by Alaric, leader of the Gothic hordes, and surrendered the following year. Alaric made Attalus, the city prefect, the new emperor and had him baptised as an Arian by a Gothic bishop. At this same period in time, Germanic tribes were still pouring across the Rhine, the Saxons had a firm foothold in Britain where Roman government was almost at an end, control of western Europe gradually passed into German hands, and the areas which had been occupied by invading tribes were on their way to becoming independent states.

Conditions in the eastern empire were only marginally better. The emperor Arcadius, son of Theodosius, was plagued by unstable alliances, political intrigues, civil unrest, and the threat of barbarian forces. His problems were not helped by the tensions within the eastern church and the fierce criticism by John Chrysostom, bishop of Constantinople, aimed at the empress Eudoxia and the imperial court. The death of Arcadius in May 408 left his son Theodosius II as his successor.

7

The Theodosian Code

*The most sacred Prince, our Lord Theodosius ... ordered the precepts of the
laws to be collected and drawn up in a compendious form of sixteen books,
which he wished to be consecrated by his most sacred name.
Which thing, the eternal Prince, our Lord Valentinian,
approved with the loyalty of a colleague and the affection of a son.*[1]

WHEN THE EASTERN EMPEROR Arcadius died, his son Theodosius
was seven years old, and ruling as regent was Anthemius, an energetic and competent Praetorian prefect. However, in 414, Pulcheria,
the emperors's sixteen-year-old sister, took control of the regency and the
education of the young Theodosius. Pulcheria was a very pious young
woman who undertook a vow of lifelong virginity. Her piety was combined with the very strong character necessary to enable her to deal with
the problems which faced her early in her reign, some of which arose
from the conflicts within the church.

When Theodosius became twenty years old, his sister Pulcheria
chose a wife for him, and in June 421 he married Athenais, the well-
educated daughter of a pagan philosopher. In deference to her Christian
husband, Athenais took the name of Eudocia and professed the Christian
faith. She named their daughter Eudoxia, after the mother of the emperor, and in January 423 was elevated to the rank of Augusta.

1. *Codice Theodosiano*, cited in Bury, *History of the Later Roman Empire*, 233.

The emperor Theodosius II was more inclined to be a scholar than a politician or a warrior, but he could not ignore the age in which he lived and reigned. He attempted to stabilise the chaotic conditions in the west by contracting his infant daughter Eudoxia to marry Valentinian, one of the claimants to the western throne, and by providing him with military support. The marriage eventually did take place in October 437, but the western empire was still far from being at peace, and Theodosius, afraid of Vandal sea power in the Mediterranean, fortified his capital city of Constantinople and made attempts to deal with the problem of Africa, where a virtually independent Vandal kingdom with an established Arian church had been founded. His military success was limited and his domestic life was similarly troubled.

In 438, the empress Eudocia went on pilgrimage to Jerusalem, returning the following year, but rivalry between her and her sister-in-law Pulcheria had been growing in the eastern court. This rivalry, manipulated by a eunuch, Chrysaphius, an imperial advisor and political opportunist, resulted eventually in Pulcheria retiring completely from public life and Eudocia moving permanently to Jerusalem under the suspicion, probably unfounded, of having been unfaithful to her husband. Theodosius, separated from the two most powerful women in his family, was left to the unchallenged influence of Chrysaphius.

Theodosius II was not as enthusiastic about warfare and conquest as he was about order and learning, and so it was in keeping with his character to authorise the project which is usually referred to as the Theodosian code. There was nothing spontaneous about this compendium of laws, since it was the culmination of a process which had been going on for a considerable time. It took sixty-nine years between an initial proposal and its official validation in both east and west.[2] The first proposal to codify the laws was made in 369, but it was filed and forgotten. In March 429, Theodosius II set up a code commission, and the compilation of laws took eight-years to complete. Opportunity was taken at the wedding of Valentinian and Eudoxia at Constantinople in 438 to present the Code as a symbol of the unity between the eastern and western empires. It was presented in the name of both emperors, but in fact when the project began, Valentinian was only ten years old. The Code covered the imperial edicts from the time of Constantine onwards, and its significance was the

2. Harries and Wood, *Theodosian Code*, 3.

clear indication it provided of the way in which the theological development of the church was reflected in the law of the empire.

Theodosius I, in 380, had already determined that Nicene orthodoxy was the only expression of religious faith legally permitted in the Roman empire, and by the reign of Theodosius II, the language of Christian doctrine was reinforced by imperial sanction. The law of God and the law of the empire were, in some cases, indistinguishable, and to disobey imperial law was an act of sacrilege.[3] Although the bishops had no official legal standing in government affairs, the emperor was inclined to decree what the bishops had decided.

In practice, however, the official faith of the church was as much the product of political infighting as of theological enquiry, and the spiritual leaders were far from unanimous in their decisions about the burning issues of the day. Although the deity and humanity of Christ had been established at Nicea, a subsequent controversy arose about how this deity and humanity were related. The emperor Theodosius had to deal with divisions over acceptable formulae expressing the two natures of Christ and also with the parallel problem of monks acting independently of episcopal authority, while being only too aware of the pressing claims of the bishop of Rome to decide the doctrine of the church in both west and east. Rival churchmen condemned one another and rejected statements from opposing camps, and so Theodosius called a general council of the church in August 449. Pope Leo declared it to be unnecessary but was pragmatic enough to send a "Tome" portraying Christ as one person with two hypostatic natures whose distinct properties were both preserved. Leo's formula was rejected and he furiously demanded another council, but Theodosius would accept no more arguments. With some degree of imperial pressure, a doctrine of Christ's one incarnate nature became recognised as the faith of the whole church.

When Theodosius died in a riding accident in July 450, there were no sons to succeed him, and so the western emperor Valentinian III might have expected to rule in both east and west, but in practical terms this was almost impossible, since eastern subjects would not have accepted a western emperor. Accordingly, on his deathbed, Theodosius, with the agreement of Pulcheria, nominated Marcian, one of his military leaders, as successor. To make this choice more credible, Pulcheria became the nominal wife of Marcian the new emperor, and almost his first act was

3. Ibid., 147.

to execute Chrysaphius, who had been the power behind the throne for the last years of Theodosius's reign. Marcian also contacted Pope Leo to hold the council Leo had been demanding. This took place at Chalcedon in 451. Here a compromise formula expressing the nature of Christ was hammered out, where Christ was declared to be one person with two natures, human and divine, without confusion or separation. Many eastern bishops were far from comfortable with the new orthodoxy, but the alliance of pope and emperor was too powerful to be resisted. The doctrinal settlement at Chalcedon was yet another attempt at unity, but in fact it became a root of division which weakened the eastern church for centuries.

Marcian reigned until January 457, but his death left the matter of his successor unclear. Military and political power lay with the army, but a general called Aspar, the most powerful soldier, was both barbarian and Arian, and therefore could not take the imperial throne. It was Aspar who chose another soldier who was an orthodox Christian, and made him Emperor Leo I on 7 February 457. Aspar perhaps believed that Leo would be fairly easily manipulated, but the new emperor was able to express his own authority throughout the pressures of his reign while holding fast to the orthodoxy established at Chalcedon. He died 3 February 474 to be succeeded by his grandson Leo II. At the same time, the church in the west was experiencing its own share of turmoil about faith and order. A controversy arose about the place of the human will in the scheme of salvation. Pelagius, a British theologian, taught that men had freedom to choose between good and evil, while his greatest protagonists, Augustine and the African church, held that without divine grace men were unable to choose good. Pope Zozimus at first supported Pelagius, but under African pressure changed his approval to condemnation, and Pelagius was banished from Rome. This kind of ambivalence from the bishop of Rome gave the impression of someone whose authority was on a poor foundation, and this impression was not diminished by the willingness of some of the western bishops to challenge a papal decision when a church council met at Turin in September 417. The bishop of Marseilles at one point felt confident enough to defy both pope and council and was excommunicated as a result, which condition he simply ignored. The greatest threat, however, to papal authority in the west was the growing status and political power of the Metropolitan See of Arles, and so in 444, Pope Leo I persuaded emperor Valentinian III to confirm a papal decree to reduce the see of Arles from its metropolitan status. The edict of Valentinian to confirm the papal decree went further. He ordered that all provincial bishops must have the approval of the bishop of Rome in any important decisions they might make. The emperor in the west was all too aware that his own empire was collapsing, and papal authority seemed like the glue that might hold it together. It was, in fact, the ground of another conflict which would trouble the west for centuries. At this point in history, the emperor made the pope, but the day would come when the pope would make the emperor.

8

Zeno to Anastasius

We therefore endeavour night and day by every means, by prayer,
by strenuous exertions, by legislation, to promote in every part
the increase of the holy Catholic and Apostolic Church,
the undefiled and immortal mother of our realm.[1]

WHEN THE EASTERN EMPEROR Leo I died in 474, his grandson, the
new emperor Leo II, was six years old, the child of Leo's daughter
Ariadne and her husband Zeno, who was the obvious regent to rule in
the child's name. Zeno was raised to imperial rank almost immediately,
but the child died in November the same year. As the new emperor, Zeno
was reasonably effective in keeping external enemies at bay by military
and diplomatic activity, however, his mother-in-law, the Augusta Verina, widow of Leo I, had an eye on the imperial throne. She was able
to persuade Zeno that there was a plot against his life. This was almost
certainly the truth, because she herself was responsible for it. He fled for
safety with a section of his Isaurian guard for protection and escaped to
Isauria. Verina organised the slaughter of the remaining guard, intending
to marry her lover Patricius and rule as emperor and empress. However,
her plotting came to nothing when in fact the Senate chose instead her
brother Basiliscus.

As a new Augustus, Basiliscus immediately made his wife Zeno-
nis an Augusta and also conferred imperial rank on his son Marcus.

1. *Henotikon of Zeno*, cited in Bettenson, *Documents*, 123.

Patricius was quickly executed as a possible rival, but Basiliscus himself lasted less than two years. He quickly made himself unpopular with the eastern church when, as a Monophysite, he issued a decree condemning the council of Chalcedon. He further enraged Acacius the patriarch of Constantinople by removing some of the Asian sees from patriarchal authority. Acacius stirred up such a level of opposition against the emperor that Basiliscus had to leave the city. He did, however, seek to stabilise his position by attempting to get rid of Zeno once and for all and sent two generals, Illus and Trocundes, to find Zeno in Isauria and kill him. Basiliscus's unpopularity, however, was so widespread that even this scheme failed. The two generals found Zeno but joined forces with him, as did Armatus, a third military commander sent on the same mission. Zeno and his newfound allies returned to Constantinople in triumph in 476 to execute Basiliscus and his entire family.

In the eastern empire at this time, loyalties were easily won and lost. Armatus was made master of soldiers for life by Zeno, but Illus persuaded the emperor that this was a mistake and so Armatus was assassinated. Illus became a powerful influence in imperial affairs, and Zeno could not afford to lose his support. The Germanic groups which had been displaced by the Isaurians were certainly no longer the power they had once been, but they were not entirely obliterated, and Zeno needed the strength of Illus to prevent any resurgence of Gothic power. The support of Illus was influenced by his appointment as Patrician and Consul in 478. In the meantime, the empress Verina, as dangerous as ever, attempted to arrange the assassination of Illus but failed. Zeno, remembering the way his mother-in-law had manipulated his own flight from Constantinople, was pragmatic enough to see that Illus and Verina could not live in the same city. She was taken to Tarsus, imprisoned in a castle, and forced to become a nun. A champion arose, however, in the shape of Marcian, son of the western emperor Anthemius. He had married Leontia, the younger daughter of Leo I, and was therefore Verina's other son-in-law. He attempted to overthrow Zeno and Illus but failed. His punishment was to be forced into the priesthood in Cappadocia, while his wife Leontia fled to a convent. Zeno's wife, Ariadne, pleaded that her mother Verina be allowed to return, but Illus objected strongly to this, and so Ariadne, clearly her mother's daughter, tried to arrange his assassination. The plot once again failed, but Illus saw the writing on the wall. He put space between himself and the dangerous imperial family he served by moving to

Antioch as master of soldiers in the east. He also harboured the suspicion that Zeno himself had been part of the latest attempt on his life and the suspicion grew into outright hostility. Illus needed weapons in what he saw would be a conflict with Zeno.

The theological struggle to define the nature of Christ had split the church in Egypt, and Illus hoped he might find some support from those who resented Zeno's attempt to impose order on the church. In a document which became known as the Henoticon, Zeno, in an attempt to unite the Catholics and the Monophysites, decreed that the creeds of Nicea and Constantinople were the bases for faith and that anything contrary to these creeds must be rejected whether taught at Chalcedon or elsewhere. In doing this, Zeno was deliberately setting aside Leo's Tome and the Chalcedonian formula. This strategy certainly pleased the Monophysites, giving them the chance to condemn Leo and Chalcedon, but it alienated the orthodox Christians. His attempt to impose unity certainly caused division among the Egyptians, but not enough to provoke any substantial support for Illus. However, one source of influence Illus did possess was in the person of Longinus, the brother of Zeno. Longinus was held by Illus as a hostage, and when Zeno demanded his release in 484, Illus refused. Zeno retaliated by banishing all Illus's supporters from Constantinople and giving their property to his fellow Isaurians. In response to this, Illus went to war.

Marcian, the son-in-law of Verina, was recalled from his priestly exile in Cappadocia and proclaimed by Illus to be emperor in place of Zeno. Illus hoped for military support from the Persians, the traditional enemies of the eastern empire, but was disappointed. In a desperate attempt to defeat Zeno he even formed an alliance with his old enemy Verina. Marcian was deposed and Verina returned to imperial rank. A patrician called Leontius was crowned by Verina as yet another emperor, and news of this event spread all over the east, gaining a measure of support. Zeno determined to end the conflict and was able to obtain troops from his old rivals the Goths. A battle was fought. Zeno was victorious, and Verina, Illus, and Leontius, the rival and short-lived emperor, fled to Isauria, where Verina died very soon after their arrival. In 488, Zeno's army captured and executed Illus and Leontius. Zeno was still very much in command.

In his attempt to bring about unity within the empire in the east by means of agreed doctrinal formulae, Zeno was failing to recognise a deeper source of controversy which lay just below the surface of the theological debate. Zeno followed the tradition of previous Roman emperors by asserting imperial authority over the church in its doctrinal statements. In the west, the bishop of Rome claimed that right for himself as the successor to Peter. A synod held in Rome in 484 excommunicated the patriarchs of Constantinople and Alexandria for their support of the emperors initiative and as a demonstration of papal authority over the whole church.

Shortly before the death of the eastern emperor Leo I, Gundobad, the Burgundian military commander who controlled Italy, put a Roman nobleman called Glycerius on the imperial throne in the west at Ravenna on 5 March 473. Leo refused to accept this and chose instead Julius Nepos, the military governor of Dalmatia, to rule the west. Nepos and a military force from the east set out for Italy. Gundobad returned to Burgundy, and his puppet Glycerius was deposed and made Bishop of Salona. Nepos became emperor in Rome, 24 June 474. However, like his predecessor, the reign of Nepos was short-lived. The vacuum in military authority caused by the exit of Gundobad was filled by a seasoned soldier called Orestes, who had ambitions for his son Romulus. In August 475, Nepos fled at the approach of Orestes, who set his son on the throne in October 475. Romulus was the nominal ruler in the west, under the control of his father, but was never recognised in Constantinople or in Gaul. Zeno, who succeeded Leo I at Constantinople, continued to regard Nepos as the legitimate emperor in the west.

When Orestes set his son on the imperial throne he had the support of his German soldiers, but within a year that support was eroded. The troops were looking for a homeland and wanted to be given part of Italy in which to settle. The refusal of Orestes to grant this request brought about a rebellion led by a senior officer, Odovacar. Orestes was killed and his son Romulus banished. At this point, two appeals were made to the eastern emperor Zeno. Nepos requested the support of Zeno to reinstate him as emperor in the west, while Odovacar, who refused to recognise Nepos as a realistic claimant to the throne, urged Zeno to be the single emperor of both west and east while Odovacar would exercise military rule in the west as master of soldiers. Zeno tried to please both men. In 476, he did appoint Odovacar to the military post but demanded that he accept Nepos as his emperor. This was refused, but when Nepos died 480, the situation was left as Odovacar had requested.

In spite of the ongoing tension and suspicion between Zeno and Odovacar, the latter managed to gain the support of the Roman Senate. He also extricated Sicily from the grasp of Gaiseric the Vandal king and defended Italy from invasion by the Rugians. Zeno, however, harboured the suspicion that Odovacar had supported Illus in his rebellion against him in 484, and so in 488, Zeno sent a Gothic commander called Theoderic to invade Italy and remove Odovacar. Theoderic had had a very stormy relationship with Zeno over the years, when loyalty was given and betrayed for political or military success, or simply for money, but at the time of the rebellion of Illus, Theoderic was allied with Zeno, and so in 488, Theoderic set out for Rome at the head of an army of one hundred thousand men. In fact, Theoderic had to deal with hostile forces on the way and did not reach Italy till August 489. After a year of fighting, Odovacar was finally defeated in August 490. Theoderic controlled Italy and Sicily and enforced the support of the Roman Senate.

The rule of Theoderic was far from peaceful. Gundobad, ruler of the Burgundians and past military commander of Italy, now returned to launch an invasion of northern Italy, and while Theoderic moved to resist this, the African Vandals attempted unsuccessfully to regain Sicily. The defeated Odovacar, who had survived the battle and had locked himself inside the city of Ravenna, in February 493 was tricked into an agreement to rule Italy jointly with Theoderic. The treaty was mediated by the bishop of Ravenna, but as soon as Odovacar opened the city to Theoderic, he and his family were murdered and his surviving soldiers slaughtered.

The intentions of Theoderic were harsh. He planned to deprive all the Italians who had withheld their support from him of their civil rights and was only dissuaded by the intercession of Epiphanius, the bishop of Ticinum, who also negotiated the release of prisoners and the reduction of taxes on a country devastated by extensive warfare.

When Zeno died in April 491, the man chosen by Ariadne, his Augusta, as her husband's successor was Anastasius, who came from a background of Arian and Manichean worship, and so he held unorthodox views of the Christian faith. He was certainly unacceptable to Euphemius, the patriarch of Constantinople, but Ariadne and the Senate were determined, and so, having signed a declaration of orthodoxy, he was crowned emperor by a reluctant Euphemius and married Ariadne in May 491.

Anastasius was a new broom. He confiscated Zeno's property, forced Zeno's brother Longinus into the clergy, and expelled the Isaurians from the capital. This action provoked a minor rebellion which was soon quashed. The new emperor also had to deal with outbreaks of opposition in the east, but his greatest military problem was the repeated invasion of the empire by the Bulgarians from beyond the Danube.

Relations between Anastasius and Euphemius were always strained. The emperor was officially a Monophysite, but the patriarch was a strict Chalcedonian. Euphemius had planned to arouse opposition against Patriarch Peter of Alexandria and his successor Athanasius because both these men rejected Chalcedon and Leo's Tome. In this scheme, Euphemius sought support from Pope Felix, but the patriarchs of Alexandria and Jerusalem retaliated by persuading Anastasius that Euphemius was a heretic. A council was held at Constantinople in 496 which condemned and deposed Euphemius. This was followed by a period of appointments and depositions as opposing parties struggled for supremacy. The patriarch Macedonius, who replaced Euphemius, was in fact another Chalcedonian, but he was willing to sign the Henotikon to secure his appointment. When his true convictions became known he was deposed and banished. His place was taken by a genuine Monophysite called Timothy who, in November 512, caused a riot by introducing Monophysite elements into the liturgy in the church of Saint Sophia. The riot grew into rebellion which required military control, but even the army could not prevent the crowd from electing Areobundus as a rival emperor. Areobundus had a fairly fragile claim to imperial rank, being married to Juliana Anicia, the granddaughter of the emperor Valentinian III, and he chose to abdicate rather than face the wrath of Anastasius.

The emperor Anastasius was determined to deal with the opposition once and for all. He removed another Chalcedonian, Flavian the patriarch of Antioch and replaced him with Severus who intended to make Antioch a stronghold of Monophysite doctrine. A synod was called at Tyre in 513 where the Henotikon was affirmed, and the Chalcedonians began to feel the weight of imperial disapproval. Anastasius's troubles, however, were far from over.

Two of the deposed patriarchs, Macedonius and Flavian, found a military ally in Vitalian, the commander of a body of federate troops. These soldiers were recruited mainly from the Bulgarians, who needed very little persuasion to strike a blow against imperial authority. Claiming that they were being deprived of their lawful provisions, Vitalian and his soldiers set out in 513 as a rebel army intent on capturing Constantinople. They found moral justification for their action by portraying themselves as the champions of the orthodox faith. Anastasius tried to deal with the crisis by diplomatic means. He sent a team of negotiators with gifts and promises, which persuaded Vitalian to withdraw his threat for a while at least. However, another negotiator who approached Vitalian to continue the bargaining was assassinated. Nothing remained but warfare. Vitalian was declared to be "an enemy of the republic" and an army was sent against him. This proved to be no more successful than the negotiations. Vitalian and his troops continued to enlarge the territory they controlled, and he was only halted by the promise of a huge ransom in gold and his appointment as master of soldiers in Thrace. Agreement was also reached to hold a church council in Heraclia in July 515. Vitalian and Anastasius wrote to Pope Hormisdas, who sent his delegates to the council, but because no agreement could be reached about an agenda, the council never actually met. The two protagonists prepared again to resume hostilities, and this time Vitalian was defeated and had to flee for safety.

In 515, the empress Ariadne died, and Anastasius, her husband, also died three years later. When the emperor Zeno sent his Gothic commander Theoderic to invade Italy in 488, it took until 490 for that conquest to be accomplished, and when Anastasius succeeded Zeno as emperor in 491, he was far from sure of how his own relationship with Theoderic would develop. However, he was willing to confirm Theoderic as master of soldiers and governor of Italy. In that land, the civil offices were held by Romans, but the army was firmly in the hands of the Goths. Officially, Anastasius was emperor of both west and east, but in fact Theoderic ruled Italy as a king. Theoderic struggled to keep the peace between the different groups in his kingdom. Sometimes he used military force, and at other times he arranged marriages to confirm political alliances. However, religious factors added to his problems. When it became necessary to take military action against the Franks, Clovis, the Frankish leader, portrayed himself as the champion of the orthodox church struggling for the faith against the Arian Theoderic. Since Theoderic was, officially at least, the subject of Anastasius, the conflict was translated into a religious contest between the orthodox western church led by Rome and the eastern Monophysite church led by Constantinople. In addition, the Roman Senate was split over the rule of Theoderic. Some senators were willing to accept his authority as a practical necessity, but there was also a group which opposed him because he was an Arian and also in some sense represented a rival church. The internal conflict came to a head when Pope Anastasius died in 498 and a papal election became necessary.

In November 498, those who were willing to accept a measure of compromise on religious issues elected Laurentius as the new pope. The others, who would not give an inch in terms of religious orthodoxy, elected Pope Symmachus. Both these men were enthroned in Rome on the same day, and the rivalry between the opposing factions ended in bloodshed. The following year, Theoderic, as king, was asked to make a choice. He favoured Symmachus because Symmachus carried with him the support of a body of clergy; however, Laurentius remained in Rome and continued to claim his own election was valid. Symmachus's theology might have been better than that of his rival, but his behaviour was not. He quickly displayed a tendency towards arrogance and aggression, so much so that he even alienated his supporter Theoderic. But in the end, both the military power and the Monophysite church of the east were perceived as a threat to the west, and so Symmachus prevailed as being more orthodox.

Theoderic made Ravenna his capital and built a new church there for his fellow Arians. In spite of the conflicting forces at work in Italy, Theoderic's efforts to preserve the peace were not wholly unsuccessful.

9

Justin and Justinian

The emperor now lays claim to an initiative in church policy,
patriarchs and bishops are his lieutenants in religious affairs
as his generals are for the army, his silentiaries for the civil administration.[1]

WHEN THE EASTERN EMPEROR Anastasius died in 518 he had not
named a successor, and there was a popular fear that the wrong
man might take the throne. The Senate were pressured to make a decision, and at the age of sixty-six an Illyrian career soldier called Justin
was crowned by the patriarch John in Constantinople. His wife, who
had once been his concubine, took the name Euphemia and became the
Augusta. Perhaps the most important thing about the new emperor in
the eyes of the church, was that he was determined to mend fences with
the west. He sought to unify the church by establishing the orthodoxy
of Leo's Tome and the decisions of Chalcedon, and his efforts gained the
support of some, but not all, of the eastern bishops. As a result, many
Monophysite monks and clergy were exiled, but links with Pope Hormisdas were confirmed.

On his death in August 527, he was succeeded by his nephew Justinian, who continued the attempts to build church unity. Justinian called
councils and arranged the preparation of new formulae, which he hoped
would be acceptable to everyone. His success in this endeavour was limited not only by the political complexities of the times but also by the support of his wife Theodora for the Monophysite cause. The empress, who

1. Hughes, *History of the Church*, Vol.1, 285.

was a formidable woman by any standards, wanted to see a pope who was sympathetic to her own views, and she succeeded in having Vigilius, a candidate of her choice, elected to the papal office. The see of Rome was very unstable at this point. Papal elections were hotly contested by rival groups of clergy. Popes died fairly soon after election and a battle for the control of Italy was being fought between Gothic armies and Imperial forces. The papacy of Vigilius was anything but uneventful. During his term of office he was rejected by the Roman clergy and excommunicated by the African church because of what they perceived as disloyalty to the position taken by Chalcedon. Vigilius narrowly escaped being arrested by the emperor and then effected a reconciliation before being excommunicated once again by imperial decree. All these trials had kept him away from the city of Rome for nine years, but when he eventually set off to return, he died in June 555 on the journey home.

The affairs of Justinian demonstrate a man who possessed a measure of skill and determination in all that he did. He restored imperial power to a considerable extent in Africa, Italy, and Spain. He enforced the Christian faith throughout his empire, compelling pagan kings to be baptised as Christians. He excluded pagans from public office and closed pagan schools. His view, however, of the church was very different from that of the bishop Ambrose, who had disciplined Theodosius I, a previous imperial lawmaker. Justinian saw the church as the religious face of his empire. He was both the political and religious head of his people, and the bishops of the church were his junior officers. One of his lasting achievements was the revision of civil and religious legislation, which was published in December 533 in fifty books of law. These covered imperial regulations and decrees since Hadrian's reign and were built to some extent at least on the Theodosian Code. Justinian's view of all human relationships was shaped by the way he saw his own imperial rule, and so it was hardly surprising that by the time of his death in 565, the Christian faith had become a spiritual rule that could, where necessary, be imposed by force on all his subjects. Personal trust in Christ tended to become outward obedience to the laws of the church and formal acceptance of its official theological statements. The strength of imperial authority over the church was, however, less easily enforced in the west than in the east because of the greater political and military turbulence. By the middle of the sixth century, the Roman empire was a thing of the past in the west. and the new barbarian kingdoms did not conform either to the imperial or the papal view of orthodoxy.

10

An Empire Reborn

Carolus serenissimus Augustus, a Deo coronatus,
magnus et pacificus imperator, Romanum gubernans imperium,
qui et per misericordiam Dei rex Francorum et Langobardorum.[1]

Let the ministers of the altar of God adorn their ministry
by good behaviour, and likewise the other orders who observe a rule,
and the congregations of monks.... And let schools be established
in which boys may learn to read.[2]

T HE THORNY PROBLEM OF authority in church and state was never
solved satisfactorily. National, political, and religious tensions kept
tearing the fabric of empire in all kinds of ways. The patriarchs of the
major religious centres of the eastern church competed for status with
one another and with the bishop of Rome. The traditional distrust by
Egypt of the government at Constantinople grew stronger. A succession
of popes attempted to achieve authority over the church in both east and
west with varying degrees of success. Doctrinal statements were used as
weapons in church conflicts. Emperors succeeded one another without
ever achieving the real unity of the empire which they sought. Less than
a century after the death of Justinian, Pope Martin I was arrested by the
imperial police and brought to Constantinople, where he was tried and

1. Bryce, *Holy Roman Empire*, 400.
2. *Admonitio generalis*, Charlemagne, cited in Bettenson, *Documents*, 135.

sentenced to death for the crime of treason. In 663 the emperor was assassinated while on tour of his western empire. The seventh century came to a close with a rebellion against one of his successors in Constantinople and the eighth century began with the murder of yet another emperor.

In the west, the religious loyalties of the kingdoms tended to change with whichever group was in power. Gaul had been occupied by tribes which were Arian, but when it passed into the control of the Franks, who were rapidly becoming the major military force in Europe, it became orthodox. Clovis, the Frankish king, had been baptised into the catholic church, and under his rule a veneer of Christianity spread across a society which was still largely pagan at heart. The bishops of the church, however, became important political figures in a time when the biggest landowner in Gaul was the church itself. These bishops were far from the best pastors, since they were crown appointed and their appointment reflected political loyalty rather than spiritual worth.

Relations between church and state waxed hot and cold during the eighth century. In 726, the emperor Leo III issued an edict forbidding images in church buildings. The eastern Monophysite church had never been comfortable with images of Christ, since these emphasised his human nature, and so the destruction of images spread rapidly in the east. The western church seemed to regard images as visual aids for worshippers, and therefore permissible for people who had little access to books. In time, the dispute led to both military and ecclesiastical conflict between Rome and the churches of the east. In fact, it took most of the century to work out a compromise.

The other great problem for the western rulers in the eighth century was the Mohammedan invasion of Europe. These warriors, many of whom had once been Christian, were in Spain by 711 and across the Pyrenees into Gaul soon afterwards. Foremost in the battle against the invaders was the king of the Franks, Charles Martel, who had no hesitancy in using the wealth accumulated by a largely corrupt church as a war chest.[3]

His successors maintained an uneasy relationship with the church, since on one hand there was rivalry between clerical and military leaders, but on the other hand kings sought papal confirmation of their authority, thereby investing the papal office with much greater political influence. It was about this time that the pope began to be seen as a prince in his own

3. Hughes, *History of the Church*, Vol. 2, 128.

right, and Pope Stephen II even entertained unfulfilled ambitions of ruling the whole of Italy. In troubled days when popes and kings supported and betrayed one another at a fairly rapid pace, the desperate need was for strong and capable leadership in church and state, and in fact two men of such outstanding leadership qualities were about to appear on the stage of history.

In June 767, Pepin, the son of Charles Martel, died, to be succeeded by his own son Charlemagne, and in the reign of Charlemagne, Adrian I became pope and formed a more stable relationship with the Frankish monarch. Adrian was a reformer who achieved a measure of success in his attempts to rid the church of the violence and corruption that had become so characteristic of recent activities. Charlemagne had the appearance, initially at least, of a deliverer. During his reign he restored lapsed episcopal sees and encouraged a trained and educated clergy. He used civil law to enforce episcopal decrees. He attempted to establish schools in every parish and encouraged foreign scholars to come to Gaul. His military achievements were no less effective, as he pushed his boundaries to cover almost all of western Europe. He completely subdued the Lombards, who had exercised a powerful grip on Italy for such a long time, and at first indicated his willingness to recognise the pope as ruler of north and central Italy. It appeared that the papal territories were to be free from the control of secular rulers, but in fact Charlemagne installed his son Pepin as the Italian king and began to instruct the pope in the appointment of political offices in the papal states. Adrian was skilful enough to avoid military conflict with Charlemagne, and so by careful negotiation he managed to retain a large measure of independence.[4]

Unfortunately, Adrian died in 795 and was succeeded by Pope Leo III, who had little of his predecessor's skill or popularity. So unpopular was this pope that he was fortunate to survive an assassination attempt in 799. He turned to Charlemagne for protection and support, and so the king sent a commission of politicians and bishops to conduct an enquiry into the matter. The strength of opposition to Leo was such that the enquiry became a trial, not of those who had plotted the assassination, but of the pope himself. The situation became so confused that no one could impose a solution except the king in person, and so in 800, Charlemagne was found in the city of Rome to ensure the vindication of Leo. In December of that year, a huge assembly was convened in St. Peters to

4. Ibid., 147.

deal with the problem of Leo III and the Roman see, and on Christmas day, perhaps the most powerful men in the Western world came together to worship the incarnate Lord. On this occasion, however, it was not a spiritual but a political action which one historian later described as "the deed . . . which was to haunt the imagination of the next five hundred hears."[5] A political resurrection was about to take place.

The Church of St. Peter in Rome was very different from the cathedrals of northern Europe. Built by Constantine himself, it was comparatively spacious and plain in its elegance. The clergy sat in semicircular tiers, with the bishop's throne in the centre. Bryce gives a description of the event:

> From that chair the Pope now rose, as the reading of the gospel ended, advanced to where Charles, . . . who had exchanged his simple Frankish dress for the sandals and the chlamis of a Roman Patrician, . . . knelt in prayer by the high altar, and as in the sight of all he placed upon the brow of the barbarian chieftain the diadem of the Ceasars, then knelt in obeisance before him, the church rang to the shout of the multitude, again free, again the lords and centre of the world, "Karolo Augusto a Deo coronato magno et pacifico imperatori vita et victoria." In that shout echoed by the Franks without, was pronounced the union, so long in preparation, so mighty in its consequences, of the Roman and the Teuton, of the memories and the civilization of the South with the fresh energies of the North, and from that moment modern history begins.[6]

Charlemagne is said to have claimed that this coronation was a surprise to him, but this is extremely unlikely. The whole occasion was almost certainly planned. The sober fact was that the new emperor and the pope needed each other. The church in the east was strongly resistant to the idea of papal supremacy, and even in the west there were leading clerics who were too powerful for the comfort of the pope. The iconoclastic struggle was a threat, and in Europe the control of Leo III over the papal estates was far from secure. Leo needed the political and military strength of Charlemagne to stabilize his position. The emperor on the other hand needed the mark of divine sanction for what was already a de facto empire in the west. His claim to a legitimate imperial crown would hardly be acknowledged by the empress Irene in Constantinople. She was

5. Ibid., 145.
6. Bryce, *Holy Roman Empire*, 49.

a determined and ruthless woman who had deposed and blinded her own son to take his throne. The western Roman empire had come to an end in the fifth century, and from that point till the time of Charlemagne, a single imperial ruler had reigned from Constantinople. The possibility of Charlemagne gaining a crown by the negotiation of a marriage with the empress Irene had been explored but came to nothing. The ceremony at St. Peter's Church in AD 800 not only gave the new emperor the sanction of heaven, but bound together the western empire and church into a single unit. That, at least, was clear to emperor and pope. What was not so clear was the question of which one had authority over the other. The "False Decretals" which were "providentially" discovered in Spain and published about midway through the ninth century were a collection of falsified and fictitious documents, including the "Donation of Constantine." Their purpose was to show that both spiritual and temporal power had been placed in the hands of the bishop of Rome by Constantine, and they were an attempt to establish the authority of the pope as head of both church and state. These were accepted as genuine, at least by churchmen, for centuries, until fully exposed as forgeries in 1588. They were used in the struggles between pope and emperor, which continued to trouble Europe for centuries, and reflect the lengths to which church leaders would go in order to win that contest.

There can be no doubt that Charlemagne saw himself as the defender and upholder of Christian orthodoxy, and although successive popes were involved to some extent in the affairs of the eastern church and empire in the ninth and tenth centuries, the gulf between east and west was by now virtually unbridgeable. Charlemagne and his successors in the west imposed the Christian faith throughout the Holy Roman Empire. Conquered enemies were made to submit not only to the secular imperial power but also to the Christian church. The emperor was God appointed and therefore ruled by divine authority. Like former Roman emperors, monarchs saw the church not as an independent spiritual body but as the visible religious expression of the spiritual life of the empire. The imperial crown continued to be placed on royal heads by the pope, but emperors and even powerful families continued to control election to the papal office.

Throughout a period of turbulent political and ecclesiastical conflict, there was nevertheless some measure of genuine spiritual advancement. There were periods of liturgical and moral reformation. Clergy became better educated and better trained. Doctrinal issues were examined and debated. Monastic houses flourished and produced teachers and preachers. However, election to the papal office produced a wide variety of candidates. Nicholas I, early in the ninth century, demonstrated a zeal for the training of missionaries and the evangelisation of the heathen. Benedict IX, elected in the eleventh century, was ten years old when he took office and sold his claim to the papacy to his godfather Gregory VI.[7]

The tension between church and state within the Holy Roman Empire continued to increase and erupted in relation to specific issues like the dispute over who had the right to choose and invest bishops with the symbols of their spiritual office. Where local citizens were strongly in favour of one side or the other, armed conflict broke out and rebellion had to be suppressed. For this reason, the battle between pope and emperor was more than a war of words.

The eleventh-century German emperor Henry IV intended to rule with an imperial authority which tolerated no opposition. His determined and forceful style alienated both the nobility and the ordinary people of his realm. His ruthless suppression of a rebellion in Saxony provoked an appeal for help from his desperate people to Pope Gregory VII. Henry responded to this in 1076 by calling a synod which deposed the pope, and Gregory retaliated by excommunicating Henry. The use of excommunication as a political weapon was in some ways more to be feared than a battalion of troops, since it gave the blessing of the church to anyone who might have the military force to overthrow the excommunicated monarch. The decree issued by Gregory spelled out the position in which Henry would find himself.

> God has given me authority to bind and to loose upon earth. Wherefore, filled with this confidence, for the honour and defence of thy Church, in the name of God Almighty, by thy power and thy authority, I deprive Henry the king, son of Henry the emperor, who with unheard-of pride has risen against thy Church, of all authority in the kingdom of the Teutons and in Italy. I release all Christians from their oaths of fidelity sworn to him or that they shall swear to him. I forbid any person to do him any of the service due to kings. . . . I bind him with the chain of anathema so that the whole world may know that upon

7. Pullan, *From Justinian to Luther*, 105.

this rock the Son of the Living God has built his Church and
that the gates of hell shall not prevail against it.[8]

Henry's opponents were encouraged and invigorated. His bishops deserted him. The pope was to be invited to preside at a council in Germany early in 1077. Henry was beaten and he knew it. After the pope had
actually set out for the German council, Henry left to intercept him on
the journey. They met at Canossa in the Apennines, where Henry is said
to have waited in the snow for three days before the pope would receive
his humble confession of repentance and contrition. In the end, Henry
had to return to Germany and fight to establish authority again, and the
meeting at Canossa was not the last time Henry and Gregory would find
themselves meeting as enemies, but the whole incident brought before
the western world a clearer understanding of the struggle that had been
simmering for centuries between church and state and what was the prize
each of the contestants sought to gain.

8. Hughes, *History of the Church*, 2:229.

11

The Vicar of God

Over all He has set one whom He has appointed as His Vicar on earth,
so that, as every knee is bowed to Jesus, of things in heaven,
and things in earth and things under the earth, so all men should obey
His Vicar and strive that there may be one fold and one shepherd.
All secular kings for the sake of God so venerate this Vicar, that unless they
seek to serve him devotedly they doubt if they are reigning properly.[1]

THE STRUGGLE FOR POWER between king and pope in eleventh-century Europe was not a simple issue of sheer political or military force. Monarch and pope alike wanted to build on a sound legal foundation. Each wanted to claim that the foundation on which their authority rested was laid by God and that their God-given authority was expressed in civil and church law. These two kinds of law were certainly not in separate boxes, because the secular government, often in the person of the king or his executives, might well rule in church affairs, while the church enacted regulations which governed the ordinary lives of men and used the civil powers to enforce them. The harder popes had to strive to control national rulers, the more their theological pronouncements took on a strong legal flavour, and this process engendered a huge international body of experts in collecting, making, and interpreting canon law. The relationship between the pope and church lawyers appeared to move in

1. Pope Innocent III to King John of England, 21 April 1214, cited in Cheney and Semple, *Selected Letters of Pope Innocent III*, 1772.

a circle. Popes issued theological statements, and the canonists turned these into laws, which became papal decrees, which in turn had to be interpreted accurately and applied by the lawyers again.[2]

Sources of tension between civil and ecclesiastical powers certainly arose in matters of administration and finance rather than doctrine, and so kings tended to be more wary about taxes due to the church or the appointment of church officials who exercised political power within the borders of their realm. However, ecclesiastical rulers like Pope Gregory VII, who was himself a church reformer and an enthusiastic canonist, had no hesitation in using kings and civil rulers as instruments of his reforms. He had a particular reason to be grateful to, and to be concerned with, the rulers of Normandy, since it was the Normans occupying Sicily and the south of Italy who reinstalled him as pope after he had been despatched by his old enemy the emperor, King Henry IV. Later, as a disillusioned man, Gregory chose to end his days among the Norman community in Salerno. On one occasion, to William, duke of Normandy, who became known as William the Conqueror and who gained the crown of England, Gregory wrote,

> If then on that terrible day of judgement it is I who must repre-
> sent you before the just judge whom no lies deceive and who is
> the creator of all creatures, your wisdom will itself understand
> how I must most attentively watch over your salvation and how
> you, in turn, because of your salvation and that you may come to
> the land of the living, must and ought to obey me without delay.[3]

Under this kind of pressure it cannot be surprising if the Norman king of England was willing to cooperate in reforming what was then a slovenly English church. Bishops and abbots that William considered to be careless and unworthy of their office were replaced, in some cases by foreigners. Lanfranc, who was a Benedictine scholar of international repute and had been advisor to William when he was still duke of Normandy, was made archbishop of Canterbury. This new broom in the English church brought in Norman clergy who were enthusiastic instruments of the reforming policies of Pope Gregory VII.

While the relationship between William and the pope seemed to be characterised by cooperation, the king was not entirely ready to surrender royal authority to the church. He was careful to separate civil from

2. Ullmann, *Medieval Papalism*, 20.
3. Hughes, *History of the Church*, 2:225.

church courts in order to emphasise that they administered a different body of law. Neither would he recognise papal authority over his subjects without his express permission, and many decisions of the English church required royal approval. The struggle for supremacy between church and state was as real as ever, even if its expression was kept under better control.

As the eleventh century drew to a close, the measure of cooperation between church and state in England deteriorated greatly. Lanfranc, as archbishop of Canterbury, was followed by Anselm, who had been the Abbot of Bec in Normandy. William the Conqueror was succeeded by William Rufus, who in turn passed the crown to Henry I in 1100. The underlying tensions were not helped by Anselm's criticism of court morals and the royal acquisition of his estates while he was out of the country. When Anselm came back to England, King Henry was willing to return the estates to the archbishop, but demanded official recognition of his royal authority to do so. Anselm refused, and the matter was referred to the pope, Paschal II, who would not give a specific judgement but did excommunicate all who broke canon law. Henry himself came under the threat of excommunication and was forced to accept a settlement in 1107 that no bishops or abbots could be invested by a layman.

When Henry II came to the throne, the Norman influence was still visible in the appointment as chancellor of Thomas Becket, the son of a Norman family in England. At first, Thomas pleased his monarch greatly, and at Henry's insistence was elected archbishop of Canterbury. However, when he began to question the king's method of raising taxes and the royal interference in church courts, he aroused Henry's displeasure. Clerics accused of crimes were brought in the first instance before the king's court, and although a trial may have been conducted in a court of the church, it was the king's court which punished the criminal, when found guilty. Henry II also held onto the right established by William the Conqueror of requiring the royal consent for the election of a bishop. The struggle for supremacy between church and state was still alive and well in England. The relationship between Henry and Thomas Becket became so strained that Thomas fled the country to the continent to gain the support of Pope Alexander III and Louis, king of France. Since the pope was already locked in a dispute with the German emperor Barbarossa over the same issue of church and state, he enthusiastically gave his support to Thomas in his conflict with Henry. The English king, however, unimpressed with the views of Pope Alexander, in 1170 used the occasion of Thomas's absence to make a clear assertion of his kingly rights. In order to make sure of the succession of his son, Henry III, the king arranged his son's coronation as joint king while Thomas the archbishop of Canterbury was still abroad. The ceremony was carried out by Roger the archbishop of York, and conspicuous by their absence were not only Thomas, the senior cleric in England, but also Margaret, wife of Henry III and daughter of King Louis of France. The statement could not have been more clear. In response, the pope suspended all the English clergy who had taken part in the coronation, including archbishop Roger himself, and the situation went from bad to worse when Thomas, having returned to England, was murdered, possibly with the knowledge of Henry II.

Fifteen years earlier, the struggle between pope and emperor in Europe had seemed to be abated to some extent when Pope Adrian IV, in 1155, crowned Frederick I Barbarossa as Holy Roman Emperor in St. Peter's in Rome, but this feeble alliance did not last when the pope sought formal confirmation that the imperial crown was something to be given or withheld by papal authority. The problem was clearly not going to be settled permanently by military might alone, and in time a renewed emphasis was placed on an old argument, i.e., the correct understanding of the will of God.

As the twelfth century came to a close, popes and kings were embroiled in church conflicts at home, crusades abroad, and the endless struggle between church and state. One monarch who came closest to turning the imperial title into a reality was the German emperor Henry VI, son of Barbarossa. By political alliance and marriage, shrewd diplomacy, military energy, and the ruthless treatment of his enemies, Henry appeared to have the empire and the papacy under his control. His uncle, Richard I, king of England, was captured on his way home from the crusade in Palestine and held to ransom by the emperor. Part of the conditions for his release was the surrender of the English crown in 1194 to Henry, who then formally returned it to him as his imperial overlord. However, even emperors are mortal, and in 1197, Henry VI died, not on the battlefield but of a fever, leaving as heir to the imperial throne his three-year-old infant son. The irony of the situation was that the ward chosen to care for the young prince was ninety-year-old Pope Celestine III. The death of Henry set off a new competition among the European rulers to succeed to his imperial title, since few of them were prepared to recognise the hereditary rights of a child. The rivalry of the secular princes weakened the strength of the state in its conflict with the church, and the balance of power in that struggle was about to change. Pope Celestine III died within months of Henry VI, and in 1198, a young cardinal was elected as the new pope and took the name of Innocent III.

The concept of papal supremacy was about to be given a whole new dimension. Innocent's predecessors had seen themselves as the vicars of the Apostle Peter, but Innocent demanded recognition as the vicar of God. He brought to his office a wide area of expertise in canon law. As pope he required absolute obedience throughout the church, but his perception of his authority was boundless. This understanding, powerfully nourished by the canonists, was built on a theological foundation. God's authority over the whole world was absolute, and since the pope was his vicar on earth, then papal authority must be the same. This was God's answer to the conflict between church and state. God had ordained them both, but the emperor and the pope were not equal rulers. Constantine and his successors might have seen the church as the religious face of the empire, and this was certainly the position reinforced by Charlemagne, but the truth, as the canonists saw it, was otherwise. When Ambrose, Bishop of Milan in the fourth century, brought the emperor Theodosius literally to his knees and kept him waiting for months at the Cathedral in Milan to receive forgiveness for his sin, this had been an early example of the power which Innocent III believed God had put into his hand. The church controlled the state and not the other way round. Kings and emperors might indeed have a God-given authority, but it was received from the hands of God's vicar on earth.

Innocent, however, was not content simply to have the theological agreement of princes to his views. He wanted the political aspect of the relationship to be as clear as the spiritual aspect. He intended the rulers of Europe to recognise him as their feudal superior and themselves as his political vassals. Some of the smaller kingdoms in Europe, like Sicily and Portugal, were already in that position. Innocent was determined to demonstrate his power, and intervened in wars, political settlements, marriages, alliances, and was eager to arbitrate in the matter of royal succession. Since it was the pope who crowned the Holy Roman Emperor, he undoubtedly could crown lesser kings, and it was possible for a monarch with a dubious claim to have that claim legitimised by submission to the pope. One of those who resisted the power of Innocent for as long as possible was King John of England, but the power of the pope to control not only the minds of men but the armies of Europe, in time made this resistance impractical.

In 1206, there was a dispute between the English bishops and the monks of the cathedral monastery of Christchurch about who had the right to choose a candidate to fill the vacant office of archbishop of Canterbury. John had chosen the bishop of Norwich as his own candidate, but Innocent overruled them all, and decreed that Stephen Langton must fill the vacant see. Langton was an Englishman who had been educated in France, was recognised as an outstanding scholar, and became a cardinal in 1206. John refused to accept him, and so Innocent put England under an interdict. Further pressure was added when John himself was excommunicated in 1209 and declared to be deposed from the throne in 1212. All this he might have ignored, but two other very important factors made John's resistance collapse. John's relationship to his own barons was far from harmonious at the time, and King Philip of France was planning to invade England and enforce the deposition. John had no choice but to submit. Innocent wrote to John expressing his thanks to God for the ministry of the Holy Spirit in guiding him so prudently and piously to promote his own interests and those of the church. He also quotes in the letter the exact wording of John's official attested submission:

> John, by the grace of God King of England, Lord of Ireland, Duke of Normandy and Aquitaine, count of Anjou, to all the faithful of Christ who may see this charter, greeting in the Lord. By this charter attested by our golden seal we wish it to be known to you all that, having in many things offended God and Holy Church our mother and being therefore in the utmost need of divine mercy and possessing nothing but ourselves and our kingdoms that we can offer worthily as due amends to God and the Church, we desire to humble ourselves for the sake of Him who for us humbled Himself even unto death; and inspired by the grace of the Holy Spirit—not induced by force nor compelled by fear, but of our own good and spontaneous will and on the general advice of our barons—we offer and freely yield to God, and to SS Peter and Paul His apostles, and to the Holy Roman Church our mother, and to our lord Pope Innocent III and his catholic successors, the whole kingdom of England and the whole kingdom of Ireland with all their rights and appurtenances for the remission of our sins and the sins of our whole family, both the living and the dead. And now, receiving back

these kingdoms from God and the Roman church and holding
them as feudatory vassal, in the presence of our venerable father
lord Nicholas, bishop of Tusculum, legate of the Apostolic See,
and of Pandulf, subdeacon and member of household to our
lord the Pope, we have pledged and sworn our fealty henceforth
to our lord aforesaid, Pope Innocent III, and to his catholic successors, and to the Roman church, in the terms herein under
stated; and we have publicly paid liege homage for the said kingdoms to God, and to the Holy Apostles Peter and Paul, and to
the Roman church, and to our lord aforesaid, Pope Innocent III,
at the hands of the said legate who accepts our homage in place
and instead of our said lord the Pope; and we bind in perpetuity
our successors and legitimate heirs that without question they
must similarly render fealty and acknowledge to the Supreme
Pontiff holding office at the time and to the Roman church. As a
token of this our perpetual offering and concession we will and
decree that out of the proper and special revenues of our said
kingdoms, in lieu of all service and payment which we should
render for them, the Roman Church is to receive annually,
without prejudice to the payment of Peter's pence, one thousand marks sterling. . . . Desiring all these terms to be exactly
as stated, to be forever ratified and valid, we bind ourselves and
our successors not to contravene them; and if we or any of our
successors shall presume to contravene them, then, no matter
who he be, unless on due warning he come to his senses, let him
lose the title to the kingdom and let this document of our offer
remain ever valid. . . . So help me God and the Holy Gospels of
God whereon I swear.[4]

This humiliating submission of the king might have brought about peace
between John and Pope Innocent, but his quarrels with his barons were
far from over. The growing discontent with the barons had erupted into
civil war by 1215, and in June of that year John was compelled to accept the terms the barons set out in the Magna Carta. Having accepted
this settlement, however, when John almost immediately appealed to the
pope, Innocent released him from any obligation to keep the agreement,
because John had entered it without the consent of his feudal overlord
and therefore it was not binding on him as vassal of Innocent III. Both
John and the pope died the following year in 1216, and the succession of
the king's son, Henry III, might have been uncertain but for the protec-
tive and stabilising power which John had resisted for so long, namely the

4. Cheney and Semple, *Selected Letters of Pope Innocent III*, 178.

authority of the bishop of Rome. In fact, the arrangement by which King John recognised the authority of the pope over his kingdom was more of a truce than a permanent settlement, because in the following century, in 1365, the English Parliament legislated to ensure that disputes over benefices were decided by the royal court and did not fall under the jurisdiction of the church. This was especially significant since at this time the influence of the Reformer John Wycliffe was beginning to be felt. Wycliffe was a theological, ecclesiastical, and political revolutionary who taught that the king should disendow a sinful church and return it to a purer poverty. A further indication of the weakening of the control of the state by the church was the fact that the tribute promised by King John to Pope Innocent III had not been paid for thirty-three years. The current pope, Urban V, demanded immediate payment with the threat that should it be refused, the penalties spelled out in John's submission would be brought into effect. The result of this threat was to unite the whole of England in a determination to deny what John had surrendered. It was claimed that John had acted without the consent of his people and therefore his agreement was illegal and void. The possibility was considered that the wealth of the church should be turned over to the state, and although this did not immediately happen, the seeds were sown that would come to fruition in the not-too-distant future.

Although Wycliffe's role in the political life of England was kept within bounds his influence abroad was considerable, and this coincided with a spirit of general unease about the church and its government. Kings and popes continued to battle for supreme power. The balance swung one way and then the other. In the reign of Philip IV, King of France, which spanned the thirteenth and fourteenth centuries, the king had clearly and deliberately denied the right of the pope to rule in the secular world. As was often the case, the issue of levying taxes was a matter of specific disagreement. When a Frenchman, Clement V, became pope in 1305, he was very much under the influence of the French king and, in fact, the pope and the entire papal administration was moved from Rome to Avignon. The location of the papacy at Avignon lasted for seventy years and involved seven popes; however, since England and France were in a state of more or less constant rivalry, which could break out into open war as it did in 1338, Englishmen had an additional reason to be resentful of the authoritarian claims of French popes who were in a position to appoint and tax English clerics. King Edward III of England was wary of adopting legal procedures against papal influence, but eventually Acts of Parliament were passed which kept the appointment of English clerics and the distribution of church finances within England. In fact, a compromise was worked out whereby the laws were in force but did not have to be applied. The pope and king had an unofficial agreement that the pope would only appoint clerics which the king had chosen.

The atmosphere during the Avignon papacy was one of ecclesiastical wheeling and dealing. Church offices were bought and sold. Men received stipends for spiritual responsibilities they had no intention of fulfilling. Bishops from other lands gravitated to Avignon in hope of promotion. Some were appointed as bishops for financial gain without ever having been ordained as priests, while others were priests with almost no training for their office. The historian Philip Hughes writes,

> The terrible abuses which in the end accompanied the system everywhere did more than anything else to bring about that indifference of Catholics to the cause of the church as such, which is, perhaps, the chief single cause of the collapse of Catholicism in the sixteenth century.[5]

There were serious attempts made to reform the system—e.g., when Benedict XII became pope there was a general flight from Avignon of corrupt church officials who saw the writing on the wall and fled while they could. This pope also turned his face from the use of military force to gain his purposes. Others of the Avignon popes achieved a fearsome reputation for their treatment of those who aroused their wrath. Bridget of Sweden, who founded the new religious Order of St. Bridget, wrote of Pope Innocent VI,

> Pope Innocent, more abominable than Jewish usurers, a greater traitor than Judas, more cruel than Pilot . . . has been cast into hell like a weighty stone. His cardinals have been consumed by the very fire that devoured Sodom.[6]

Bridget, who was never slow to scourge unworthy clerics, had a major influence on the papacy in her day, and after consulting her and seeking her advice, Pope Gregory XI left Avignon for Rome on 13 September 1376. The struggle between church and state was far from over.

---

5. Hughes, *History of the Church*, 3:174.
6. Ibid., 187.

12

Daughter of Rome

Subject to the apostolic see as a special daughter with no intermediary.[1]

THE ELEVENTH-CENTURY OCCUPATION OF England by the Normans did not leave her northern neighbour unaffected. Malcolm III, the Scottish king, was not infrequently employed in raiding into the disputed borderlands across the Tweed, and in 1070, William the Conqueror came north on a punitive mission with a fleet and an army, and at Abernethy compelled Malcolm to agree to a treaty. Arguments raged for many years about exactly what conditions Malcolm had accepted in the treaty; however, in practical terms it seemed to be worthless, since both the Scottish king and his son Edward died on yet another military expedition into Northumberland in 1093. Malcolm's English Queen Margaret died, it was said, of grief four days later.

The queen, whose personal piety seems to have been completely genuine, had a refining influence on the Scottish court and church. Although there might have been initially a measure of resistance from the strong Celtic element in the church, it was the influence of Margaret which brought Scottish church life closer to the pattern of the church in Europe. She built a new church in Dunfermline, encouraged the cult of St. Andrew, and brought a small group of monks from Canterbury to found a Benedictine priory.

After the death of Malcolm, competition for the Scottish crown left, at first, Malcolm's brother Donald on the throne, but in 1097, an army led

1. Cited by Carson, in *Oxford Companion to British History.*

by Edgar, who was Malcolm's son and also the vassal of King William Rufus of England, defeated and captured Donald, who was compelled to end his life as a Cluniac monk. Edgar reigned as William's vassal until 1107, when he was succeeded by his brother Alexander, who continued to look to the English sovereign as his feudal superior, and in 1100 had married Sybil, the daughter of Henry I, king of England. However, subjection to the English throne was not absolute, because in the reign of Alexander, signs began to appear of a slow movement towards consolidation and independence in Scottish political and religious life. New castles were built. Augustinians arrived from Yorkshire and began to have an increasing influence on the Scottish church. The see of St. Andrews, which had been supervised from York, saw the appointment of a new bishop.

When Alexander died in 1124, he was followed by his brother David, who although a son of the Scottish royal line had been brought up as an Anglo-Norman at the English court. As the youngest son of the pious Queen Margaret, David founded many monasteries and encouraged his leading nobles to do the same. He reorganised his bishops, succeeded in making St. Andrews an archbishopric, and set about extracting the sees of Glasgow and St. Andrews from the control of Canterbury and York. Perhaps the most important religious change that took place in the reign of David was the development of the parish church system and the collection of tithes associated with it. The other feature of an energetic reign was David's encouragement of Norman knights to settle in northwest England and southwest Scotland in a political system based on the Norman model. Several Norman families were settled in this way, but among the land distribution none was more significant than the allocation of a large tract of land to the family "de Brus" at Annandale.

Because of his Norman background and dependence on the English crown, it was perhaps surprising to find David leading a huge Scottish army in an unsuccessful invasion of northern England in 1138. He also had to contend with a number of rebellions in his own country, and when he died in 1153, the succession was far from clear. David's grandson Malcolm IV reigned until 1165, followed by his brother William until 1214. A serious attempt was being made to weld the disparate elements in the north and west into a single country, but this was not helped by the lack of definition in the line of succession, nor by William's largely unsuccessful squabbles over border territory with England, nor by the fact that so many of the Scottish aristocracy held lands outside of Scotland. William did not marry until 1186, when he was forty-three years old, and his first legitimate heir was his son Alexander, born in 1198. Alexander II came to the throne in 1214 and was followed by his son Alexander III in 1249, who was eleven years old. Both these kings married English princesses, but when Alexander III died in an accident in 1286, three of his children who might have been his heirs had predeceased him, and the heir to the throne of Scotland was his granddaughter Margaret, the child of his daughter, also Margaret, and her husband, Eric II, king of Norway. The little "Maid of Norway" was still in that country, and because of her age, preparation had to be made to govern Scotland.

Six guardians were chosen. They were four nobles, and the bishops of St. Andrews and Glasgow. In consultation with Edward I of England, a treaty was arranged by which the little princess would marry Edward's son when they were of age. This was not a union of England and Scotland but was to be a joint reign over two separate and independent kingdoms. However, this carefully planned solution to the stressful relationship between the two countries came to nothing when the little Maid of Norway died at Orkney on her journey to Scotland in September 1290, leaving thirteen candidates claiming succession to the Scottish crown.[2] Of course, Edward of England demanded recognition as feudal superior of Scotland, and this claim was easier to establish because of the rivalry among so many Scottish candidates for the throne. A panel of arbiters was set up which Edward controlled, and in November 1292, John Balliol was made king of Scotland by a legal process which involved clear recognition of the Scottish monarch as Edward's vassal. In the years which followed, Edward took more than one opportunity to demonstrate his power over the Scots, and this was dramatically portrayed at Montrose in 1296, when Edward symbolically removed the symbols of kingship from John Balliol. Relations between the two countries were not too far from open warfare.

During this difficult period of humiliation and oppression, Scotland had been reinforcing her bonds with France. An alliance which promised mutual military assistance was arranged, as well as the future marriage of the son of John Balliol to the niece of Philip IV of France. The timing could not have been worse for Edward of England. He was at war with France and demanded Scottish forces to support his war effort. Scottish troops did in fact gather into an army, but its purpose was the invasion

2. Lynch, *Scotland*, 115.

of England in 1296. However, the Scottish army was vastly outnumbered by the English forces, and by July of the same year, King John and his advisors were prisoners in the Tower of London. Almost immediately, a group of English officials were set up to govern Scotland. The result was not, however, the peace Edward hoped for. His war with France was not going well and some of his own subjects were objecting to the taxes and manpower they had to supply for the war effort. The Scots took the opportunity to rebel against English rule on several occasions, and even though these were crushed, the occupation of Scotland proved to be difficult and expensive to maintain. One strand of Edward's policy was the appointment of English clergy to Scottish benefices, but this proved to be impracticable, since the church in Scotland saw political and ecclesiastical independence as mutually beneficial, and in general terms this view was supported by the papacy.

There had been for centuries strong links between the church and Scottish monarchy. While the exact division of authority was not spelled out, there is evidence that the church, in some sense at least, pronounced divine blessing on the coronation of kings from as far back as the days of Columba in the sixth century.[3] A further record in the Chronicle of the Kings of Alba describes a ceremony which took place early in the tenth century at Scone, which indicates some sort of covenant between crown and church:

> In the vi year king Constantin and bishop Cellach pledged to keep the laws and disciplines of the faith and the rights of the Church and the Gospels partier cum Scottis on the Hill of Belief next to the royal cuitas of Scone. From that day the hill earned its name, that is the Hill of Belief.[4]

A patriotic myth was born and carefully nourished to present the legend of a long line of Scottish kings loyal to the church and supportive of the papacy, and while this concept owed more to pious imagination and political expediency than to historical accuracy, there was a strand of truth woven into the mythical tapestry.

In the sixth and seventh centuries, Pope Gregory the Great, as part of his strategy for the evangelisation of the British Isles, had divided the entire land into two provinces under the control of the bishops of London and York. However, when Celestine III became pope in March 1191,

3. Ibid., 93.
4. Wolf, *Pictland to Alba*, 134.

at the age of eighty-five, he had to deal with the overwhelming energy and authority of the German emperor Henry VI, who was determined to rule both church and empire like the Roman emperors of former days. It was this emperor who captured Richard I of England and compelled the recognition of himself as the imperial overlord. Pope Celestine III, in an action not altogether unrelated to the problem of churches controlled by secular rulers, issued the bull Cum Universi as a proof and recognition of Scottish loyalty to the Roman see. The Scottish church had always seen itself as an integral part of Western Christendom, and this was confirmed by the bull in which it was asserted that "the Scottish church is subject to the apostolic see as a special daughter with no intermediary." Throughout Europe there were bishoprics under the direct control of the pope, but Scotland was the only ecclesiastical province with this special relationship. In practical terms this meant that the Scottish church was free to conduct its own affairs without interference from the archbishops of York or Canterbury, and that only delegates sent directly from Rome could speak for the pope The exceptions to this rule were the see of Galloway, which remained under the authority of York, and that of The Isles which was governed by the Norwegian archbishop of Trondheim.[5] The bull, which was issued again by Popes Innocent III and Honorius III in the thirteenth century, certainly protected the Scottish church from English control, but it was found that direct control from Rome was not an unmixed blessing. In conflict with England, Scottish kings could find themselves opposing papal support for English overlordship and having to repent under threat of financial penalties. In 1251, Henry III of England wanted to raise taxes in Scotland to finance his crusade in Palestine. Pope Innocent IV vetoed this at first, but then agreed. However, instead of supporting the crusade, a decision was taken to use the tax to pay part of the price for the kingdom of Sicily, which the pope sold to Henry III for his son. Throughout the thirteenth century, several similar taxes were demanded from Scotland with papal support. Some were refused and some were paid with great reluctance and were diverted to the English crown. While the pope made serious attempts to gain the cooperation of the Scottish clergy, there were a number of occasions when papal authority overruled Scottish preferences, and while these incidents may have damaged the special relationship, it was never broken. The Scottish church continued to look to Rome to guarantee her freedom, and in

5. Brown, *Wars of Scotland*, 124.

Scotland, church and crown continued to support one another. It was the recognition of Scotland as a single province of the Western church which helped to define the political unity of the emerging nation.

During this period, while the "special relationship" prevented any official rule of the church by the state, in fact the king had great influence over the appointment to positions of ecclesiastical authority. This tended to make the church a route to political power, and not a few ambitious men followed this course. Leading Scottish bishops demonstrated consistent loyalty to the crown even when it might not have been expected for them to do so, taking an active part in both the political and military events of their day.

Michael Brown writes,

> Clergy played a vital role in sanctioning warfare to the wider population. This was never more vital than in the months and years after Robert Bruce's seizure of the throne. A usurper, a homicide and an excommunicant, Robert's qualifications as a royal leader were hardly those supported conventionally by the church. However in February and March 1306, Wishart legitimised Bruce's claim to the kingship, absolving him of his sins, administering an oath in which Robert promised to follow "the direction of the clergy of Scotland" and producing from his wardrobe and treasury the vestments and royal banner used in the inauguration of the new king.[6]

The support of the leaders of the Scottish church for the crown certainly did not endear them to the Plantagenet kings of England nor the English clergy, and that support was not always uniform in degree, but that it was a vital element in the continuing demand for the independence of Scotland cannot be denied.

6. Brown, *Wars of Scotland*, 311.

13

The Stewart Dynasty

> Unfortunately for Scotland, a hundred years had to pass
> before a worthy successor sat on the throne of Bruce.[1]

THE SUPPORT OF THE Scottish nobility for Robert I was expressed in
the Declaration of Arbroath in 1320, which was a document addressed to the pope. The ecclesiastical face of national independence
seemed to have been assured by the papal bull "Super Anxietatibus" in
1176, separating the Scottish church from the control of the archbishop
of York. The special relationship to the apostolic see was set out in the bull
Cum Universi of 1192, and this was followed by another bull, Quidam
Vestrum in 1225, giving the Scottish church the right to hold provincial
councils although there was no metropolitan see.

Robert I died in 1329, to be succeeded by his son David II, whose
reign, in spite of his father's success, was far from untroubled. Seven years
were spent in exile in France and eleven as a prisoner in England. He was
released in 1357 on the promise of a ransom which the Scottish government never fully paid, and peace with England was only secured by an
arrangement whereby a son of the English king should succeed David on
the Scottish throne. However, the arrangement came to nothing, and in
1371, David was succeeded by Robert Stewart, the grandson of Robert
the Bruce. This monarch was the first of a royal dynasty which was to last
until the end of the seventeenth century.

---

1. Mackie, *Short History of Scotland*, 149.

Robert II seemed to lack personal authority, and control of his kingdom was largely administered through his sons. Conflict with England trundled on with armies crossing the borders, captives taken, and ransoms paid. The internal affairs of Scotland were likewise troubled by the rivalry amongst the king's sons, and when Robert II died in 1390, the throne passed to his son John, earl of Carrick, who changed his name to Robert III and whose inheritance was not gained without military force. Robert's brother Alexander, the infamous and fierce "Wolf of Badenoch," had attacked Elgin and Forres, burning Elgin Cathedral, and the new king's coronation was in fact delayed by his attempts to pacify conditions in the region of Moray. The Scottish bishops were caught up in the political struggles. Alexander was, for his crimes, excommunicated by Bishop Bur of Moray but later reinstated by Bishop Trail of St. Andrews.[2] The Wolf continued to exercise considerable power in the north of the realm and remained a thorn in the side of his brothers and other political rivals. Robert III was past the vigour of his youth, being fifty-three years old when he came to the throne, nevertheless, gradually there seemed to be a greater measure of control over his kingdom.

The successor to Robert III was James, although he was not the eldest of the king's sons. In 1406, this young prince was sent to France for his education and his safety from rival claimants to the throne. His ship, however, was captured by English pirates before he reached his destination, and while he was a prisoner in England, his father the king died. The Scottish government recognised him as king in his absence although he remained a prisoner for eighteen years. While he was imprisoned, Robert Stewart, the duke of Albany and brother of the late king, was appointed as governor at the age of sixty-six. Relationships with England continued to be stormy and it was suspected in some quarters that Albany was in no hurry to have James released from captivity. Albany died in 1420 to be succeeded, as governor, by his son Murdoch. The new governorship was a mixture of success and failure, but Murdoch did negotiate the return of James in 1424 to become James I, king of Scotland. Michael Lynch cites the description of the restored monarch as a "king unleashed."[3]

The new monarch lost no time in dealing with those who might seem to be a political threat. Even before his coronation he arrested Murdoch's son, and later executed Murdoch himself and two of his sons. In

2. Boardman, *Early Stewart Kings*, 176.
3. Lynch, *Scotland*, 144.

1428, he called a gathering of Highland leaders at Inverness and put fifty of them into prison. This kind of action could only arouse hostility, which might have been kept under control had it not been for the combination of military ineptitude and increasing taxation which accompanied it. In spite of a secure line of succession in the birth of a son and closer alliance with France, a plot organised by the chamberlain of his household brought about the king's assassination in February 1437. The church could only condemn the murder, and Lynch comments, "The resuscitation of the reputation of James I began early when the visiting bishop of Urbino kissed the wounds on the corpse and proclaimed the dead king a martyr for the commonwealth."[4] While the king was far from popular with his subjects, neither was his murder, and so the assassins were quickly brought to justice and executed.

The son and heir of James I, at the age of seven years, was crowned James II by the bishop of Dunblane at Holyrood Abbey in March 1437. In view of the many years that must elapse before the little king could exercise personal authority, there was a problem in choosing a governor to rule the nation. Furthermore, among the leading families who might be expected to provide someone to fill such an office there was a shortage of adult candidates, while other suitable members of the Scottish nobility were prisoners in England. A struggle developed to control the king in which the two most powerful contenders were the queen dowager and the Earl of Douglas. In such a time of political instability, the church, which was strongly supportive of the crown and could usually be relied upon to exercise a controlling influence, was perhaps less influential than might have been expected because the attention of Scottish churchmen was focused on the ecclesiastical wrangling going on at the Council of Basel. This assembly trudged on from 1431 until 1449. One of the main sources of conflict at Basel was the continuing assertion that ultimate authority in the church lay not with the pope but with a general council, and at Basel the council was determined that the pope should recognise its legitimacy as the authoritative body. It was decreed that "all ecclesiastical persons" should, when summoned, attend such councils, and,

> if the Roman Pontiff or other above-mentioned persons fail to do this, or in any way take means to impede change, prorogue or dissolve the council, and shall not have repented with real satisfaction within four months, thereafter the pope will

4. Ibid., 146.

114

be automatically suspended from the papal administration and . . . the papal administration will devolve by law upon the sacred council. If they persist with hardened hearts . . . for a further two months . . . then the general council shall proceed against both the Roman pontiff and the above-mentioned persons up to and including the penalty of deprivation.[5]

The year after the coronation of James II of Scotland, the French king, Charles VIII, at the city of Bourges, convened a synod at which it was confirmed that "the authority of the general council is superior to that of the pope in all that pertains to the faith, the extirpation of schism and the reform of the Church in both head and members."[6]

The Scottish church, as the "special daughter of Rome," and at the same time the political ally of France against England, could hardly be blamed for allowing the focus of their attention to drift to some degree from domestic affairs. However in 1449, as the Council of Basel came to an end, the church was once again concerned with Scottish matters, when the nation saw the marriage of James II to Mary of Gueldres, the niece of the Duke of Burgundy, and the young bride, as a strong supporter of the church and patron of an austere group of Franciscans called the Observants, did much to reinforce the bond between church and crown.

James began to display a measure of ruthlessness in exerting royal control over some of his most powerful subjects, and when, in 1452, he stabbed and killed the Earl of Douglas in Stirling, the incident almost brought about civil war. In spite of this being averted, within a few years the king had well nigh destroyed the power of the Douglas family, and James, by means of the annexation of lands and property, the shrewd allocation of political honours, and the marriage of members of the royal family to powerful men, brought about a new level of stability in Scotland. So confident was the king that he set about the capture of the Isle of Man and the castle of Roxborough, both of which were under English control. In August 1460, at the siege of Roxborough, James II died when one of his own canons exploded. The siege was successful, but within days his son and heir, aged nine, was crowned at Kelso Abbey and became James III, king of Scotland.

In the early years of James III, the government of the nation was strongly influenced by Mary, his widowed mother, who had been

5. Council of Basel, Session 11, 27 April 1433.
6. Pragmatic Sanction of Bourges, 1438, clause 2.

appointed his guardian in 1461. The other major influence was James Kennedy, bishop of St. Andrews. In the English War of the Roses, the sympathies of the Scots and of Bishop Kennedy were with the Lancastrians, but Mary the queen mother was inclined to seek support for the Yorkists. However, in March 1461, the Lancastrian King Henry VI of England was decisively defeated by his Yorkist enemies and fled to Scotland with Margaret, his queen, and his son Edward. His arrival in Scotland was made more acceptable because he brought with him, and delivered into Scottish hands, the surrender of the town of Berwick, which had been under English control. The Yorkist Edward IV now ruled England and demonstrated his resentment of Scottish Lancastrian support by conspiring with magnates in the south and west of Scotland who were fomenting opposition to the Scottish crown. The influence of the queen mother, Mary of Gueldres, helped to avoid open warfare, and Edward was fairly soon embroiled in a split within his own ranks. A difference in government between Edward and the Earl of Warwick, one of his earliest and strongest supporters, developed into civil war. Warwick, with French help, forced Edward to flee to the Netherlands and restored the Lancastrian Henry VI to the English throne. However, Edward, with the support of Burgundians, returned in force in March 1471 and was able to gain a complete victory over Warwick and Henry VI.

Henry's wife, Margaret, was captured. His son, Edward, was killed, and Henry himself was later murdered. In this later civil war in England, which finally ended the Wars of the Roses, the Scots offered the Lancastrians no assistance. Mary the Scottish queen mother had died in 1463, as well as Bishop Kennedy two years later.

The influence of the church on Scottish politics and national life is illustrated by the career of Bishop Kennedy. As the grandson of Robert III and nephew of James I, he was appointed bishop of Dunkeld in 1437. In spite of this being a royal appointment, it did receive papal confirmation, and Kennedy remained firmly committed to the authority of the pope in the conciliarist dispute. In 1440, he became bishop of St. Andrews, and while opinions vary as to his qualities as a Christian leader, his influence in national affairs was considerable, especially after the death of the queen mother. Within three years of Kennedy's death, the seventeen-year-old James III began his personal rule in 1468, and in 1469 was married to the twelve-year-old Princess Margaret of Denmark and Norway. The failure to receive Margaret's dowry in full brought the successful assertion of Scottish claims to the Western Isles, the Orkneys, and the Shetlands. It is doubtful if the young king had the strength of character to deal with the pressures of Scottish political life during his reign. He was almost continually under threat from stronger powerbrokers, notably his brothers, the Duke of Albany and the Earl of Mar. There was also an ongoing tension between the Scottish government and the papacy for the control of ecclesiastical appointments and church income, and in James's reign a number of measures were taken to bring these under crown control. Patrick Graham, the nephew of James Kennedy, became bishop of St. Andrews in 1465, and when in 1472 the see was elevated to metropolitan status, with Graham as the first archbishop, the whole process was effected in Rome by authority of Pope Sixtus IV without any attempt to gain the agreement of James III and his government. When Graham returned to Scotland the following year, a levy was imposed on his property, his authority was ignored, and in time he was charged with heresy. His health broke under this pressure and he died in 1478, to be replaced by William Scheves, whose loyalty to the crown was unquestioned. The church in Scotland was an essential part of the royal administration, and its officers had to recognise this fact. For much of the reign of James III, the king was greatly influenced by the wrong men. He had gathered around him a number of companions whose interests were artistic rather than political and whose personal relationships to the king were abhorrent to his government. This group persuaded James to arrest his brothers, the Duke of Albany and the Earl of Mar, in 1479. Mar died in prison, but Albany escaped and fled to France. Within a few years, Albany returned, supported by Edward IV of England and other allies. His success in Scotland was made possible by the unpopularity of the king among so many of his nobles, and Lynch comments that Margaret the queen was probably also involved in the rebellion.[7] In the conflict, the king's companions were captured and hanged from Lauder bridge and James himself was imprisoned in Edinburgh castle. His captors, however, were divided in their loyalties, and James was able to leave the castle and even negotiate a temporary truce with Albany. However, in 1483, Albany and the Earl of Douglas attempted yet another unsuccessful bid for power in the conquest of Scotland. They were defeated at Lochmaben. Douglas was imprisoned for the rest of his life. Albany fled again to safety in France but was involved in a fatal accident there two years later. In all

7. Lynch, *Scotland*, 157.

these troubled circumstances James seems to have been unable to learn the skills of royal government. His lifestyle remained unchanged, the trust of his political leaders was limited, and in 1488 some of his nobles launched yet another attempt to remove him from the throne with the support of his heir, the future James IV. The young prince, who believed that his position as future king was threatened by a younger brother, was at first in the custody of James but escaped to join the rebels. Battle was joined at Sauchieburn, and the king's forces were defeated. James fled from the field, and one account of his death records that he was murdered by a man who pretended to be a priest called to give him the sacrament.[8] Fifteen days later, James IV was crowned at Scone, and his coronation marked the beginning of a very different kind of reign. The new king was only fifteen years old when he was crowned, but he was not slow to learn from the mistakes of the past. He had been used by his father as a second-rate player in the game of proposed matrimonial alliances with England.[9] However, as he matured, he began to exert firmer control over his realm. He was energetic in dealing with rebellious nobles and he exploited to the full the rights of the crown to property and funds. Unlike his father, he showed concern for the administration of justice to all of his subjects, and there was an overall rise in the national prosperity. The art of printing and the growth of learning were other factors in the reign of James IV. The king himself spoke six languages and encouraged the patronage of poets and musicians at court, while in parallel to this there was fostered the cult of "honour" which helped to unite his nobles. In his dealings with England, James was more confident than his predecessor. He spend a great deal of money in building his navy, and even when the two nations were officially at peace, Scots and English ships mounted acts of piracy against one another. The king seemed at times to go out of his way to shake the stability of English politics. In 1495, an imposter called Perkin Warbeck arrived in Scotland from Ireland. Brought up in Antwerp, Warbeck in earlier days had come into contact with exiled supporters of the English Yorkists headed by Margaret, duchess of Burgundy and sister to English King Edward IV. Alert to any opportunity to damage Henry VII, the exiled Yorkists persuaded Warbeck to masquerade as Richard, one of sons of Edward IV supposedly murdered in the Tower of London. European rulers similarly opposed to Henry and the house of

8. Rait, *Making of Scotland*, 124.
9. Macdougall, *James IV*, 13.

Tudor supplied him with men and ships to invade England. The attempt was unsuccessful, as was a similar adventure in Ireland, and so Warbeck crossed over to Scotland and James IV. It can hardly be supposed that James believed the claims of his guest to the English throne were genuine, but nevertheless he publicly acknowledged him as Prince Richard of England, arranged his marriage to the daughter of the Earl of Huntly, and assisted him in a fruitless invasion of Northumberland. In September 1497, Warbeck attempted his last invasion of England in Cornwall, and for a time found the support of local rebels, who were fairly soon crushed by Henry's troops. He surrendered, and in 1499 was hanged for his attempt to escape from the Tower. Such an impostor was hardly a serious threat to Henry VII, but he was at least one of the factors which made an alliance with James IV seem expedient. This resulted in the marriage of James to Henry's daughter Margaret at Holyrood in 1503, and the union of the "Thistle and the Rose" left their son, Arthur, born in 1509, second in line to the English throne.

James was nothing if not ambitious, and his traditional animosity against England and sympathy with France led him to become embroiled in machinations of the Holy League. The extremely vigorous and warlike Pope Julius II, in an attempt to control the complex elements in European politics, formed a league with Louis XII of France, Ferdinand II of Aragon, and Maximilian I, the Holy Roman Emperor. Political loyalties, however, tended to change fairly easily, and allies became enemies with amazing speed. By November 1510, Henry VIII, king of England, who had succeeded his father the previous year, was proposing to unite with the pope against France, which left James IV contemplating a conflict between Julius and Louis, his two most important allies in Europe. In spite of James's attempts to mediate in the growing hostility, Julius, in 1511, formed the "Holy League," which created an alliance in which he lined up with the Venetians, Ferdinand, Maximilian, and Henry, against France. France was placed under a papal interdict and the French bishops tried to have Julius deposed.

James held a council in Edinburgh early in 1512 to confirm his alliance with France and perhaps thereby persuade Henry to abandon any attempt to invade that country. James also dallied with the notion of going on crusade and hoped that a grateful Louis might help him to achieve that aim. The crusade never came to pass, but what did become clear was the firm intention of Henry to be at war with France. In addition to the loyalty of James to his French ally, there was also his claim to the English throne. The succession of the Tudor line was by no means secure, and King Louis of France supported James's claim, should Henry VIII fail to provide an heir. The atmosphere grew worse as Henry claimed both the French throne and the overlordship of Scotland. A peace treaty with England had been in place, at least nominally, since 1502, and had been renewed in 1509. Nevertheless, in August 1513, James, with the support of almost all his subjects and his English queen, and reinforced by French aid, led his army across the border into England. Pope Julius II, just before he died in February the same year, had promised the excommunication of the Scottish king if he attacked England, and this threat was activated by the next pope, Leo X, when James went to war.

Although the Scots seemed at first to be destined for success, the end result was a disaster. On 9 September, the battle of Flodden left James dead on the field together with many of his nobles, a number of clergy including his illegitimate son Alexander Stewart, who was the archbishop of St. Andrews and chancellor of Scotland, and thousands of Scottish soldiers. The support of leading Scottish churchmen for their monarch was a reflection of the importance James IV placed on the church as an institution. His loyalty to the church and the Roman see were recognised in 1507, when he received two symbolic papal gifts, the blessed Sword and Hat.[10] In the eyes of his subjects this was a specific mark of papal, and therefore divine, favour, and for more than three centuries no Scottish monarch had received such an honour. However, since church leaders had a vital role to play in Parliament, the nomination to senior positions was in the hands of the king subject to papal recognition, and in practical terms, James controlled the church. Politically and financially the church served the crown. It was, therefore, a devastating blow to church as well as state when the confidence and enthusiasm of the Scots were so badly damaged at Flodden. However, as bad as it was, the situation left both kingdom and church injured but far from dead.

10. Macdougall, *James IV*, 196.

14

The Reek of Patrick Hamilton

The reek of Patrick Hamilton affected all it blew on.[1]

K ING JAMES V OF Scotland was born in April 1512 and therefore was less than two years old when his father died at Flodden. He was crowned in the Chapel Royal at Stirling in September 1513, twelve days after his father's death. A council of regency was formed, Archbishop James Beaton of Glasgow became chancellor, and the widowed Queen Margaret was regent and guardian of her son. In spite of the outstanding English victory at Flodden, Henry VIII, whose attention was focussed on European tensions and developments, did not send his armies to follow up their triumph with a full scale invasion of Scotland, and so the Scottish government found breathing space in which some degree of order could be established. Bishop Elphinstone of Aberdeen was perhaps the most capable administrator and cleric in Scotland and the obvious choice to become the new archbishop of St. Andrews, but he died in 1514, and Andrew Forman, bishop of Moray, was able, with papal approval, to negotiate his way into the leadership of the Scottish church. Although Margaret had publicly supported her husband's invasion of England, her position as the queen regent was open to suspicion because she maintained a fairly close and dependent relationship with her brother, Henry VIII. She wrote to him saying that only lack of funds forced her to agree with her council and that whatever steps gained her agreement would not

1. Attributed to John Lindsay, servant of archbishop David Beaton, at the execution of one of Hamilton's disciples. Forbush, *Fox's Book of Martyrs*, 198.

take place without his guidance. Her separation from him, she claimed, was due to the responsibilities of motherhood and her pregnancy with the second child of her dead husband. The child, in fact, died in infancy, and her regency was terminated by her marriage in August to Archibald Douglas, the nineteen-year-old earl of Angus. This wedding was anything but a royal celebration. Henry did not even know of it until September, and it certainly did not have the approval of the queen's council. Angus was a "Douglas" and suspect on that ground alone, and he was also a known supporter of Henry VIII. Scottish loyalty was split between queen and council. The council sent for John, the duke of Albany, to become the new governor of Scotland and guardian of the young king, although Albany, for all practical purposes, was a Frenchman. He was certainly in line for the Scottish throne, but his French land holdings, his interests, and his service to the French crown made him an unusual choice to be Scottish regent. A further problem was that Albany spoke not a word of Scots, but when he arrived in May 1515, he began to build a gratifying measure of support in spite of some degree of opposition. Margaret and Angus fled to England, leaving the young James V in the care of Albany. A growing coalition, encouraged by Henry VIII, did attempt unsuccessfully to remove the king from Albany's guardianship and actually took up arms against the new regent, but his sincere concern for the young king, his efforts to maintain law and order, and his support of the rights of the Scottish crown to make church appointments won him increasing support. Neither was he noticeably vindictive in dealing with his opponents. Some were pardoned, and Angus, whose marriage to Margaret was rapidly becoming stormy, was able to return to Scotland and was restored to the council by March 1516. In June 1517, Albany returned to France, where the alliance between Scotland and France was confirmed with the new French King Francis I, and immediately after Albany left Scotland, Margaret returned. The absence of the regent seemed to be the signal for all kinds of squabbling to break out in the borders, and even in Edinburgh there was fighting in the streets. Men who feared for the stability of the whole country sent urgently for the return of Albany from France. Margaret by this time, desperate to be rid of Angus, wanted a divorce, and since Albany was related to Pope Leo X, she hoped he could influence the pope to grant an annulment. For Margaret, Albany had changed from enemy to ally much to the displeasure of Henry VIII, who saw the alliance as a personal betrayal. Angus, casting himself on Albany's mercy, was exiled to France. The strong alliance between Scotland and her French ally came with a price. The Scots had no appetite for renewed war with England, but a Scottish invasion of England was very much on the agenda of the king of France. To encourage this, Albany went to France late in 1522 and brought back to Scotland in September 1523 a fairly substantial French army. Even this, however, failed to generate the invasion of England, and having used up a considerable supply of Scottish food and fuel, the French troops, to the great relief of the Scots, left six weeks later. Nursing his disappointment and frustration, Albany went back to France in the late spring of 1524. He would never see Scotland again. Margaret, in March 1526, married James Stewart, who would become Lord Methven, while her ex-husband Angus, who had been brought back from France by Henry VIII, was again in Scotland and again a member of council. As the young king grew older it became less simple to control his location and his activities. A matter of weeks after Albany returned to France for the last time, in July 1524, the Earl of Arran and Margaret arranged for James V to be personally invested with the symbols of monarchy and to attend the council, where his authority to govern was formally recognised. An arrangement was in place whereby the king would remain in the custody of a number of his leading magnates in rotation, but while under the control of Angus in June 1526, a second investiture of the king took place, the outcome of which was to leave the king virtually a prisoner, Angus very much in control, and the rest of the Scots powerless in political terms. The council almost ceased to function. Angus began to install many of his Douglas kinsmen into important offices and became chancellor himself in 1527. As long as he held the king, he seemed to be invincible. In May 1528, James escaped and fled to Stirling Castle, which Margaret his mother gave over to him in exchange for his recognition of her third marriage to Lord Methven. In July, he returned to Edinburgh with Arran and a number of other powerful men in support. Angus fled Edinburgh, and when Parliament met without him he was charged with treason and declared to be an outlaw. An attempt to squeeze him out of Tantallon Castle did not succeed, but the Douglases did receive permission to move to England if they gave up their strongholds. From this point onwards, James V was to a much greater extent in charge of his own life. In January 1537, James gained a wife and a substantial dowry. He married Madeleine, the daughter of Francis I, however this young queen was in very poor health and in fact died in Scotland in July of the same year. James did not remain a widower for long, and in 1538 he found a second bride and another dowry when he married Mary of Guise, a recently widowed French noblewoman. The young king lost little time in demonstrating his royal authority. Troublemakers in the borders were brought to heel. Some were hanged and at least one was burned at the stake. It has been suggested that the vindictiveness of the king towards those he regarded as his enemies made the latter years a "reign of terror," and that execution at the stake had been something unusual in Scotland. It became, however, a form of punishment that was to be repeated more than once. In July 1537, Lady Janet Douglas, aged thirty-three, the sister of the Earl of Angus, the king's stepfather, died at the stake, accused of being part of a plot to murder the king. There was wide and justified suspicion that the charge had been brought as a political manoeuvre, and the practical result was certainly a financial gain for the crown. Like his mother, James V had more than a little respect for the views of his uncle Henry VIII. The English monarch had formally broken with the papacy in 1534 and hoped to persuade his Scottish nephew to take the same action. James, however, in spite of the obvious financial gain from the confiscation of church lands and funds, refused to follow the example of England, much to the approval of his French allies and the pope. His loyalty to the Roman see gained him papal approval of increased taxes levied on the church, which was very much under royal control. The church itself was at the time involved in a conflict of authority between James Beaton the archbishop of St. Andrews and Gavin Dunbar, archbishop of Glasgow. Neither James nor his clergy seemed to give enough weight to the "Lutheran heresies" which were already taking root in Scotland, and since the king's control of the church was achieved, at least in part, by the appointment of his family members to the most prestigious and lucrative posts, James was opposed to any suggestion of rocking the ecclesiastical boat. A law against heresy had been in force since 1525, and in the next decade a number of offenders were accused of this crime. Some recanted and some were burned at the stake, but by far the most influential execution was that of Patrick Hamilton. The great-grandson of King James II of Scotland, Hamilton studied at Paris and Louvain, where he was very much influenced by the Reformation going on in Europe. He returned to Scotland and began further studies at St. Andrews in October 1524, where he was quickly engaged in debating and preaching his Reformed convictions. Early in 1527, archbishop Beaton demanded his appearance to answer the change of heresy, and Hamilton fled to Germany. After visiting Luther in Wittenberg and spending some time at the University of Marburg, he returned to Scotland later the same year to receive an invitation from Beaton to attend a conference at St. Andrews. It cannot be supposed that Hamilton was unaware of the dangers involved, but he did go to St. Andrews and enjoyed a short period of freedom to preach and debate the doctrines of the Reformation. Within weeks, however, Hamilton was arrested and tried before a church council as a heretic. In February 1528, he died at the stake in St. Andrews, and his martyrdom probably drew more attention to the Reformed faith than his preaching. Those seeking the reformation of the church were found among clergy and nobility alike. The loyalty of James to the Roman church was a continuing irritation to Henry VIII. The English king became convinced that an invasion from France was likely, and so he continued to try to persuade James to separate the Scottish Church from the pope. At this time, some Scottish Lutherans, concerned for their safety, were starting to cross the border into England, while English Roman Catholics came over to Scotland. Henry was encouraged by the apparent willingness of James to consult with him, and so a meeting was arranged in York in 1541 between the two monarchs. There was, however, a suspicion among the Scottish councilors that some kind of treachery was planned, and so James did not appear. After two weeks of waiting, an enraged Henry returned to London convinced he had been deliberately insulted. The following year, Henry intended to launch a preemptive strike on France and demanded an assurance from James that the Scots would not attack England while he was absent. Since this promise amounted to a denial of the Scottish-French alliance, James refused to provide any such assurance. Henry's reaction was to renew the former English claim to be supreme ruler over both countries and war was then inevitable. Battles were fought at more than one location. An English force crossed the border but was defeated at Haddon Rig, but in spite of this success for the Scots, James seems to have had trouble generating enthusiasm to invade England. The Scots military leadership was rearranged and the army, divided into several groups, intended to attack at different points along the border. Scots support for the war proved far from uniform, and some border men in fact attacked and killed their fellow Scots. They captured others and gave them as prisoners to the English. The end came at Solway Moss on 24 November 1542 with the complete rout of the Scottish army. James himself was not at the battle but with another section of the army at Lochmaben. He returned to Falkland and died there on 14 December. Several explanations have been offered for his death, ranging from a depressing lack of will to live to the possibility of cholera, but whatever the cause, his death left Scotland with no male heir. His two sons borne by Mary of Guise had both died in April 1541, and a daughter, Mary, born in December 1542, would inherit not only her father's throne but a kingdom where political and religious pressures would combine to bring her reign and her life to a tragic end.

15

Mary, Queen of Scots

I am yll at ease and glad to write unto you when other folke be asleep, seeing
that I cannot doo as they doo, according to my desyre, that is between your
arms, my dear lyfe, whom I beseech God to preserve from all yall,
and send you good rest as I go to seek myne.[1]

MARY WAS BORN ON 8 December 1542, and her father, James V, died six days later, leaving the immediate task of finding a guardian for the infant queen and a regent to rule until she came of age. James Hamilton, the second earl of Arran and great-grandson of King James II, was appointed regent in January 1543. David Beaton, the archbishop of St. Andrews, who had been made a Cardinal in 1538, became chancellor a week later, and from the beginning these two men were at loggerheads. Beaton was implacably opposed to any reform of the church and wholly committed to the alliance with France. Arran was sympathetic to the Reformation, being in favour of an alliance with Protestant England, and in the first Parliament of Arran's regency, in March 1543, an act was passed permitting the use of the Bible in the common tongue. Beaton, who was blamed in some quarters for the recent disaster at Solway Moss, was accused of deliberately misrepresenting the decision of the dying king to ensure that Arran should not be part of the government.[2] It was also unlikely that Arran could forgive Beaton, ever an enthusiastic hunter of

1. Extract from the second of the "Casket Letters" alleged to have been written by Mary Queen of Scots to the Earl of Bothwell.
2. Donaldson, *Scotland*, 63.

heretics, for accusing him of that very crime during the reign of the late king. In spite of the mutual hostility, some kind of compromise seemed possible initially, but by the end of January, Arran had imprisoned the cardinal.

It was clear that major changes were to be expected. Arran had a group of supporters whose desire for the reform of the church made them look to England for some kind of example and help. Nobles who had been taken to England as prisoners after the battle of Solway Moss were allowed to return to Scotland. Angus, the stepfather of James V, ended his fourteen-year exile in France and England and was permitted to return home. Those who came back were expected to reinforce Arran and the group pressing for reform and to help to establish an agreement whereby Edward, the five-year-old son of Henry VIII, should in time marry the infant Mary. Arran, next in line to the throne, continued to demonstrate his approval of a limited measure of church reform, but meantime, Cardinal Beaton was able to negotiate the exchange of one prison for another, until by March 1543 his "prison" was his own castle at St. Andrews. Beaton found an ally in Mary of Guise, the king's widow, and began to sow discord in the ranks of the pro-English group. With the future queen still an infant, a great deal of plotting and planning revolved round the possibilities that lay ahead. Would she survive to reach marriageable age? Would she be able to produce an heir? Would the independence of Scotland be assured if she married Prince Edward of England, or would that be achieved by the marriage of Mary to one of Arran's sons?

A further factor in the political game was the location of the little princess. In the summer of 1543, Mary and her mother were moved from Linlithgow to Stirling, as being more secure against any attempt to take her out of Scotland. It was well known that Henry wanted her to grow up in England, and terms of a treaty were proposed by which Mary and Edward would be married by proxy and then Mary would move to England when she reached the age of ten. All kinds of inducements were offered to Arran if he could successfully arrange this, and military support was promised if the opposition became too powerful. The sticking point, however, was Henry's insistence that the Scottish-French alliance must end. At first Arran agreed to the terms, but then almost immediately, aware of the growing support for Beaton and his allies, he changed his allegiance and joined them. Arran's son became a hostage in Beaton's castle at St. Andrews to guarantee his loyalty. Beaton was again appointed as chancellor, and in December the arrangement with England was formally rejected and the alliance with France confirmed. With Beaton firmly in charge of the church, the prosecution of clergy and laymen who embraced the Reformed faith continued with renewed vigour.

Arran's "about face" had the effect of hardening the resistance of those Scots who still hoped for an alliance with Henry, and trust among the Scottish politicians was in very short supply. When Mary was crowned on 9 September 1543, the pro-English party took action, and one of its leaders was Matthew Stewart, the fourth earl of Lennox. Lennox was the great-great-grandson of King James II and next in line to the throne after Arran. He was a staunch Roman Catholic but decided to ally himself with Henry because he reasoned that, since Arran had deserted Henry's cause, the English king would then uphold Lennox in his own claim to the Scottish throne. Most of his early life had been spent in England and he had experience of military service in France. At this point, French funds and weapons had been sent secretly to Scotland to be used in a possible armed conflict between Beaton and the Reformed nobles. These were now delivered to Lennox by the French in the mistaken view that he was still in favour of the Scottish-French alliance.

By the end of 1543, Lennox and his allies had gathered an army fortified by the French supplies. Cardinal Beaton made an attempt to avoid open conflict by proposing an arrangement whereby both Arran and Lennox would achieve positions of great power and influence while giving complete loyalty to the queen and her government. There were so many complications to this proposal that it was never realistic, and early in 1544 the pro-English army went to war, capturing Glasgow and Paisley, but then found themselves under siege in Glasgow. In April, the rebels realised that their position was hopeless, and so they surrendered to government forces. By May, Lennox had fled back to England, where he strengthened his ties to Henry by his marriage in July to Henry's niece, Margaret Douglas, the daughter of Margaret Tudor and her second husband, the Earl of Angus. At this point, "Bluff King Hal" had come to the end of whatever little patience he possessed.

Since diplomacy and intrigue had produced very few favourable results for Henry, he was left with no alternative but military force. In May 1544, an English army sailed up the firth of Forth, landed at Newhaven, and captured Leith. The English troops then marched to Edinburgh and burned part of the city before turning south towards Berwick, devastating land and property as they went. Further raids continued during the rest of the year and into 1545. Angus, the stepfather of James V, was able to gain a heroic reputation by one victory over an English army at Ancrum Moor, but the overall picture was one of intense suffering and loss for southern Scotland and a growing resentment against the government, which seemed unable to defend its own people. Scotland was a divided country, both politically and in terms of its religious loyalties. Some who had been indecisive began to think that an alliance with England was the only practical option left to the Scots. Others began to think that Arran could no longer continue as regent, and waiting in the wings was a powerful and decisive alternative, Mary of Guise.

In June 1544, a group of Scottish leaders gathered in Stirling to replace Arran with Mary of Guise as regent. This group agreed that Mary should take Arran's place, but they agreed about little else. Some were for England and others for France. Some were for the Reformation and others resisted it. Arran and his remaining supporters called a parliament in Edinburgh on 6 November. Mary called her own parliament at Stirling six days later. Arran thundered that all who attended the gathering at Stirling should be charged with treason. Calmer voices appealed for national unity in the face of English aggression, and an uneasy truce was reached with no one anxious to rock the boat. In the meantime, more than one politician was planning for the future. Arran tried to gather support for the marriage of the infant queen to his son, and a number of both clergy and laymen favoured this plan. In June 1545, another French army arrived in Scotland to oppose further English incursions. Lennox, again campaigning for Henry, rallied some of the clans of the western isles and began raiding the mainland. These tactics, however, tended to die out due to lack of strong leadership. Henry also encouraged all who would oppose the Scottish government by offering monetary gifts, but this was countered by similar bribery from his opponents. The factor which brought about the greatest change in Scotland was neither bribery nor warfare but the change in the Scottish church. As the doctrines of the Reformation grew in popularity, it became harder to silence "heretics," since the boundaries of orthodoxy tended to be moveable. One of the most influential of the Reformed preachers was George Wishart, who returned from England to Scotland in 1543 in the company of a group of commissioners whose purpose was to arrange the treaty between Henry and the Scots that would remove Queen Mary to England and marry her to Henry's son Edward. Although this was rejected by the Scottish Parliament, the association of Wishart with such a proposal brought it more popular support than it might otherwise have gained. This Reformer was thirty-three years old when Cardinal Beaton ordered his arrest. Wishart had fled Scotland eight years earlier with the charge of heresy hanging over his head. He studied in Switzerland and Germany before returning first to Cambridge and then to his native land. His arrest and imprisonment as a heretic was followed by his execution in March 1546. John Knox, his friend and disciple, wrote of the execution,

> When he came to the fire, he sat down upon his knees, and rose up again; and thrice he said these words: "O Thou Saviour of the World, Have mercy upon me! Father of Heaven, I commend my spirit into Thy holy hands." Then he turned to the people and said: "I beseech you, Christian Brethren and Sisters, be not offended at the Word of God, for the affliction and torments which ye see prepared for me. But I exhort you, love the Word of God and suffer patiently, and with a comfortable heart, for the Word's sake, which is your undoubted salvation and everlasting comfort."[3]

Eight weeks after the death of Wishart, a group of his supporters broke into the castle of St. Andrews, killed Cardinal Beaton, and took possession of the castle. Although the death of Beaton gave the regent Arran more room to manoeuvre, his response to the event was not easy to decide. The rebels had gained not only possession of the castle but also of Arran's son, who was still there as a hostage for his father's good behaviour. While Arran probably shed few tears over the death of Beaton, neither could he ignore the event which had political as well as religious implications. A siege was mounted against the rebels but without success. Nor was the siege so intense as to exclude periods of negotiation and access to the castle. A number of men supportive of the Reformation and Henry's future plans were able to join the rebels, including John Knox in April 1547.

Arran attempted to control the situation with as little national upheaval as possible. Some damage was done to church property in parts of the country, but the rebellion did not become nationwide. He did not accept the plan to have the young queen marry the English Prince Edward, but neither would he accept French help for his cause, because

---

3. Knox, *Reformation in Scotland*, 64.

he did not want an increased measure of French influence in Scottish affairs. However, in August 1546, a truce was agreed with the rebels, and in December, weakened by lack of food and disease, they were willing to surrender on condition of papal absolution and indemnity against punishment. This condition was not assured, and so the siege dragged on. Arran's half brother, John Hamilton, who was the abbot of Paisley, was selected as the new archbishop of St. Andrews, and until he took control, the affairs of the diocese were in the hands of the vicar-general, John Winram, who was already noted for his reforming sympathies.

Early in 1547, Henry VIII died, and his death was followed by that of his old rival Francis I of France a few months later. The new situation quickly had effect on Scotland. Henry II, the new king of France, fearful of English help for the rebels, was determined to reinforce the Scottish-French alliance. He sent warships to the coast of Fife, and French naval gunners brought the siege of St. Andrews to an inglorious end in July of the same year. Some of the rebels were imprisoned and others, including John Knox, became galley slaves until their release in 1549.

The end of the reign of Henry VIII did not bring about the end of English ambitions to control Scotland. Henry's heir was Edward VII, the son of his third marriage to Jane Seymour. The nine-year-old Edward was crowned in February 1547, and the regency council which ruled in his name was dominated by his uncle, Edward Seymour, the duke of Somerset. Somerset was an enthusiastic soldier, and by September he had led a powerful army over the border and won a decisive victory over a larger but less effective Scots army at Pinkie. Somerset's troops trampled their way back to England leaving a chain of garrisons whose headquarters was at Haddington and which depended to some extent on the support of Scots sympathetic to a Reformed England. Somerset encouraged such sympathy by trying to portray his recent invasion as an attempt to free Scotland from her bondage to Rome and bring about the spiritual liberty of the Reformation. In this he was partly successful, and a number of Scottish lairds committed themselves to his cause. The regent Arran and the Scots council looked towards France for support, but Arran's authority among his fellow Scots was eroded by his obvious intention to promote the cause of his Hamilton kinsmen in a confused and damaged nation. Henry II of France was only too aware that in any bargain made with the Scots he had a clear advantage. He gained the removal of the young queen to France, the agreement that she should marry his heir, and French occupation of Scottish garrisons. The Scots gained a French army which landed at Leith in midsummer 1548, and joined by Scottish troops, the English garrison at Haddington was quickly under siege. Henry promised that the French presence in Scotland should not undermine Scottish law or liberty, and at the end of July, Mary the queen sailed from Dumbarton for France. In February 1549, Arran's cooperation was rewarded when he became duke of Chatelherault. However, the English occupation of Scottish strongholds proved to be an expensive and unstable business, and when Henry's troops in France attacked the English garrison at Boulogne, the English forces in Scotland left for home. The English regency council was trying to deal with local rebellions in East Anglia and Cornwall while trying to stabilise a division in its own ranks, and the struggle to dominate Scotland was just too costly to maintain. England was compelled to make peace with France in March 1550 and with Scotland in June 1551.

While French forces had brought the Scottish conflict with England to a final conclusion, the French presence in their homeland made many Scots uneasy. Henry II boasted, "I have pacified the kingdom of Scotland, which I hold and possess with such authority and obedience as I do in France."[4] There were certainly some immediate advantages for a number of Scots. The prisoners captured after the siege of St. Andrews castle were now released. Some Scottish nobles found themselves the recipients of honours and better incomes. A number of men largely sympathetic to the Reformation were persuaded to accompany Mary of Guise to France in 1550 to be courted and bribed by King Henry, whose efforts to gain their support was far from wasted. In November the following year, Mary of Guise returned to Scotland to play a major part in bringing that country under almost complete French control. Arran remained regent but had little real influence over the French resident.[5]

The death of Cardinal Beaton and the end of hostilities with England brought an opportunity for a number of church reforms, but these were mainly in the realm of discipline and administration rather than doctrine. Perhaps the most important step was the provision of a new catechism in the common tongue. This was carefully composed in terms which avoided radical doctrinal change but were open to Reformed interpretation. During this time of change, Arran was able to hold on to

4. Dawson, *Scotland Re-formed*, 173.
5. Donaldson, *Scotland*, 81.

his regency partly because his sympathies lay more with England than with France, and in any attempt to remove him, English support for Arran could not be ruled out. However, Edward VI died in July 1553 and was succeeded by Mary Tudor, the daughter of Henry VIII's first wife, Catherine of Aragon. Mary, the new English monarch, was a staunch Roman Catholic and no friend at all to a Scottish regent with reforming sympathies.

Arran's official term of office was due to end when Mary the Scottish queen reached her thirteenth birthday, but in December 1553, at the beginning of Mary's twelfth year, the French government began negotiations to persuade Arran to accept an earlier resignation. A number of inducements were offered, financial and dynastic, and in April 1554, the regency of Scotland was transferred to Mary of Guise, the mother of the queen, which brought Scottish affairs even further under French control, and significantly she was crowned in Edinburgh by a representative of the French government.[6] Henry II of France saw in the young Scottish queen an opportunity to extend French rule not only to Scotland but to England also, since there was a question of legitimacy linked to the children of Henry VIII, and Mary Queen of Scots had a claim to the English throne as the great-granddaughter of Henry VII.

The new regent, Mary of Guise, tried to balance leniency towards the growing numbers of Reformed preachers with the appointment of a growing number of Frenchmen in positions of influence in Scotland. While a number of preachers, John Knox among them, were free to exercise their ministry, the presence of French troops and a new range of taxes to support several projects could hardly be popular. One of the taxes imposed was to finance the marriage of the queen to the French dauphin, which eventually took place 24 April 1558. By this marriage, the French king became king of Scotland should Mary die without an heir, and Scotland accepted the debt it owed to France for the expense of its defence and the nurture of its queen. The party of commissioners that Mary of Guise sent to France to negotiate her daughter's marriage settlement contained a small group of Reformed noblemen. Her tolerance for these men and their spiritual leaders arose from her perception that the Reformation in Scotland was more thorough and radical than that in England, and her hope was that the enthusiasm of this Scottish movement might make the conditions in England less stable. However, at the same time as the Scots

6. Dawson, *Scotland Re-formed*, 179.

nobles went to France, a covenant was prepared in Scotland in December 1557 which committed those who signed it to work for the recognition of a Reformed church. Covenants with a military or political basis were not unheard of, and this first covenant did not attract the commitment of as many nobles as its designers hoped for, but its significance lay in its religious components. It offered protection for Reformed ministers who preached God's word and administered the sacraments.

Since this was a step beyond the toleration of Reformed preachers who ministered in private houses, John Hamilton, Arran's half brother and the current archbishop of St. Andrews, did two things. He urged the Earl of Argyll, perhaps the most powerful of the Scottish nobles, to oppose the emerging Reformed church and he executed Walter Mylne, an eighty-year-old Reformed minister. Neither action was profitable. Argyll confirmed his support for the Reformers, and the death of Mylne aroused great resentment. In spite of these things, some degree of hope still remained that a measure of reformation in the church could be found which would gain the acceptance of all parties. Events outside Scotland, however, made this impossible.

Edward VI, king of England, had died in 1553, aged sixteen. On July 10 of that year, Lady Jane Grey was proclaimed queen but was deposed nine days later to be succeeded by Mary Tudor, the daughter of Henry VIII and his first wife Catherine of Aragon. Mary was a devout Roman Catholic who married Philip of Spain, although Parliament would never permit him to become king. During her reign, English Protestants were fiercely persecuted, earning her the title of "Bloody Mary." Mary had a half sister, Elizabeth, the daughter of Henry VIII and Anne Boleyn, and since it was his infatuation with Anne Boleyn which caused Henry to divorce Mary's mother, Catherine, Mary harboured a lifelong hatred of Anne Boleyn and her daughter Elizabeth. In spite of this, she was persuaded, possibly by her husband Philip, with extreme reluctance to recognise Elizabeth as her heir. Mary herself had no children, and in fact her husband deserted her in 1555 when he returned to Spain, where in 1556 he became King Philip II. A bitter and devastated woman, Mary Tudor died, aged forty-two, in November 1558, to be succeeded by her half sister Elizabeth I, queen of England and Ireland.

The reign of Elizabeth in England brought the repeal of many of the laws passed by the government of Mary Tudor, and it became clear that the Reformation in England was not going to be reversed. It was equally clear to the regent of Scotland, Mary of Guise, that toleration of the Scottish Reformers was no longer a stick with which to beat a Roman Catholic England, and so the policy of tolerance for the Reformation in Scotland evaporated, especially as the Reformers became more militant. John Knox, who had visited Scotland between 1555 and 1556, returned permanently from his base in Geneva, landing at Leith on 2 May 1559.

In January 1559, Scottish friars had been warned that on 12 May they must leave their houses which would then become shelters for the poor and those who were unable to work. At the same time, citizens of Perth and Dundee together with many of the "gentlemen" in the surrounding parts declared themselves to be Protestant and ready to protect the Reformed ministers. Mary of Guise was compelled to act, and demanded the Reformed ministers to appear in Stirling on 10 May. They answered the summons but travelled with a large crowd of militant supporters. This threatening group was persuaded to halt in their journey to Stirling, but the ministers, remaining with their supporters, were declared outlaws when they did not appear. At this point, Knox arrived at Perth, and his sermon in St. John's Church castigating idolatry led to a riot in which a number of church properties were damaged. News was also received that the townspeople in Ayr had become Protestant. On 24 May, government forces gathered at Stirling to deal with the rebellion, but immediately Reformation supporters formed an opposing force at Perth. Open conflict was avoided, and although the regent garrisoned the city, her troops were Scottish and not French. However, over the following months, the government forces and what had become "the Congregation" of those seeking to establish the Reformation in Scotland challenged one another, occupying and re-occupying whatever parts of the country each side could control. By the month of July, Edinburgh was in the hands of the Reformers and John Knox was preaching in St. Giles, even though the regent's forces occupied the port of Leith. A form of truce was agreed by which the city would be allowed to choose which form of religion it favoured and to remain free of government troops. This condition was not as favourable to the Reformers as it seemed at first. Outbursts of reforming enthusiasm were not the same as steady determination, and in August, Knox was forced to leave St. Giles in the charge of John Willock, his deputy. Knox wrote of him, "For the comfort of the Brethren and continuance of the Kirk in Edinburgh, was left there our dear brother John Willock, who, for his faithful labours and bold courage in that battle, deserveth immortal praise."[7] The presence of the Reformers in the city did not prevent Mary, the regent, attending mass at the palace of Holyrood and increasing the garrison at Leith.

It was an unforeseen factor which raised the temperature of the tension between the Roman Catholic royal family and the Scots Reformers. On 10 June 1559, Henry II of France, and father-in-law to the young Scottish queen, was fatally injured in a jousting tournament. He died on 10 July. His son, the dauphin, became King Francis II, who together with his wife Mary, Queen of Scots, now ruled their Franco-Scottish dominions. Affairs in Scotland, however, were fast becoming more troubled. The two leading noblemen of the Congregation were the Earl of Argyll and James Stewart, who was earl of Moray and an illegitimate son of King James V. Moray was commendator of the priory of St. Andrews, and so these two lords of the Congregation set out with a small body of troops to encourage the Reformation in the ecclesiastical capital of Scotland. Knox preached in St. Andrews parish church on 11 June on the theme of "the cleansing of the temple," after which all images were removed from church buildings and the houses of the Franciscans and the Dominicans were destroyed.[8] The regent Mary received this news at Falkland Palace and sent a detachment of troops to St. Andrews, where they confronted a newly reinforced Protestant company. A truce was negotiated, but the military aspect of the Reformation process continued to expand. The Congregation recaptured Perth from the garrison stationed there by the regent. Stirling followed, and by the end of June, the army of the Congregation was in Edinburgh.

When the news of the death of Henry II and the accession of Francis II to the French throne reached the Reformers it seemed that the struggle in Scotland must now involve both France and England. To encourage English support, the Congregation held a council to formally depose the regent Mary of Guise on 21 October 1559, but made no decision to appoint a successor. In practical terms, her removal was not an easy matter to accomplish, since the army of the Congregation was a hastily assembled makeshift force, whereas the regent's troops were professional French soldiers. Furthermore, the Reformed army were assembled from fairly distant parts of the country and could not afford to remain far from home indefinitely. Neither could armies be sustained without money, and

7. Knox, *History of the Reformation*, 182.
8. Dawson, *Politics of Religion*, 93.

in fact some of the troops of the Congregation mutinied because they had not been paid. Argyll tried to rally the islesmen and Highlanders by warning them that Scotland could easily become a French colony, but taking advantage of this confusion, the French garrison at Leith recaptured Edinburgh, and the Reformation cause began to look uncertain. The regent's French troops had been reinforced in August, and Elizabeth, the English queen, seemed reluctant to get involved in what had the appearance of a rebellion against royal authority. However, on 23 January 1560, English ships did sail into the Firth of Forth with the intention of cutting off the French forces, now operating in Fife, from their base at Leith and their supply lines from France. By March, an English army had crossed the border as an expression of English commitment to protect the law and liberty of Scotland from French aggression. The English troops made their headquarters east of the city of Edinburgh, the regent took refuge in the castle, and the French garrison at Leith was quickly under siege.

Negotiations began yet again to reach an agreement about the future of Scotland, and in fact two envoys travelled from France and were meeting with English representatives when the regent Mary died on 11 June. The death of the regent made it easier for the French and English commissioners to formulate some kind of truce, which became known as the Treaty of Edinburgh. It was agreed that almost all the French and English troops should leave Scotland. Queen Mary should reject the use of English arms and recognise Elisabeth as the legitimate English sovereign. A new Scottish council should be formed and, since none of the Lords of the Congregation liked the appearance of unlawful rebellion against the crown, the emphasis would be on church reform rather than military opposition. In August, the Scottish Parliament met to accept a new Confession of Faith prepared by Knox and his colleagues which rejected papacy and the mass.

What did not form part of the new arrangement was any complete reorganisation of church structure and finance. Leading church offices were for the most part in the hands of the strongest political families, and change was difficult to effect. Most of the bishops did not join the Reformers but continued to control funds and church appointments as before. Kirk sessions began to multiply locally but operated under no national authority. An attempt to get the French to formally accept the decisions of the Scottish Parliament was rejected, likewise the attempt to have Queen Elisabeth marry the Earl of Arran, son of the former regent.

In December 1560, Francis II of France died at the age of seventeen. Mary the queen was now alone in France and marriageable. The Lord James Stewart, her half brother and a leader of the Congregation, visited Mary in France in April 1561. Her return to Scotland and the nature of her rule were considered in great detail. She was warned against any attempt at changing the Reformed church and urged to exercise care in choosing those who would be her chief advisors. Mary landed at Leith on 19 August 1561, and on the following Sunday attended mass in her chapel at Holyrood, much to the displeasure of John Knox and the protesters who tried to prevent it taking place. The protesters were especially irked because it was Argyll and Lord James who defended the queen's right to attend mass in her private chapel.

Mary's immediate responsibility was the formation of her new privy council, and this was chosen to attempt to reconcile the rival elements in the Scottish government. George Gordon, the earl of Huntly, who had succeeded Cardinal Beaton as chancellor, was confirmed in that office. Huntly, who had offered to lead a Catholic military campaign on behalf of the queen, was more loyal to Mary and the crown than to the Lords of the Congregation. There were moderates like William Maitland of Lethington, who became Mary's secretary of state, and whose primary goal was a genuine friendship with Queen Elizabeth and a mutual recognition by Elizabeth and Mary of the legitimacy of their respective rules. There were also extremists who would have forced Mary into the Reformed church and a marriage with Arran, and this group had the support of John Knox.[9]

Mary made a serious attempt to live amicably with the Reformed church in spite of Knox's unchanging distrust. The prosecution of a number of priests and bishops who continued to say mass took place. On 19 May 1563, they were put on trial and imprisoned. At the same time, financial provision was being made for Reformed ministers and their churches. The church assemblies were composed of representatives of both church and nation and tended to operate like an unofficial parliament. It is significant, however, that whatever structure or machinery the church erected was seen as deriving its authority from the government. The appointments to clerical offices were made by the authority of the Parliament. Members of the council were the "godly magistrates" whose approval was necessary for the church. The First Book of Discipline,

9. Donaldson, *Scotland*, 107.

which outlined the doctrine and government of the Reformed church, was commissioned on 29 April 1560 by "the Great Council of Scotland now admitted to the regiment by the providence of God," and its purpose was not simply to guide the affairs of the church but "for common order and uniformity to be observed in this realm." The idea of a monarch whose faith was not that of her subjects was not one which appealed to Knox, and he could never be content with a ruler practicing her religion as if it were something outside the church of the nation. In the "First Head" of the Book of Discipline there is a list of the feasts and holy days observed by the Roman Catholic church, which Knox soundly condemns, and continues,

> which things, because in God's scriptures they neither have commandment nor assurance, we judge them utterly to be abolished from this realm, affirming further, that the obstinate maintainers and teachers of such abominations ought not to escape the punishment of the civil magistrate.[10]

It was clear that the queen and John Knox would not find much common ground on which a compromise could be built.

In addition to her problems with the Scottish government and church, Mary had to deal with her relationship to Elizabeth. Mary wanted Elizabeth's promise that she would succeed to the English throne, and as long as Elizabeth remained unmarried and childless that outcome became more likely. Within weeks of Mary's arrival in Scotland, Lethington was at the English court trying to arrange the conditions for Mary's succession, the most important of which was Elizabeth's approval of any husband Mary might take. In 1564, Elizabeth suggested Robert Dudley, the earl of Leicester, as a husband for Mary, although the relationship between Leicester and Elizabeth herself bordered on the scandalous and made Mary's agreement less than likely. A second candidate was Henry Stewart, Lord Darnley. He was the son of the Earl of Lennox, who had fought for Henry VIII against his fellow Scots and had to flee to England as a result. His son Darnley had therefore been brought up in England, and as the grandson of Margaret Tudor, had himself a claim to the English throne. The prospect of Darnley becoming Mary's husband paved the way for the return of his father, Lennox, to Scotland in September 1564, followed by Darnley himself early in 1565.

10. Concluding statement of the First Head, *First Book of Discipline (1560)*, based on Laing, *Works of John Knox*, 1865.

Elizabeth at this point had given no formal acceptance of Mary as her successor, and in fact announced her disapproval of the proposed marriage. The uniting of two people, each of whom had a claim to the English throne, made Elizabeth distinctly nervous. The union nevertheless took place in July 1565, and Darnley was proclaimed king before an uncomfortable Scottish nobility. Although Darnley was Protestant, at least in nominal terms, the marriage service was Roman Catholic. Mary hoped her marriage to a Protestant husband might alleviate some of the anxieties of the Reformed church, but there were several important Scottish politicians who saw Darnley as a threat. Maitland's efforts to win some kind of settled agreement from Elizabeth about the succession were now hopelessly undermined. Lord James the earl of Moray, Argyll, and the Hamiltons could not accept the influence which Darnley and his father Lennox would have over the queen, and by the month of August, Moray and his allies were in rebellion and declared to be outlaws.

Those who supported Moray were not as many as he might have hoped for. Mary's attempts to woo her Reformed subjects were not entirely unsuccessful, and she gathered a number of Protestant nobles to her cause, including James Hepburn, the earl of Bothwell. The support of Bothwell was not an unmixed blessing, since he was a man who appeared to be without moral scruples of any kind. He had a reputation for violence and jealousy, and his previous lifestyle had resulted in periods of imprisonment and exile. Five years before his reappearance in Scotland he had become engaged to a Norwegian noblewoman, but after relieving her father of a very large dowry, he then abandoned his bride-to-be. When Mary called him back to Scotland in July 1565, he was in France, from where he returned to become, in September, part of her council.

The events following Moray's rebellion became known as the "Chaseabout Raid" for obvious reasons. The rebels gathered in Ayr while Mary and her army left Edinburgh on 26 August to confront them. The rebels, however, "dodged" the royal army and marched back to Edinburgh where they soon realised that they were anything but welcome. Moray and his allies then moved south to Dumfries to be replaced in the capital city once again by Mary and her troops. Both Mary and Moray looked outside of Scotland for support, but neither found as much help as they hoped for. Moray gained no military encouragement from Elizabeth, although she did permit him to find asylum in England. Mary, perhaps unwisely, appealed for help to Philip of Spain and to the pope, which undermined the support of her Protestant subjects. In addition, her husband Darnley, while the General Assembly of the church was in session at Christmas 1565, returned to the Catholic church. After mass at Mary's chapel in Holyrood, he was invested with the French Order of St. Michael and then boasted that he had returned the whole nation to the true faith.[11] It was also noticeable that as her Scottish supporters deserted her, foreigners took their place. At the same time, the queen became aware that Darnely, her husband, would never make a reliable king. The factor which united Mary's remaining Protestant nobles and her ineffective husband was their resentment of those foreigners who seemed to enjoy the close confidence of the queen. They were convinced that such a relationship belonged to native Scotsmen, and the object of their focused animosity was the Italian David Rizzio.

Rizzio was in fact a musician who arrived in Scotland in 1561. It was his artistic talent which first brought him to the attention of the queen, who encouraged artists at court, but as time went by he became the administrator of her French household and a very close advisor. There were rumours, almost certainly unfounded, of an adulterous relationship with Mary, but the associated gossip and Darnley's suspicion that Rizzio had persuaded Mary to withhold the crown matrimonial from her king-consort, drove Darnley to collude with James Douglas, the earl of Morton, to murder Rizzio. The other strand of justification for such a violent course of action was a growing fear that the queen intended to reverse the work of the Reformation. On 9 March 1566, armed men entered Holyrood. The queen was threatened at gunpoint and Rizzio was brutally murdered. Bothwell and some of the others present were able to escape, and when the news was broadcast, Moray and the other Chase About rebels who had been waiting outside the city rode into Edinburgh.

It was a measure of the queen's personal charm and self-control that she was able to do two things. She negotiated the terms of a pardon with Moray and the other rebels and she was also able to persuade Darnley that his alliance with those who carried out the murder of Rizzio was not in his long-term interests. Three days after the murder, Darnley and the queen, who was seven months pregnant with his child, escaped from Edinburgh and fled to Bothwell's castle at Dunbar. On learning of Mary's successful escape, Moray and the rebels left Edinburgh afraid of what Mary might now be able to accomplish, and since John Knox had

11. Lynch, *Scotland*, 214.

indicated his approval of Rizzio's death, he also left the city on the same day for Ayrshire. By 18 March, Mary and an army were back in Edinburgh. The next day the privy council demanded that the rebels be put on trial for their actions, but they were already in England.

On 19 June 1566, the son, James, who would become the first monarch of Scotland, England, and Ireland, was born. There is little doubt that Darnley was his father, but it soon became apparent that Mary retained no affection for her husband, and a growing suspicion surfaced that her relationship with Bothwell was adulterous. In December 1566, the little prince was baptised at Stirling. The Roman Catholic ceremony was arranged by Bothwell, and Darnley, who had moved to Glasgow, was not present. The baptism was followed by a celebration and pageant designed to symbolise the unity of Catholic and Protestant nobility under the crown. The reality was rather different. It had become a matter of some urgency that the situation between Mary and her estranged husband be dealt with, because the birth of Prince James opened up new possibilities in terms of the succession. The future was not easy to predict. Darnley began written correspondence with the pope and the king of Spain posing as an enthusiastic Roman Catholic, while Mary bestowed funds and property on her Reformed church. At the same time, however, she ensured that John Hamilton, the archbishop of St. Andrews, was restored to his clerical office, where he would be in a position to nullify the marriages between Darnley and herself, and Bothwell and his wife. The intention to marry Bothwell seemed to be clear.

It was at this point a new factor entered an already confused situation. Mary was convinced that she was again pregnant, and the child could not be her husband's, although it must be made to appear to be so. On 20 January 1567, she visited Darnley in Glasgow for five days and brought him back with her to Edinburgh. In returning to Edinburgh, Darnley was surrounded by groups of enemies. Those who murdered Rizzio had already been pardoned and they bitterly resented his desertion with the queen immediately after the deed was done. There were nobles who believed it imperative that Darnley's influence must come to an end one way or another, and there was Bothwell who wanted to marry his wife. When Darnley returned to Edinburgh he was unwell, and arrangements for his convalescence were made in the Old Provost's House within the quadrangle of the Kirk o' Field. In the evening of 9 February, the queen, accompanied by Argyll, went to visit the invalid, and in the early hours of the following morning the house was destroyed by an explosion. An adequate explanation of this act of regicide and the identity of its perpetrators has never been found. Part of the mystery arose from the discovery of the bodies of Darnley and his servant not in the demolished house but in the garden outside. They had not been killed by the explosion. They had been strangled.

Mary and Bothwell were perhaps the too obvious suspects. Immediately after the Kirk o' Field incident Argyll tried to calm the anxious government, and in March he took the infant Prince James to the safety of Stirling Castle. Moray, unsure of what might happen next, fled the country. Lennox was determined to avenge the murder of his son, and Bothwell was indeed put on trial on 12 April. The trial was directed by Argyll, but Bothwell's supporters flooded into Edinburgh in such numbers that his acquittal was inevitable. On 7 May the archbishop of St. Andrews declared Bothwell's marriage to be null, and on 15 May he was married to Mary at Holyrood in a marriage service of the Reformed church. There was some doubt among the Scottish nobles as to exactly how enthusiastic Mary was about this marriage. Between Bothwell's trial and his marriage, he took Mary into his custody on 24 April, and it was not clear whether this took place by abduction or by consent. There were those who believed that Mary's marriage was forced and had been preceded by abduction and rape. A number of the Scottish lords had agreed to "rescue" Mary before the marriage took place, and when it was too late, they now formed an armed force to engage in battle with the troops raised by Mary and Bothwell. The two armies met at Carberry, just outside Edinburgh, on 15 June 1567, and it was plain that Mary's troops were hopelessly outnumbered. Bothwell escaped from the battlefield, Mary surrendered and was imprisoned in the castle on the island in Loch Leven. Bothwell was now a fugitive. He reached Orkney, then Shetland, and then Norway, where his past caught up with him. Recognised as the unscrupulous rascal who had cheated and deceived his gullible victims in the past, he was arrested and imprisoned in Denmark, where he died in 1578.

Mary, even as a prisoner, proved difficult to deal with. The confederate lords who had captured her were not sure what to do with her. Some wanted her to be executed for the murder of Darnley and her adulterous relationship with Bothwell. Others, notably Argyll, were horrified at such a course and almost immediately began to look for ways to protect and set her at liberty again. An important factor in deciding Mary's future was the likely response of Elizabeth to the Scottish situation. However, on 24 July 1567, Mary, weakened both physically and psychologically by a recent miscarriage, signed an abdication in favour of her son. Moray, now returned from his earlier flight, was appointed regent. The coronation of the infant prince as King James VI took place in Stirling on 29 July, attended by few of the nobility and no foreign dignitaries at all.[12] There gradually emerged two distinct groups, one to support the new king and his regent, and the other to restore Mary to the throne.

Moray called a parliament in December at which those former acts to establish the Reformation, which had never received Mary's royal approval, were now ratified. The church indicated support for the new government with its greatest scholar, George Buchannan, providing the strongest moral justification for the right to resist or remove unworthy rulers. However, support for Moray among the members of council was uneasy, and the escape of Mary from Lochleven on 2 May 1568 was enough to bring a considerable force of armed men to her cause. The queen's army, led by Argyll, met Moray's troops at Langside in Glasgow on 13 May, and Mary was defeated. It was not such a rout that her forces could not have regrouped to continue the ongoing struggle, but Mary herself fled into England to throw herself on the mercy of Elizabeth. There were two reasons why Mary might have hoped for English help. Elizabeth so far had refused to recognise Moray as ruler of Scotland, and furthermore, the arrest and imprisonment of a reigning queen was not an example that Elizabeth could live with comfortably.

Elizabeth promised her support for Mary's restoration on condition that Moray would have the opportunity to present evidence of Mary's guilt and answer for his own act of rebellion against his sovereign. An investigation of evidence from both parties was held when the representatives of Elizabeth, Mary, and Moray met at York in October, at Westminster in November, and at Hampton Court in December 1568. The implications of such an investigation were complicated for all who took part in it. Mary's advocates did not seem to be completely convinced of her innocence, while Moray's representatives had one eye on their own future should Mary be restored to power. The leader of the English group was the Duke of Norfolk, who had hopes of marrying the Scottish queen himself whenever she could be divorced from Bothwell. In time, Moray

12. Dawson, *Scotland Re-formed*, 267.

was given the impression that a guilty verdict was not completely unacceptable to Elizabeth, and so he formally accused Mary of the murder of Darnley. Perhaps the most important evidence he had for this accusation was the "Casket Letters." This was a series of eight letters alleged to have been written by Mary which, if genuine, seemed to implicate her in the murder of her former husband. The result of this investigation was inconclusive. Moray was not proved to be a rebel who raised his sword against his lawful queen, but neither was Mary proved to be an adulteress who helped to murder her husband.

When Moray returned to Scotland at the end of 1568, his popularity was in decline. The investigation of Queen Mary had been orchestrated by William Cecil, Elizabeth's most trusted advisor, and the need for Moray to justify himself to the English crown gave the impression that Elizabeth had a legitimate right to make judgements about Scottish affairs. Moray gave further evidence of his subjection to English authority when he arrested the Earl of Northumberland, who had taken part in a rebellion against Elizabeth and escaped over the border to Scotland to seek asylum. The future for Scotland seemed unpredictable. In July 1569, a fairly small Scottish Parliament in Perth considered and then rejected a proposal that Mary should be divorced from Bothwell and return to Scotland as the wife of the Duke of Norfolk, and in January 1570, the regent Moray was shot and killed in Linlithgow by a member of the Hamilton family. His death provoked an even greater measure of political confusion, and Elizabeth decided to intervene to try to bring about some measure of stability. In May 1570, a body of English troops appeared in order to assist the supporters of King James in their continuing struggle with Mary's forces, but with no decisive result. The king's party, feeling the need of English support, appealed to Elizabeth to choose the new regent to succeed Moray, and her choice fell on Lennox, who was still thirsting for vengeance against the murderers of Darnley, his son. The appointment did nothing to end the civil conflict, although the number of Mary's supporters in the Scottish nobility showed signs of diminishing as one and another left her ranks to support the young King James. The queen was, however, not completely bereft of energetic allies. Sir William Kirkcaldy of Grange, who was a leading Protestant soldier, was nevertheless a firm defender of his Roman Catholic queen, and as governor held and fortified Edinburgh Castle in the queen's name. He also appeared at a parliament held in Stirling in August 1571 and attempted, unsuccessfully, to capture a number of the lords who were in attendance. It was during this attempt that the regent Lennox was killed. John Erskine, earl of Mar, became regent in Lennox's place but died in October 1572, to be succeeded in turn by James Douglas, earl of Morton, on 24 November of the same year, the day that John Knox died.[13]

Morton's efforts to promote common cause with England were unquestionable and made him acceptable to Elizabeth for that reason. In addition, the outbreak of violence against Protestants in France in the St. Bartholemew's Eve Massacre of 24 August 1572 raised at least the possibility of French intervention on behalf of Scotland's deposed Roman Catholic queen. While suspicion of "popish plots" were a feature of the age, the real threat to Elizabeth could not be ignored. In April 1570, Pope Pius V had issued the bull Regnans in Excelsis, which declared Elizabeth to be a heretic, excommunicated, and deprived her of the title to the English crown, while condemning all who recognised and obeyed her to the same excommunication. It was this condemnation of Elizabeth which encouraged a Florentine banker called Ridolfi to arrange a plot to murder the queen and replace her with Mary Queen of Scots as the wife of the Duke of Norfolk. When this was discovered, the English Parliament were certain that Mary was part of the plot and demanded her execution. Elizabeth was not yet ready to execute Mary, but Norfolk did suffer this fate in June 1572.

It was against this background that Elizabeth's government was compelled to increase their support for King James. Greater pressure was applied to force a further group of Scottish nobles to change their allegiance from Mary to her son. Mary's cause was clearly failing. By autumn, control of the city of Edinburgh had passed from Mary's forces into the hands of the king's men, and the castle was under siege. On 28 May 1573, with the help of English men and cannons, the castle fell, and Mary's loyal defender Kirkcaldy of Grange was hanged.

The regent Morton was now firmly in control. He managed to achieve a measure of success in dealing with lawbreakers in the Highland and border regions while his cooperation with England continued. Political and clerical leaders were pledged in allegiance to the young James VI as head of a Reformed church and state, and the goods of the church were at least one component in the rewards directed towards those who had loyally supported the king. The nation was certainly at peace again

13. Lynch, *Scotland*, 222.

after the civil war, but a number of the church's leaders were already focusing more sharply on the principles which should guide a thoroughly Reformed church, and their leader was a man called Andrew Melville.

16

The Wisest Fool[1]

There is twa kings and twa kingdomes in Scotland. Thair is Chryst Jesus the King, and his kingdome the Kirk, whase subject King James the Saxt is, and of whase kingdome nocht a king nor a lord nor a heid bot a member. And they whome Chryst hes callit and commandit to watch over his Kirk and govern his spirituall kingdome hes sufficient power of him.[2]

IN MARCH 1578, A number of Scottish nobles, resentful of the power of the regent Morton, persuaded the young King James to form a council to act in his own name and bring the regency to an end. Morton had been an unashamed Anglophile, and a considerable measure of Scottish law was based on the English model; however, the expected development of Scotland as an English client state did not take place.[3] While Morton's commitment to Protestantism was clear enough, his commitment to Presbyterianism was not. The clergy were required to take an oath to recognise the king as "supreme governor of the realm as well in things temporal as in the conservation and purgation of religion,"[4] and bishops continued to exercise considerable control over church affairs and revenues. Resentment of conditions in the church and a desire for further

1. The Wisest Fool in Christendom, a title said to have been given to James VI and I by Sir Anthony Weldon, an English courtier.
2. Andrew Melville to James VI, cited in Rait, *Making of Scotland*, 163.
3. Lynch, *Scotland*, 226.
4. Donaldson, *Scotland*, 167.

reform were expressed through the growing influence of a returned exile called Andrew Melville.

Melville was a native of the county of Angus who distinguished himself at the University of St. Andrews before pursuing further studies and gaining a reputation as a gifted teacher in France and Geneva. His contact with Protestant refugees and scholars in that city shaped the development of his views on the relationship between church and state, and he returned to Scotland in 1574 to be the principal of Glasgow University. Melville not only attracted scholars from Europe to study under his direction, but he introduced new methods of teaching to Scottish university life. In 1580 he moved to St. Andrews, and although never a parish minister himself, he had, as an educator, a great deal of influence over the training of the clergy. Melville had a very firm conviction about the separation of church and state which affected some of the most basic practices of the church. He held that the church must be governed not by crown-appointed bishops, but by presbyteries composed of ministers, teachers, and elders. Clergy must not hold office in civil government, but were to act as the moral and spiritual conscience of the nation. Most critical for a government which was financially straitened was the idea that the church had the sole right to the management of church property and funding. As Melville's influence continued to grow, his conflict with the king and Parliament was inevitable. At one of their encounters, the regent Morton is said to have remarked to Melville, "There will never be quietness in this country till half a dozen of you be hanged or banished."[5]

When the king was persuaded to end the regency, Morton was able to hold on to a measure of influence by an alliance with the Earl of Mar. This young man was a fellow student of the king and possessed the hereditary right of royal guardianship. He now exercised this right to have control of the king's safety, and in April 1578 brought James to Stirling Castle, where he was joined by Morton. A conflict over who should be responsible for the king's location and security rumbled on for a number of years, but the greatest danger to Morton came not from his current political rivals but from a different source altogether.

In September 1579, Esme Stewart arrived in Scotland from France. Stewart was a first cousin of Lord Darnley, the king's father, and in practical terms was a French Roman Catholic. The thirteen-year-old monarch was profoundly impressed and influenced by Stewart, who as

5. Ibid., 169.

a worldly-wise and sophisticated companion rapidly demonstrated the control he had over the king. In June 1580, Stewart became a member of the privy council and a willing ally of Morton's political opponents. By December of the same year, Morton found himself under arrest and accused of being involved in the murder of Darnley. His execution took place in June 1581. Esme Stewart had become a powerful figure in Scottish affairs. He was made commendator of Arbroath, keeper of Dumbarton Castle, earl of Lennox, and finally duke of Lennox in August 1581.

Lennox appeared to be a man whose religious loyalties were fairly flexible and he seemed quite ready to change his support from the Roman Catholic church to the Reformed church, but in spite of this, his move to Scotland and his obvious influence with the king made him look like someone who might still be useful to the interests of the papacy and of Queen Mary, still a prisoner of Elizabeth in England. In 1581 Mary, with the assistance of the Duke of Guise, who was leader of the French Catholics, attempted to arrange her restoration as joint monarch of Scotland to rule with her son James. The arrangement came to nothing, but this overture to the king, coming with the involvement of Guise, who was known to have considered the possibility of Spanish intervention in Scotland, did nothing to calm the continuing fears and suspicions of Scottish nobles and clergy committed to a Reformed church and nation. A number of Jesuit missionaries in Scotland further raised the temperature when they brought back to Paris exaggerated reports of Scottish support for a proposed Catholic uprising. In spite of his profession of the Reformed faith, the new duke of Lennox was suspected of being a Catholic agent who could well use his influence to persuade the king himself to become Catholic. Tension between the kirk and the government continued to grow. King James and Lennox both signed the "King's Confession" in 1581, which was clearly anti-Catholic in tone and content, but this did not quieten Presbyterian fears, since a more practical indication of government policy was the refusal to recognise the authority of the Kirk's General Assembly and its opposition to a church ruled by bishops. Lennox continued to arrange appointments to church offices and to control the revenues attached to them until opposition to his rule could be contained no longer.

In August 1582, the king was on a hunting party in Perthshire when he was "captured" by a group of nobles who took him to Ruthven Castle. This action certainly encouraged the General Assembly of the Kirk, and it was hoped that during his enforced stay at Ruthven, the king might be persuaded to accept a Presbyterian form of church government. Losing control of the king meant a change in the political authority of Lennox, who returned to France where, to the king's great sorrow, he died in May 1583. James blamed his captors for the death of Lennox, and any hope of the king becoming an enthusiastic Presbyterian were dashed when he escaped in June the same year. In the absence of Lennox, a new and possibly even more powerful figure was to emerge in the struggle between king and kirk.

James Stewart, the earl of Arran and brother-in-law of John Knox, emerged as the new leader of the king's government and was appointed chancellor in May 1584, but his lack of support from England inclined his allies to encourage the king to look for help from European sources. Indeed, King James did enter into correspondence with the Duke of Guise and the pope, indicating his support for the release of his mother, Mary. Arran accepted the reformation of the church, but like the king was opposed to the radical presbyterianism of men like Andrew Melville, and the Reformer was one of a number of ministers who had to flee to England to escape imprisonment in March 1584. In May of the same year, the Scottish Parliament passed a body of legislation which became known as the "Black Acts." These affirmed the supreme power of the king, the authority of the bishops, and their combined rejection of presbyterian church government. Arran's hopes of support from English bishops, however, came to little, because Elizabeth, at this point, still looked on the radical Scottish Reformers as a bulwark against Catholic pressure. She was, however, willing to enter a political league with Scotland in July 1585, which brought with it £4000 annually from the English crown.[6]

Although Arran was still in power in Scottish political affairs, opposition to his authority was growing. A number of important English statesmen did not trust him, and allies of Melville and the exiled Scottish lords and Reformers were plotting his downfall. In July 1585, Arran was blamed for a border skirmish which resulted in the death of a young English nobleman. King James was almost persuaded to have Arran arrested, and even though this did not in fact take place, Elizabeth's release and return of the exiled Scottish Lords from England made his position impossible, and he was forced to flee. In July 1586, the English league with Scotland was confirmed, each nation promising recognition of the

6. Ibid., 182.

other's monarchy and defence of the other's security. The unity expressed in the league was to be tested to considerable extent in coming days.

In the autumn of 1586, Mary Queen of Scots, still a prisoner in England, was accused of being part of a plot to assassinate Elizabeth. Her execution in February 1587 provoked a predictable reaction among sympathetic Scots. Some clamoured for vengeance, and border raids broke out, but James himself was forced to accept his mother's death, since he was negotiating for a formal recognition of himself as Elizabeth's heir. The death of Mary was seen in rather a different light, however, in France and Spain. She was viewed there as a martyr who had died for the Catholic cause and her death was the excuse needed by Philip II of Spain to launch the armada against England. James wisely resisted the temptation to join in any military conflict with England, since such a move would inevitably lead to alliance with France and Spain, and this seemed dangerously unprofitable to a Protestant Scottish king. Indeed, James was considerably relieved when the Spanish invasion of England failed. Dawson writes,

> Scottish Protestants, including James VI, rejoiced as "God's wind blew" and scattered the fleet. They looked forward with hope, but no sure expectation to a presaged new age when God's providential mercies would transform Scotland into a holy people, the new Israel ruled by its godly king.[7]

The ambition of James VI to rule Scotland and England was his paramount concern, and his choice of a suitable bride was also influenced by this aim. In 1589, a Scottish mission sailed to Denmark to negotiate a marriage with Anne, the daughter of the Danish king, Frederick II. Denmark had no quarrel with Spain and seemed sympathetic to the claims of James to the English throne, and so Anne and James were married at first by proxy at Copenhagen in August 1589, when James was twenty-three years old and his bride aged fourteen. However, when Anne set out for Scotland, her journey was interrupted by storms, and she had to remain at Oslo, where James married her in person in November of the same year. The newlyweds landed at Leith in May 1590.

James had learned enough from his own experience of being manipulated by powerful politicians to be aware of the damage caused by conflict within his realm, and so he made considerable effort to conciliate the opposing factions. As a Protestant king he maintained communication

7. Dawson, *Scotland Re-formed*, 325.

with the pope and avoided extreme measures in dealing with his Roman Catholic subjects. In spite of this there arose a number of problems that could not be ignored. In February 1589, a series of letters were intercepted in which the Earl of Huntly and some of his allies lamented the failure of the Spanish attempt to invade England and promised military support for any future attempt. Although he was required to serve only a nominal term of imprisonment for this offence, Huntly again tried unsuccessfully to engage in armed rebellion on more than one occasion in the future and was responsible for the murder of the Earl of Moray. He simply could not let things rest, and at the end of 1592, a Roman Catholic called George Kerr confessed to a plot which promised the support of Huntly and others for a Spanish invasion of the west of Scotland. Even then, James, having dealt with any military threat from his northern earls, treated them with great leniency. In March 1595, however, an unrepentant Huntly was driven out of Scotland.

One of those most opposed to the activities of the rebellious Catholic nobles was Francis Stewart, the earl of Bothwell. He was an extremely vigorous but unpredictable man. Bothwell was a kinsman of the murdered Earl of Moray and a natural opponent of Catholic conspiracies, yet his behaviour was so erratic that he himself spent much time and effort in rebellious activities against the king, and even, on one occasion in 1594, formed an unlikely alliance with Huntly which resulted in Huntly's imprisonment and Bothwell's exile.

During this period of time, James was only too glad of whatever support he could get from the Kirk. In the conflict with the northern Catholic lords, the Presbytery of Edinburgh provided troops to support James, and Andrew Melville accompanied his monarch on one of the expeditions against the rebels, while in 1596, the king was still confident enough of Presbyterian approval to apply to the General Assembly for funds.[8] Robert Bruce, an Edinburgh minister, and the Reformer Melville had both taken part in the coronation of Queen Anne, and the Golden Act of May 1592 did recognise a presbyterian form of church government even if there was no immediate financial provision for the Reformed church. In spite of these measures, the Presbyterians were never wholly rid of the suspicion that James was too sympathetic to the Roman Catholic church. His leniency towards the northern rebels was not forgotten, and in 1596, Huntly was not only permitted to return to Scotland but was allowed

8. Rait, *Making of Scotland*, 163.

to recover his estates. He seemed to become completely restored to the favour of the king and became a marquis in April 1599. His religious conformity was accepted when he professed his conversion to the Reformed faith and was received into the Kirk. The Reformed church in Scotland had indeed been growing in confidence during the previous years and had no hesitation in lecturing everyone, including the royal family, about appropriate language, church attendance, and stewardship of time.[9] The government was likewise accused of spiritual negligence on occasions, and the minister of St. Andrews, David Black, was bold enough to launch a personal attack on Queen Elizabeth, accusing her of atheism. It was time for James to assert royal authority.

In December 1596, the king and his government were in Edinburgh when the city erupted in a riot based on a spurious report that a Catholic mob intended to massacre James and his councilors. James was furious and blamed the Kirk's ministers for the tumult. He arrested the Edinburgh ministers and locked them up in the castle, ruling that they would not be restored to their charges until they recognised his authority. The incident was simply one symptom in a growing power struggle between king and church which lasted not only till the end of James's own reign but into those of his successors.

The king's own views about his authority were formed partly in reaction against those of George Buchannan, the scholar who had been his childhood tutor. Buchannan, in his treatise "De Jure Regni apud Scotos," argued that the king held his throne by authority of the people, and like them was subject to human and divine law. Buchannan even considered the possibility of the execution of a king, should he become a wicked tyrant. James was less than flattered to have such a treatise dedicated to himself, and in fact had it condemned by his government in 1584. He was also aware that his lifelong ambition to succeed Elizabeth on the English throne was not acceptable to all his subjects, and so he advocated the view that kings were chosen by God, received their authority from God, and were responsible to God alone and not to their subjects. This view was expressed clearly enough in two documents written by the king. In 1598, James wrote "The True Law of Free Monarchies." In contradiction of Buchannan, he writes, "It follows of necessity that the Kings were the authors and the makers of laws and not the laws of the Kings. . . . We daily see that in the Parliament, (which is nothing else but the head court

9. Donaldson, *Scotland*, 194.

of the King and his vassals) the laws are but craved by his subjects." He continues, "As ye see it manifest that the King is overlord of the whole land, so is he master over every person that inhabiteth the same, having power over the life and death of every one of them. . . . The King is above the law as both the author and giver of strength thereto."

The following year another document, called "Basilikon Doron," came from the king's pen. This took the form of a charge to his eldest son, Prince Henry, and gave instructions about good kingship, "Your father bids you studie here and reede. How to become a perfite King indeede." The three parts of the treatise cover a fairly wide range of activities, including advise about practical matters like control of trade, the selection of courtiers and military officers, and even details about personal appearance and hairstyles. James also deals with the qualities of a suitable wife and the necessity of her exclusion from political matters. He insists on marital faithfulness and the avoidance of any kind of immorality, pointing out the trouble caused by his own grandfather's moral failure.

There is much of genuine piety in James's instructions. His son is to spend time in the study of Scripture and reverent prayer. He is warned that his great office brings great responsibility to God, but it is also clear that for James the king is a "little God to sit on his throne," and as such he must rule the church. Accordingly, Prince Henry was warned equally against Roman Catholics and the Puritans in the Kirk who fomented sedition and calumnies. James's preference for episcopacy is undisguised, and he warns that the parity so much treasured by Presbyterian ministers cannot agree with monarchy. Henry must, with equal determination, oppose papal bishops and vain puritans. James, in 1597, was able to enforce his preference and ensure that Parliament passed the act that brought men who were bishops in all but name back into government. One of the advantages the king enjoyed was the lack of overall organisation in the Presbyterian Church. There was not yet the strength in the Kirk to resist his will.

It was also clear that the popularity of James with his ordinary subjects was growing. In August 1600, he was at the home of the Earl of Gowrie, to whom he owed £80,000. At some point, his companions were informed that the king had left the house. When they discovered fairly quickly that this was in fact untrue and that the king was still inside Gowrie House, they immediately assumed that it was another attempt to capture him and stage a coup. In what they claimed was a "rescue," the Earl of Gowrie was killed.

Since Gowrie was a firm Protestant and on excellent terms with the Presbyterian ministers, some of the clergy were suspicious of the whole affair, but when James returned to Edinburgh he was greeted with enthusiasm and great expressions of gratitude for his deliverance. Over the next decade, James's grip on church affairs became steadily tighter.

On 24 March 1603, Elizabeth died, and James's greatest ambition was realised. The English statesman Robert Cecil had been advising James for some time about the best preparation he could make for his accession to the throne of England, and within two weeks of the queen's death, James was on his way to London. Indeed, his progress towards that city had to be deliberately slow in order to avoid arriving before Elizabeth's funeral. Having promised his Scots subjects that he would return every three years, he failed to keep his word and returned only once, fourteen years later. From now on, both kirk and parliament in Scotland were to be governed by an absent monarch.

James is said to have told the English Parliament, concerning his native land, "Here I sit and govern it with my pen. I write and it is done, and by a clerk of the council I govern Scotland now, which others could not do by the sword."[10] With the threat of Catholic plotting and rebellion, in Scotland, at least, realistically in the past, James did not have the same need of Presbyterian support and began to demonstrate just how firmly he intended to control the Kirk. In July 1604, a general assembly arranged to be held in Aberdeen was suspended indefinitely by the king. A number of ministers who chose to ignore James's authority and assembled the following year were imprisoned or banished for life. Melville and a group of his colleagues were summoned to London and refused permission to return to Scotland. Melville's demands for a free general assembly were forceful enough to have him imprisoned in the tower until 1611. On his release, he spent the rest of his days at the University of Sedan in France, where he died in 1622. His nephew James Melville was allowed to travel north as far as Newcastle, but no further. Other ministers were permitted to return to Scotland, but kept under strict control. In December 1606, James called an assembly at Linlithgow, where he bullied and bribed the ministers into accepting the appointment of moderators of both presbyteries and synods who ruled these courts not for a limited time but continually. It was hard to see the difference between these moderators and diocesan bishops. The goal, however, was the restoration of a completely

10. Lynch, *Scotland*, 240.

Episcopal church, and in October 1610, three Scottish bishops were sent to London for consecration, since there were no already consecrated bishops left alive in Scotland who could have performed the ceremony.[11] Although General Assemblies were never formally prohibited, the affairs of the Kirk were administered by crown-appointed bishops, and as long as the forms of worship remained relatively unchanged, the bishops and the die-hard Presbyterians limped along in an uneasy compromise. James, however, had not yet reached his goal.

In 1614, James began to press for the observance of the major festivals of the Christian year, and the prayer book was introduced into worship in the colleges. In 1616, work was in hand for the use of two new liturgies which dealt with Sunday services, sacraments, and marriage. There was more than a little unease among the clergy at even this degree of change, but more was to follow when James came to Scotland in the summer of 1617. The king then presented what became known as the "Five Articles," which covered kneeling at communion, observance of the Christian year, private communion, private baptism, and Episcopal confirmation. After James had returned to London, an assembly was held at St. Andrews in November which rejected his proposals, but a second assembly in Perth held the following year was pressured into acceptance. In 1621, the Scottish Parliament confirmed the Perth Articles, although they were not put into practice with equal obedience in every part of the kingdom.

In all these changes to the Scottish church, James was driven by the concept of himself as a British monarch rather than the King of Scots, and although he was still a long way from reigning over one single kingdom, he saw a unity between the churches of England and Scotland as a step on the road to that end. Wisely, James introduced no further major changes to Scottish worship, and his death in March 1625 at the age of fifty-eight left the church in an uneasy peace, with the resentment of Andrew Melville's disciples simmering under the surface.

11. Donaldson, *Scotland*, 206.

17

The Road to Revolution

We believe with our hearts, confess with our mouths,
subscribe with our hands, and constantly affirm, before God
and the whole world, that this is the only true Christian faith and religion.[1]

WHEN JAMES I AND VI died on 27 March 1625, he was the first Scottish king since 1390 to leave an adult heir to succeed him.[2] His eldest son, Henry, had been created prince of Wales in June 1610 and groomed to wear the crown, but died unexpectedly in November 1612, leaving his brother Charles to inherit the throne. King Charles I was a very different kind of monarch from his father. If anything, he was even more determined to rule over a single kingdom and a single church, but he lacked James's ability to compromise and to manipulate events to achieve his purposes.

Within weeks of coming to power, Charles revoked all grants of land made by the crown or the church since 1540. Church property and income were now in the hands of the king. Lands which had previously provided income for the nobility were now controlled by others, and although compensation was paid to those who were disadvantaged under the Act of Revocation, it did not make up for the loss of prestige and power which a now resentful nobility had once held over their sub-tenants. A number of heritable offices were also brought under the king's direct control and therefore no longer remained within the same noble families.

1. *National Covenant*, 28 February 1638.
2. Stevenson, *Scottish Revolution*, 15.

It seemed to be the intention of Charles that the minor aristocracy and the church should benefit from the funds and opportunities released by the Act of Revocation. John Spottiswoode, the archbishop of St. Andrews, was appointed chancellor in 1635, and bishops began to exercise much more influence over the business which came before government and the way it was enacted. The nobility also felt very strongly the lack of the king's presence in Scotland and resented the increase in taxation and the costs of some of the projects promoted by their absentee king. Neither was Charles as diligent as he ought to have been in listening to his counsellors. In 1626, he was advised of the need to call a parliament in Scotland, but it took seven years before it met.[3]

At the same time, Charles encouraged a small but growing number of clergy who were inclined to favour some of the practices in worship which had been rejected at the Reformation. The Five Articles of Perth still expressed the official position of the Scottish Church, but these were not rigidly adhered to, and while the articles were certainly unpopular, a reluctant Reformed clergy were prepared to live with them. The chief religious advisor to Charles, however, was not a Scot but William Laud, whom Charles made archbishop of Canterbury in 1633. In that year, the king visited Scotland. It was on this occasion that his Scottish coronation took place at Holyrood Abbey. The English prayer book was in use, the clergy were compelled to dress like their English counterparts, and Charles made it clear that his decisions about church and state were not open to negotiation. A number of members of Parliament tried but failed to gain a free discussion of their grievances, and Lord Balmerino who was involved in preparing a supplication to the king was sentenced to death for treason. This sentence seemed to be a step too far even for Charles, who had enough sense to grant a royal pardon.

The other means open to the Presbyterians in the church to curb what they saw as a Romeward trend was the general assembly, but this had never been held since 1618. The followers of the kind of presbyterianism advocated by Melville and his supporters at the end of the sixteenth century had little doubt that a king who married a Roman Catholic princess the same year as he came to the throne[4] was a threat to a Reformed kirk, and their worst fears were confirmed in the aftermath

3. Donaldson, *Scotland*, 305.

4. In 1625, Charles married Henrietta Maria, the fifteen-year-old daughter of the French king Henry IV.

of the coronation visit. Archbishop Laud and Charles I were determined to bring the church in Scotland into line with that of England. At first Laud's proposal was that the Scottish church simply use the English prayer book. The Scottish bishops, however, demanded their own prayer book, and this was granted on the condition that its composition would have the approval of Charles and Archbishop Laud. Preparation for this went ahead very slowly, and before the Scottish liturgy was completed, the king authorised the publication of a book of canon laws for church life and worship, which among other things confirmed the Five Articles of Perth, arranged for the ordination of deacons, committed the Kirk to the forthcoming liturgy, but made almost no reference to kirk sessions, presbyteries, or general assemblies.

When the liturgy was eventually published in 1637, there was some small degree of recognition of Scottish practices, but its imposition on the Kirk was to prove the last straw. The book contained parts of the Apocrypha. The minister at the communion table began to look like a priest at an altar. The language hinted at Roman Catholic elements in worship, and worst of all it was a direct imposition of the king with no authority from the General Assembly. A number of meetings took place where opposition to the prayer book was considered. A treatise opposing it was to be printed and published. A "walk-out" was planned for its first use in Edinburgh. Some ministers were prepared to be outlawed for their refusal to use it.[5] All kinds of opposition was expressed in a variety of ways, but in spite it all, Charles seemed to be unaware of what would happen.

On 23 July, a well-organised demonstration took place. A service held in St. Giles Cathedral in Edinburgh was interrupted inside and surrounded outside by a mob of protesters. Guards prevented them getting inside the building, but when the bishop of Edinburgh left at the end of the service, his carriage was stoned all the way to Holyrood house, where he had to flee for safety. The protest was effective and certainly not spontaneous, and afterwards blame for the whole incident had to be apportioned when the king received a report of the riot. The bishops blamed the council for failing to take adequate precautions against such a predictable event, and the councillors blamed the bishops for forcing the prayer book on the church. Edinburgh waited for the king's reaction.

5. Stevenson, *Scottish Revolution*, 60.

The Scottish government issued grim warnings about any similar disturbances or opposition to the prayer book in future, but fear of further riots curbed any enthusiasm to continue the enforcement of the new liturgy until Charles replied to the report. His reply was clear and to the point. Those responsible for the disturbance were to be tried and punished and the introduction of the new prayer book was to go ahead as planned. The Scottish bishops found little success in forcing ministers to comply with the king's orders, and petitions from clergy and prominent laymen against the book flowed into the council. The main argument against the new liturgy seemed to be that it had no authorisation from either Parliament or General Assembly, and the privy council, desperate for some kind of compromise, let it be known that what the letter of the law demanded was the purchase of the prayer book, not its use.[6] It was becoming clear, however, that Charles had not yet grasped the seriousness of the situation in Scotland, and the council believed that the sooner he could be convinced of just how difficult things might become, the better. Accordingly, a plea was sent to the king that a delegation of councillors and bishops might be able to go to London to explain the problem in detail. Arrangements were made for the council to meet on 20 September to hear the result of the request.

When news of the proposed council meeting became generally known, many of those who opposed the prayer book began to gather in Edinburgh. Nobles, lairds, ministers, and church commissioners came to lodge petitions against its use in Scotland. On the day of the council meeting, among those present was the king's cousin, the Duke of Lennox, and he was presented with the petitions and a request to plead the cause of the petitioners with the king. Lennox, however, had scant sympathy for the petitioners, and Charles himself had scornfully rejected the proposed meeting with the delegation of councillors and bishops. Immediately after the council meeting on 20 September, the unrest began to spread. A small number of ministers travelled to parts of Scotland more distant from the capital to raise support for the petitioners. The burgh council of Edinburgh brought its own petition against the prayer book, and this influenced other burghs to do the same. A further meeting of the privy council was planned for 17 October, and the result of this was even greater numbers of people and petitions gathered in the city.

6. Stevenson, *Scottish Revolution*, 65.

Charles issued his instructions. The council must receive no more petitions. The Edinburgh crowds had to leave the city immediately, and the council and court of session must be moved out of Edinburgh entirely. The proclamation by the privy council of these royal commands was simply ignored, and the Scottish nobles ordered ministers and others to remain in the city while yet another petition was prepared. At this point in the proceedings, one or two warning bells began to ring. A section of the crowd were becoming a mob of rioters. The newest petition, which was composed by the nobles and some of the ministers, attacked not only the prayer book but the canon laws which the king had recently issued, and the bishops who were blamed for the outbreak of hostility. Not everyone wanted to increase the opposition beyond the scope of the prayer book and provoke the further wrath of the king, but most were persuaded to sign the petition, which was then circulated more widely for further signatures. The council were in a cleft stick. They tried to get the petitioners to go home to prevent any more rioting but agreed that they could choose a few representatives to remain in Edinburgh to keep abreast of developments, and developments were indeed on the way.

Petitioners formally asked the council for permission to hold meetings in other parts of the country to elect commissioners to come to Edinburgh to hear the most recent responses from the king. The council at first refused, but Sir Thomas Hope, the king's advocate, argued that the petitioners were within their rights, and his view prevailed. In fact, this election of commissioners to be sent to Edinburgh became something much more formal and organised than was first envisaged. All the nobles were involved. Commissioners were to be chosen from every county, burgh, and presbytery. The gatherings were called "tables" to avoid the implication that they were a rival version of the privy council. That same body was due to assemble in Linlithgow in December to receive Charles's latest instructions and promised to meet with the petitioners a few days later. There was, however, no good news to deliver. Charles gave a general assurance against any movement towards Roman Catholicism, but no acceptance of the specific complaints from the petitioners, some of whom were already preparing a legal defense against possible charges they might have to face. An attempt at compromise was made when the petitioners were asked to withdraw objections to the book of canon laws and the bishops while keeping the objections to the prayer book. They were also asked to present several smaller petitions rather than one inclusive document signed by them all, which carried a whiff of rebellion against the king. Not only were these requests refused, but the petitioners went on to formally refuse to recognise the authority of the bishops as members of council. All these complaints were presented to the council in a very formal written manner and a record obtained of the presentation. The council stated that the king must be informed of what had transpired, and everyone paused to await the latest royal response.

These events finally made Charles take the threat to his northern kingdom seriously, and he sent for John Stewart, the earl of Traquair. The petitioners had carefully prepared a record of all their requests and the matters arising from them, from the introduction of the prayer book onwards, and this record was now entrusted to Sir John Hamilton, who would accompany Traquair to London. Traquair hoped to persuade the king that some kind of compromise was necessary if the situation in Scotland was to be controlled, but found that Charles seemed to be blind to the inevitable consequences of his policies. Traquair returned to Scotland and called a meeting of the privy council at Stirling in February 1638 to hear a royal proclamation he had brought back from the king. In the proclamation, Charles reminded the council that the prayer book had been introduced by his personal authority, and those who rejected it were standing on the borderline of treason. Those who had opposed it and were now willing to return to their homes to live as faithful subjects of the king could expect forgiveness. Those who continued to gather in opposition would be charged with treason. The proclamation was made days later in Linlithgow and Edinburgh, but far from obeying the king's commands, the angry protesters decided that a greater gathering was necessary. Letters were set out to an even greater number of men of all ranks to come to Edinburgh. A committee of nobles, lairds, burgesses, and ministers was formed. A decision was reached to construct some kind of bond or covenant which would bind together all those who were determined to preserve a Reformed church and reject the religious policies of the king.

The final form of what became the National Covenant, also known as the Noblemen's Covenant,[7] was very carefully worded. It was based on the King's Confession of 1581 and had to possess enough flexibility to gain the support of moderates and those of more extreme views. It was first signed in Greyfriars Church on 28 February 1638 by nobles, lairds,

7. Lynch, *Scotland*, 264.

ministers, and burgh commissioners. In the days which followed, copies were signed by the citizens of Edinburgh and people in parish churches all over Scotland. It was some time before the principles of the covenant could be worked out in church life, and the aim was probably the form of moderate episcopacy which had prevailed before Charles came to the throne.[8] There remained, however, the real possibility of the covenant being interpreted in different ways. In spite of this, the National Covenant did provide a focus for Scottish independence in political and religious terms.

On 1 March, the privy council met in Stirling to consider the implications of the covenant and were realistic enough to see that it was there to stay. It was a time to wait and see. Charles sent for the Earl of Traquair and the Earl of Roxburgh to come and explain what the privy council intended to do about the situation. Archibald Campbell, who was then Lord Lorne, and later became marquis of Argyll, also went to advise the king, although he did so unofficially and without the approval of the council. Argyll had not signed the covenant and might therefore have seemed sympathetic to the king's cause, but when Traquair returned with instructions to hold a meeting of the council in Dalkeith on 6 June, its purpose was to advise the Marquis of Hamilton, who had been appointed as the king's commissioner in Scotland. Hamilton conveyed Charles's demands for obedience, which would be enforced if necessary by an English army, and he also had authority to raise Scottish troops to deal with any opposition. As an inducement to persuade the Covenanters to accept the king's authority, Charles promised to hold a parliament and a general assembly whenever peace had been restored.

The hope of peaceful negotiation was doomed from the start. A shipment of arms and ammunition for Edinburgh Castle could not be delivered and found its way secretly to the king's house at Dalkeith. Covenanters immediately suspected some kind of plot and believed that Charles was only buying time until he was strong enough to crush them altogether. Even before Hamilton reached Dalkeith, he learned that the Covenanters intended to hold a parliament and general assembly, whether the king called them or not. He continued to try to negotiate, but sent word to Charles to bring an English army and fleet to Scotland as quickly as possible. Meanwhile, the proposed council meeting was moved from Dalkeith to Holyrood house, where Hamilton planned to issue a royal

8. Donaldson, *Scotland*, 314.

proclamation and the Covenanters planned to protest against it. Wisely, Hamilton decided to withhold the proclamation in order to avoid open rebellion, and the Covenanters were not to be accused of treachery until the English fleet was under sail for Scotland. To gain more time, he left Edinburgh for London in July, urging the Covenanters to leave the city and wait till he returned. However, almost immediately, Charles authorised a new proclamation which promised a fair and reasonable use of the canons and liturgy, a free parliament, and a general assembly as soon as possible. Hamilton came back to Edinburgh and issued the proclamation, but the Covenanters were not impressed by its contents. Negotiations dragged on, but by July, both sides were preparing for open warfare. The king had hopes of support from parts of the north, from Ireland, and from the western isles, but since some of his supporters were Roman Catholics and others wanted Scotland to become a northern section of England, this prospect tended to drive the waverers into the covenanting ranks. Neither was there overwhelming support among English parliamentarians for an invasion of Scotland.

Charles, still playing for time, now attempted a diversionary tactic. He tried to persuade his opponents to exchange their zeal for the National Covenant for a recommitment to the 1560 Scots Confession of Faith composed by John Knox and his colleagues. He even called a general assembly, hoping that before it could meet, his army would have crushed the covenanting forces. There were a number of conditions attached to the proposed assembly which the Covenanters would not accept and a number of covenanting conditions which the king would not accept. Surprisingly, a compromise of sorts was reached. In September, Charles agreed to abandon the Articles of Perth, the recent canons, and the new prayer book. He would also accept certain limitations on the authority of the bishops, but all his Scottish subjects would sign the King's Confession of 1581. This policy was hardly a success, because neither the Covenanters nor the king's supporters were certain of the implications of the 1581 confession, and so many refused to sign. Neither was there complete agreement about who was eligible to be elected as a commissioner to the forthcoming assembly in Glasgow. The one body the Covenanters were determined to exclude were the bishops and ministers who had not signed the Covenant. It became clear that the future position of the bishops was one of the major issues to be dealt with, and Hamilton's willingness to hold the assembly at all was only because he knew it would go ahead whether he was there or not.

On 21 November 1638, Glasgow Cathedral was filled to capacity, and great crowds gathered outside. Hamilton's position as the king's commissioner was acknowledged, but the following day he questioned the legitimacy of some of the other commissioners before proceedings could begin. More that one man from university or presbytery was competing for the same appointment as a commissioner, and some, therefore, had to be rejected, but eventually business was under way. It became clear from the start that the Covenanters had control of which items of business would come before the assembly and which would not. Hamilton was intent on delaying matters as much as possible, and it took six days to get down to the central issues. At this stage, Hamilton knew he could delay no longer, and so he attempted to dissolve the assembly before it could do any real damage to the king's cause. He then left the gathering and commanded the privy council to proclaim the assembly to be over and to order its commissioners to go home. Of course he was ignored, and from this point onwards, assembly business proceeded apace. The previous six general assemblies were declared invalid because they had been controlled by the king and his bishops. The prayer book and the new canon laws were declared illegal. Bishops were abolished. The Perth Articles were likewise removed. Clergy were forbidden to hold political posts, and the right of the Kirk to summon general assemblies without royal permission was asserted. The decision was also taken to revise the National Covenant and include, in specific terms, the decisions made at the Glasgow assembly. Finally, an approach was made to the council and the king to formally accept the new shape of the Kirk. Hopes of this were obviously quite unrealistic, and in December, Hamilton declared all the proceedings of the Glasgow assembly to be null and void. Charles, however, attempted to continue negotiations with the Covenanters until he had gathered enough troops to begin the invasion.

The Scots were aware of the danger of an invasion from England, but also of the possibility of another from Ireland, and so in January 1639, a system of administration was set up to deal with communications and the raising of covenanting troops. Scots with military experience who were serving in continental armies were called back to begin training soldiers to defend the homeland, although a few were simple mercenaries who were willing to fight either for king or kirk.[9] The Covenanters continued to try by diplomatic means to get Charles to accept the new

---

9. Stevenson, *Scottish Revolution*, 131.

arrangements for the Scottish church, but the king had begun to portray their recent rejection of his authority as a military threat to England. In April, he called the English nobility to assemble at York with their forces to repel the invading Scots. The Covenanters made a direct appeal to the English Parliament assuring them that the new changes to the Kirk must not be interpreted as disloyalty to the king and that there was no intention of invading England. There was, moreover, in the English Parliament considerable sympathy for church reform, and the Scots were raising the possibility of closer political union with their English brethren in the faith. A Scottish paper called "Instructions for Defensive Arms," written by Alexander Henderson, the minister of Leuchars and one of the architects of the National Covenant, was printed in England and used to justify English opposition to the king.[10]

Preparations for war went ahead, and although the Covenanters planned to send ambassadors to France, Denmark, and Sweden to ask the rulers of these kingdoms to mediate with Charles, the project was abandoned because many were uneasy about foreign powers being involved in Scottish affairs. Some members of the privy council tried to persuade Charles that an invasion of Scotland would solve nothing and would only bring many who had not signed the covenant into the covenanting ranks when they saw their native land under attack. The king, however, would not be persuaded and tension continued to grow. Groups of men, mainly in the northeast of Scotland, had begun to gather to decide what they should do when the fighting began. There was posturing and threatening but no actual engagement, since Charles warned his supporters against any open conflict until his English army was ready to march into Scotland. Against this threat, the Covenanters were able to occupy the city of Aberdeen, Edinburgh castle, and almost all the lowland strongholds with no opposition at all.

The king's plans were far from complete. Anticipated help from Ireland did not materialize, and the army Charles was able to raise was neither strong enough nor experienced enough to mount a successful invasion. In spite of this, he pressed ahead with the composition of a new proclamation promising to recognise Scottish civil and religious rights and to pardon those who submitted to his authority. The exception to this royal clemency was to be a group of men deemed guilty of treason, which included a number of the covenanting nobility. These were to be

10. Ibid., 133.

outlawed, and a reward was promised to anyone who could find them and kill them. Of all the errors in judgement Charles had made this was perhaps the worst, and his horrified advisors were able to persuade him to revise and modify the proclamation, which was published at first not in Scotland but in England on 25 April at York.

The king intended to attack on two fronts. Hamilton and an army of five thousand mostly untrained men were to sail up the coast and into the Firth of Forth, while Charles led another army across the border at Berwick. Once landed in Scotland, Hamilton would publish the modified version of the royal proclamation in the hope that many of the Covenanters would accept its terms of pardon and lay down their arms. Hamilton's ships anchored off Leith but his troops stayed firmly on board. It would have been hard to discover a less enthusiastic invader than the Marquis of Hamilton. Not only did he find the most stubborn refusal of his offer of pardon, but his own mother, Lady Ann Cunningham, marchioness of Hamilton, a staunch Covenanter, vowed to shoot him herself if he tried to land. Hamilton and the Covenanters continued to exchange messages back and forth until Charles was ready to move up from the south. Charles, however, in military terms, was in a position not much better than his Scottish commander. By the end of May, the king and his forces were near the town of Berwick, and a covenanting army occupied Kelso. A detachment of English troops crossed the border to engage the Covenanters, but being outnumbered, quickly retreated back into England. At the beginning of June, the main covenanting army moved down to Duns Law, from where they offered to negotiate with the king. The offer was accepted without delay by the discouraged monarch. The result of these negotiations was an agreement that Charles would come to Scotland in the autumn for meetings of Parliament and the General Assembly. Both armies would also be disbanded. In fact, neither side disbanded, and the Covenanters were more than a little uneasy because of opposition to their cause in the northeast of Scotland. Covenanting forces led by James Graham, earl of Montrose, occupied and reoccupied the city of Aberdeen three times, but the need for a covenanting army in the north meant that their forces in the border negotiations with the king were weakened.

The parliament promised by Charles was planned for July 1639, but before it took place, the Covenanters called a convention in Edinburgh where they appointed Alexander Leslie, an experienced soldier, as commander in chief of the army of the Covenant. Suspicion of Charles was fully justified, since while dealing with the Covenanters he was, as the same time, trying to arrange forces from Ireland and the Western Isles to attack from the west.

In June, there was an attempt to negotiate a treaty. The negotiations were arranged to take place between appointed commissioners from both groups of combatants, but in fact Charles himself turned up and took control of the discussion. Among the demands made by the Covenanters were that all future church business be handled by the General Assembly and all civil matters by Parliament. Charles balked at this, but a compromise was reached giving the Covenanters freedom to worship as they chose, but recognising royal authority in civil matters. Assemblies and parliaments would meet annually or as often as necessary. Covenanters, however, thought this arrangement suspiciously vague, since Charles did not specifically recognise the Glasgow Assembly nor the abolition of bishops. He also demanded the disbanding of the army of the Covenant, to which the Covenanters reluctantly agreed, and a general assembly was arranged for 6 August, with a parliament two weeks later. Much was not clearly spelled out, and both sides accepted the truce as a temporary means of avoiding warfare. In fact, the truce pleased neither side, and when, as part of the agreement, the Covenanters handed back Edinburgh Castle to the Marquis of Hamilton, he immediately began preparing it for battle.

A further sign of the king's real intentions appeared when he issued the royal summons to the promised general assembly. Bishops and archbishops were to be included as usua,l which caused a measure of protesting on the streets of Edinburgh. Suspicions were raised even further by the king's demand that fourteen of the leading Covenanters attend him at Berwick for the curious purpose of discussing his journey to Edinburgh. As a compromise, six were permitted to go, but when they met with Charles he insisted that the remaining eight must appear also. By this stage of the negotiations, each side was accusing the other of breaking the terms of the truce, and so Charles turned his face towards London and set off for home, leaving John Stewart, the earl of Traquair, to be his commissioner at the promised assembly, since it was felt that Hamilton had lost the trust of the Covenanters. They met on 12 August, and Traquair was authorised to accept a number of compromises, like annual assemblies and the removal of the bishops, but he was also instructed to make it clear that the king would not be bound by any decisions made in his absence. The outcome nevertheless represented a considerable achievement for the Covenanters, and so on 30 August, by an act of the council, every one of the king's Scottish subjects became obliged under the law to take the Covenant. Immediately after the assembly was over, Traquair began to persuade the government to qualify and shake loose some of the assembly decisions. Charles himself was most opposed to the conclusion that episcopacy was contrary to the laws of the church in Scotland, since what was illegal in the Scottish church must be the same in that of England and Ireland.

It was soon apparent that the wind of change blowing through the church was affecting every part of Scottish life. Commissioners elected to Parliament were themselves Covenanters, almost to a man, and one of their priorities was to change the way in which the business before them was controlled. The "Lords of the Articles" had been the committee which first examined and then presented the business to be brought before the whole Parliament. In the past, such a committee was based on crown-appointed bishops who chose nobles approved by the king. The combined group then chose other commissioners, but the result was always a body of men who would do the king's bidding. Now, however, since bishops were no longer involved in government, some form of restructuring was required. The function of the Lords of the Articles was to be continued, but since bishops were no longer the foundation of this body, the question arose as to who should take their place. A compromise was reached whereby candidates would be chosen by the nobles themselves and approved by the king's commissioner. It became evident, however, that even in a parliament of Covenanters, there was no clearly worked out agreement about the future authority of the king. Indeed, the business of government proved to be so lengthy that the Lords of the Articles were still working their way through their agenda in October. Charles, in turn, refused to give royal consent to what they had already accomplished and instructed Traquair to suspend Parliament till June 1640. The Covenanters refused to recognise the king's authority in this matter, but were persuaded to leave a parliamentary committee in operation until they could agree with the king about his future role. It was not clear to everyone whether this committee was in fact a continuation of Parliament itself or not. Traquair eventually left for London in November to report to the English privy council and the English Committee for Scots affairs that nothing but force could solve the Scottish problem. Charles, hoping for funds and support to renew his military activities against the Covenanters, called an English Parliament, and the Scots were realistic enough to realise that war was inevitable. They began to raise funds, while the king sent a small detachment of English troops to reinforce Edinburgh Castle.

At the beginning of 1640, Charles and the Covenanters continued to negotiate without much hope of success on either side. Covenanters not only sent commissioners to deal with the king in London, but also a letter to Louis XIII, king of France, asking him to plead their cause with Charles. Unfortunately, even before the messenger sailed for France, a copy of the letter to Louis reached Charles, who saw it as a means of persuading his English Parliament that a military threat from Scotland was imminent. The letter was produced to the English Parliament, which met in April 1640, but it soon became clear that this body had no intention of going to war with the Scots, nor would they agree to the raising of funds for such an enterprise. Many of the English parliamentarians were sympathetic to the covenanting cause and ensured that the Scots were kept informed of all that took place in English politics. In spite of this, Charles continued to prepare for battle. In Scotland, there was no armed resistance to the Covenanters, but they deemed it necessary to send an army to occupy Aberdeen to discourage the possibility of any royalist opposition in the north. At the same time, plans were made to hold a parliament as soon as possible.

In the summer of 1640, the burning question was the precise relationship of the king to his Scottish subjects. The possibility of deposing an unworthy monarch was reluctantly considered, and politicians discussed, at least unofficially, the replacement of a king by a temporary ruler until the way ahead was clear. Parliament met on 2 June in spite of Charles's attempts to prevent it, and the result was a number of important changes to the way Scotland was governed, although the future role of the monarchy was not in fact specifically agreed. Parliament was to meet at least every three years and was to debate all important matters, not only those referred by the Lords of the Articles. This once all-important committee would meet in future only if Parliament considered it necessary and would only deal with matters referred to it by Parliament. The effect of this change was that the king's control of government through his own appointed officers was ended. When Parliament was not in session, a committee of estates was formed to make necessary decisions and prepare for the war, which crept closer every day. To confirm the integrity of these proceedings, a new covenant was drawn up for general subscription, binding Scots to recognise the Parliament's legal basis. Taxes were raised to finance the coming war, and William Hamilton, the earl of Lanark, was sent to London to inform the king of the acts passed by the new Parliament.

It was at this time the Covenanters felt it necessary to deal with men who had failed to support the cause and to demand the submission of those who, like the garrison in Edinburgh Castle, were still serving in the royal army. A leading covenanting noble like Archibald Campbell, the earl of Argyll, plundered his way through land and property belonging to prominent Royalists and was not unjustifiably accused of working for his own aggrandisement rather than for the covenanting cause. Perhaps Argyll's greatest critic was James Graham, the earl of Montrose, whose zeal for the covenant was modified by his loyalty to the crown. The division between Argyll and Montrose was not healed, but rather grew wider as time went on. A number of men who refused the covenant were arrested, and preparations for war became more urgent.

The General Assembly which was held in Aberdeen in July 1640 was unusual for several reasons. It was dominated by clergy, since the nobility were otherwise occupied in military matters. There was no commissioner present to represent the king, and one of the main subjects for debate was whether or not private meetings for prayer were dangerously incompatible with the Presbyterian Church. There was a general suspicion of any small group of people meeting together for any purpose, and the assembly ruled against prayer meetings, although this ruling was ignored in many cases. The other issue which caused division was the declared need to justify every component in worship from the Bible and therefore to purge from church services a number of practices which were not found in Scripture.

On the military front, the general view was that a decisive victory over the king's forces was necessary, and since there appeared to be no immediate indication that Charles would invade Scotland, it seemed obvious that the army of the covenant must invade England. The point of the warfare, however, was not to destroy the king, but simply to make him recognise the government and church in Scotland. A number of Scots hoped that English parliamentarians might "invite" them to cross the border, but this did not happen, since the English deemed it to be treasonable. There was, however, enough encouragement given to convince the Scots that their invasion would not be entirely unwelcome and that it would be used by the English as an occasion to deal with their own grievances against the king.

At this point, the division between Argyll and Montrose threatened to become a split in the covenanting ranks. There was a lurking fear that Argyll and his supporters might still depose Charles and rule in his place, while the more moderate Covenanters seemed to be excluded from the highest levels of consultation. Neither were all of them convinced that the invasion of England was the best course to take. In August 1640, Montrose and seventeen allies met at Cumbernauld and signed a bond to support the covenant and one another. They stressed their commitment to the entire nation, as opposed to those who were only committed to their own advancement. Whatever misgivings the moderate Covenanters might have had about the invasion, it did take place on 20 August, and the Scots troops were able to occupy Newcastle with very little resistance. The royal garrison in Edinburgh Castle surrendered in September, and the army of the covenant seemed invincible. Some of Charles's advisers even raised the possibility of the Scots reaching London in a matter of weeks. The Scots were anxious to avoid the impression that their quarrel was with the English people, and in the negotiations which followed the invasion, it was made clear that the English Parliament had to be involved in establishing a lasting peace with the king. A group of English nobles were chosen to meet the Scots at Ripon, and an agreement was reached that seemed very favourable to the Scots, largely due to the fact that the English negotiators were themselves opponents of Charles's rule. The arrangements at Ripon were to be binding for two months, and a final treaty to end all hostilities was planned for a consultation in November in London.

Far from being unwelcome as the representatives of an invading army, the Scots commissioners were received with enthusiasm by the Puritan section of the English Parliament and Scottish ministers were invited to preach in London churches. Negotiations, however, proved to be a lengthy business in spite of the king's reluctant agreement to give the Covenanters most of what they asked for on the basis of the 1640 Scottish Parliament. Charles's problems in dealing with his English Parliament were growing by the day, and he wanted the Scots out of England as soon as possible. Initially, the king's strongest English critics wanted to keep the Scots army and their commissioners in England as a lever to force their own demands on the monarch, but as time went on and the spring, then the early summer, of 1641 rolled around, the Scottish presence began to look more and more of a nuisance. The English Parliament became more confident of dealing with the king without Scottish help, and the most unwelcome element in the Scottish proposals was their attempt to make the English church Presbyterian. The Scots claimed that a unity of church worship and government would be the only foundation for political and economic peace and stability. This was a step too far, and Charles had a much greater measure of support from his Parliament in resisting such a demand. There was a reluctant agreement to the appointment of a standing commission from both Parliaments to deal with any problems between the two nations, but the king would not give clear consent to the right of the Scottish Parliament to choose the officers of state and lords of session. The matter was postponed for a future day because of a more urgent issue between Covenanters and monarch. The Covenanters intended that the Scottish Parliament should pass an Act of Oblivion, which would protect them from being accused and prosecuted for actions taken during the recent conflict. However, they did not want this kind of protection to be given to everyone. They intended those who had been opposed to covenanting rule and had supported the king to be brought to trial. Charles, in turn, was equally determined that not all Covenanters should escape retribution. He claimed that the actions of some were treasonable, but could not persuade the Scots to accept these terms. In the end, there was one new factor which pressed the negotiations to a conclusion. Charles decided to come to Scotland.

The announcement in April 1641 of the proposed royal visit was received with surprise and suspicion, but one practical result was the determination of the Scots to have the treaty with the English Parliament finalised as quickly as possible. They wanted no further wrangling with the king when he arrived, and in fact the completed treaty gained royal approval in August. It was suspected that one of the reasons for the royal visit to Scotland was to find Scottish support for the king in his quarrels with the English Parliament, and this hope was not as vain as it seemed. Charles was aware of the division in the covenanting ranks and to exploit this, some Scottish nobles were offered positions in the English court. Those who had signed the Cumbernauld bond and were supporters of Montrose had not formed a separate party and were certainly still within the covenanting ranks, but Montrose on more than one occasion had written to the king privately to assure him that if he respected the Scottish church and rightful liberty of his subjects he would find a body of men who would defend him against any that sought to depose him. A monarch with powers restricted by law seemed preferable to many, as opposed to a dictator who might ignore the rights of less powerful men.

The Scottish Parliament had some unfinished business, including the hearing of charges brought against Royalists accused of opposition to the covenanting regime, but the sitting of parliament had to be postponed several times because the king was not ready to embark on his visit to Scotland. The Scots settled finally on 17 August, assuming that the king would have arrived by that date. The charges against the Royalists focussed on the allegation that Argyll had plotted to depose the king. When Argyll and his troops had marched through Atholl in June 1640, subduing any royalist opposition, he had called local leaders to a meeting at the Ford of Lyon and compelled them to commit themselves in a bond of loyalty to the covenanting government. Montrose, always suspicious of Argyll, had sent John Stewart of Ladywell, to attend the meeting and report exactly what Argyll's intentions were concerning the king. Stewart reported that Argyll intended to depose the king, and Montrose made sure that Charles learned of this. When the accusation became known, Argyll furiously denied it, and Stewart was imprisoned, later modifying his statement by saying that Argyll had simply discussed the principle of deposing unworthy monarchs with no specific reference to Charles I. His modification of the accusation, however, did not help his own circumstances, and he was beheaded on 28 July 1641. His execution was a warning that covenanting leaders could not be attacked with impunity.

When Parliament began on 17 August, the acts passed by the Parliament of June 1640 were issued in the king's name. Significantly, the traditional ceremony where the monarch touched the acts with the royal sceptre as a sign of his approval did not take place. Parliament was making the point that the acts were law by their own authority and not that of the king. When Charles arrived, a number of royalist supporters were with him. Those who had not yet signed the covenant were excluded until they did so, and those who were facing charges were excluded completely. Agreement was reached for the army of the covenant to return from England and to be disbanded apart from three regiments. The terms of the London treaty were ratified by king and parliament, but the two elements which remained a matter of dispute were the identity of those not protected from prosecution by the Act of Oblivion and the more urgent matter to which this was linked, the appointment of officers of state, councilors, and lords of session. Agreement was eventually reached that the king would appoint these men, but only with parliamentary approval. There was a move to make Argyll the chancellor, but the king resisted this vigorously and accepted a compromise whereby a fellow clansman, John Campbell, the earl of Loudoun, was given the post.

The business of electing officers of state was to drag on for months, and the king, while desperate to find supporters and increase the number of men he could trust, did not seem to have the wisdom required to make this happen. The gap between Royalists and Covenanters was widening every day, and one prominent Royalist, Lord Ker, summoned to Parliament to apologise for insulting behaviour, answered the summons but brought hundreds of armed troops with him. A group of Royalists, led by Ludovic Lindsay, the earl of Crawford, formulated a plot to capture and possibly kill Argyll, the Marquis of Hamilton, and the Earl of Lanark. The king was suspected of knowing about the plot and failing to disclose it, and when he arrived at Parliament to protest his innocence, he was unwise enough to arrive with hundreds of armed men. The three victims of the plot believed their lives were in danger and fled from Edinburgh.[11] A committee was chosen to investigate the incident, but before Charles could be cleared of implication in the plot, a Catholic rebellion broke out in Ireland, and the king was immediately suspected of being involved in it. To the surprise of the Scottish Parliament, he asked for Scottish troops to crush the rebellion. Parliament had a good measure of sympathy with this request, since there were thousands of Scottish Presbyterians in Ireland who would be threatened by the Catholic uprising, but Parliament refused to become involved until they had consulted with the English Parliament about the matter.

As various offices were filled and committees chosen to deal with national affairs, Charles attempted to reward the Covenanters who served in this way in an attempt to buy the loyalty of former enemies, while almost ignoring those who had offered him unswerving support. Parliament dropped charges against all but the most aggressive Royalists and even released from prison some who were no longer deemed to pose a threat to the government. Charles returned to England, leaving

11. Stevenson, *Scottish Revolution*, 238.

the Covenanters well and truly in control. In spite of their position of undoubted authority, the Covenanters were realistic enough to see that the king's continuing struggle with the English Parliament would have an effect on their own security. If Charles had to submit to the English Parliament, the Scottish position would be confirmed, but if he forced his English subjects to accept royal authority, the Scots feared that all they had gained from the king would vanish like the morning mist.

18

Covenant Is King

*We shall endeavour to bring the Churches of God in the three kingdoms
to the nearest conjunction and uniformity in religion, confession of faith,
form of Church government, directory for worship and catechising, that we,
and our posterity after us, may, as brethren, live in faith and love,
and the Lord may delight to dwell in the midst of us.*[1]

IN THE IRISH REBELLION of 1641, King Charles I had asked the Scottish
Parliament to send troops to crush the Catholic uprising, although the
Scottish army in Ulster, which did not arrive until spring of 1642, did
not bring the advantage he had hoped for. Part of the English Parliament
who also wanted to see the rebellion brought to an end were happy for
this task to be undertaken by the Scots, since they believed they needed
every armed man available in England to deal with the inevitable conflict with the king. Other English parliamentarians who were not wildly
enthusiastic about the Covenanters were afraid that once established in
Ulster, they might be hard to remove back to Scotland again. Negotiation
with England about the size of the Scottish force and who would pay
for their services was a slow business. By the time the details of the arrangement were settled in July 1642, Charles was having doubts about
the whole matter and refused to ratify the agreement. However, ratified
or not, by November more than eleven thousand Scottish troops were in
Ireland. Although the Scottish army found little effective opposition, the

---

1. *Solemn League and Covenant*, sec. 1.

promised funds and provisions from England were slow to arrive because war between Parliament and the king in England had begun, and so the Scottish government had to make their own provision for the Scottish army.

The other concern of the covenanting government at the time was the prosecution of the Royalists they considered to be their greatest enemies. This proved to be no easy matter. Those responsible for the prosecution of criminals were reluctant to put prominent Royalists on trial, and in the end, only John Stewart, the earl of Traquair, was tried and found guilty of crimes, but he was never punished. There was a feeling among the Covenanters that the concessions gained from the king should be allowed to settle, and the Scots army being away from their homeland made some feel vulnerable. It was not the time to energetically pursue Royalists. In fact, the attitude of Charles himself towards his royalist allies became distinctly cool at this point because he still entertained hopes of getting the Covenanters to support him against the English Parliament. He called a meeting of the Scottish council for 25 May, hoping to persuade them to condemn the English Parliament, and indeed a number of Royalists petitioned the council for this very thing, but were ignored, while a number of Covenanters urged the council to mediate between Charles and his English Parliament, but on no account to offer the king any assistance. In July 1642, a general assembly was planned in St. Andrews, and the king appointed Charles Seton, the earl of Dunfermline, as his royal commissioner. On this occasion, the assembly took the opportunity to urge both Parliament and the king to speed up the process of working out a uniformity in church doctrine and government between the Scottish and English churches. There was also continued debate about the legitimacy of holding conventicles and prayer meetings, but fear of division in the church made the assembly stop short of a decision binding on every congregation. A committee was appointed to deal with church affairs between general assemblies, even though some assembly commissioners feared it might become too powerful.

In the summer of 1642, there was a genuine desire for a peaceful solution to national problems. Many Scots did not want to be dragged into the English civil war, but both Charles and the English Parliament looked to them for support, and in November, the Scots received a formal request for armed forces to fight on the English parliamentary side. One of the king's most implacable opponents in the English Parliament,

John Pym, even considered calling for Scottish officers to command the English army. This was followed by an informal approach for military assistance, made not to the Scottish council or any other official body, but to some leading Covenanters. Charles was deeply concerned about the trend in English affairs and wrote to the Scottish council in order to correct what he claimed was a serious misrepresentation of affairs in England.[2] His intention was to have his letter printed and distributed widely. There was considerable resistance to this intention, but in the end it was agreed by a narrow margin to do so. The Covenanters could see the writing on the wall. Their influence in the council was clearly not as great as they hoped, and so they turned to Parliament as a means of controlling events. The next Scottish Parliament, however, was not due to meet until June 1644, and so a group of commissioners was chosen to travel to England to meet with both king and Parliament to attempt to negotiate the end of the civil war, to arrange a conference of ministers from both churches in order to work towards religious uniformity, and to persuade Charles to call a parliament in Scotland. The mission was not fruitful. Charles and his allies were unwelcoming and discourteous, while the Scots returned home without negotiation with the English Parliament.

At the same time, Charles wrote to the Scottish council pointing out that the English parliamentary forces were composed almost entirely of Independents who had no intention of becoming Presbyterian, but assuring them that when he had conquered his English rebels, he would respect the laws of church and state in Scotland. The situation he faced in Scotland was far from stable. The Covenanters themselves were steadily dividing into moderates like Montrose, who was willing to take up arms for the king if necessary, and extremists like Argyll, who did not trust the king one inch and intended to make sure that Charles never regained any authority over the Scottish Parliament and church again. Charles was enough of a realist to see that it was only a matter of time until covenanting troops crossed the border unless he could defeat his parliamentary opponents quickly. However, he did not want a royalist uprising in Scotland to add to his English troubles, and so he hoped that by stringing out negotiations with the Covenanters he could keep them out of England and give himself enough time to win the civil war. Neither had he forgotten the Scottish army in Ireland, still short of money and supplies and available to be used against him when needed. The Scottish council

2. Stevenson, *Scottish Revolution*, 256.

themselves were considering the condition of the army in Ireland, and Argyll persuaded them that a convention was necessary, since the king had not yielded to their request to call a parliament. He urged the need to consider the Irish problem and the pressure the English civil war had brought to bear on Scotland. Charles, simply to make a protest, wrote to the council to forbid them to call a convention without his permission. He also sent William Hamilton, the earl of Lanark, to plead his cause at the council, and Lanark was not entirely unsuccessful, since the council sent a fairly supportive reply to the king. Charles repeated his displeasure at the calling of a convention without royal authority, but simply urged them to restrict their deliberations to finding funds and provision for the army in Ireland. This might have been possible, at least in the short term, except for the discovery of a royalist plot.

Randal MacDonnell, the earl of Antrim, was both a royalist and a Roman Catholic. He was captured by the Scots army in Ireland in May 1643 carrying papers which indicated that he was involved in a plot with Montrose and others to help the king. It was not clear exactly how far Charles himself was involved in the plot, but its very existence ended the Covenanters trust in his promises. Montrose, who had been in England to negotiate with the king and had returned, thought it wiser to go back to England, since some of his fellow plotters were arrested and charged with treason. A number of other Royalists who had advised the queen about tactics for winning the civil war in England were accused of being troublemakers, and charges were prepared against them.

When the convention got under way, the two most prominent figures were James Hamilton, now duke of Hamilton, who was the king's commissioner in Scotland, and Argyle, the undisputed leader of the more extreme Covenanters. Hamilton had the greater influence among the nobles, but the lairds and burgesses mainly followed Argyll, and the first question they had to deal with was the authority of the convention itself. Hamilton insisted that it was held by permission of the king and therefore limited to whatever he had authorised. Argyll was able to persuade the majority that, although not a parliament, the convention was authorised by the council and perfectly competent to make decisions about any matter which came before it. Hamilton seemed to be so restrained by this decision that he gave no clear lead to the Royalists present, an approach which was to become more typical of his involvement in Scottish affairs. Conscious of its own power, the convention began to consider sending troops to fight for the Parliament in England, and this was encouraged by the Scottish church, whose aim was the political and religious unity of the two kingdoms. In June 1643, an invitation was sent to Scottish ministers to attend the Westminster Assembly, which had been called by the English Parliament to direct the further reformation of the English church. Although for the Scots unity of church and state were inextricably linked, there was less enthusiasm for this among their English colleagues. This was partly because the English Parliament was too busy fighting royalist forces to give the matter the attention it deserved, but there was also a genuine reluctance to embrace the covenant and presbyterianism among some of the English churchmen. Hamilton, for his part, tried to discourage the alliance by reminding the Scots that the English Parliament had not yet paid what they owed for the maintenance of the Scots army in Ireland, and this complaint was reinforced by commissioners to the convention from that army who reported that the troops were so short of money and provisions they could no longer function as an active military unit. However, the failure of the English Parliament to meet its obligations in Ireland did not prevent a further request for a large unit of Scottish infantry and cavalry to come immediately to join the parliamentarians in England in their struggle, and while this was not unwelcome to the Scots, they did indicate that some sort of payment to the Irish army was expected. At the same time, it seemed sensible to raise a smaller group of armed forces to be ready to deal with any royalist rising in Scotland.

The General Assembly of the Church also met in August 1643, and so a royal commissioner had to be appointed. Charles did not make the choice himself but left it to the Earl of Lanark to appoint the lord advocate, Sir Thomas Hope of Craighall, as commissioner for the king. Anticipating a difficult commission there were very few envied him the post. When commissioners from the English Parliament arrived, the differences between the Scots and English churches became clear. For the Scots, a covenanted nation meant that a Presbyterian church and civil government could not be separated, but the English church was a fairly mixed multitude. For the English commissioners, the urgent priority was winning the civil war, and the question of church uniformity was on the back boiler. The Scots, while willing to send military assistance to the English Parliament, wanted it known that their assistance carried with it the clear understanding that the worship and government of the English church would be brought into line with that of the Scots. A document expressing the basis of this uniformity was prepared and accepted by the Scottish convention, the General Assembly, and the commissioners who represented the English Parliament. "The Solemn League and Covenant," like the National Covenant, contained both religious and political promises. The religious aims of English church reformation were just wide enough to admit something less than strict presbyterianism, and the promises to preserve the person and authority of the king were even wider in their interpretation. The document, however, in spite of its lack of precision, was sent off to be ratified by the English Parliament, and preparations began immediately for the invasion force which would assist English parliamentary troops. The agreement was that England would repay the Scots for the cost of this venture and the terms of a formal treaty were worked out promising mutual support and defence. By the end of August, both the Solemn League and the treaty were signed and sealed by both governments. There were, however, two important points added by the English Parliament. The Solemn League was extended to include Ireland, as well as the two original nations and the wording which described the reformation of the English church was altered to avoid the obligation to reproduce an exact copy of the church in Scotland. These alterations were deemed to be acceptable and the covenant became enforceable on all Scots. Those who refused to sign it were subject to confiscation of goods and exclusion from public office.

After making arrangements for raising the army, the convention was adjourned, leaving a committee to direct affairs until it convened again. The intention was that one part of the committee should remain in Scotland and the other part should travel with the army when it moved into England. This force was to be strengthened by half the Scots army in Ireland coming to join them, although the arrangement was complicated by the fact that the army in Ireland was still owed large sums of money for their services and the king was making his own plans to bring part of the royalist troops in Ireland over to England to improve his chances in the civil war. By September 1643, the first of the Scots army had occupied Berwick and begun to gather on the borders, although numbers of troops were held in reserve because of the threat of royalist activity in the northeast and rumours of opposition from Ireland. Nevertheless, in January 1644 it was a confident, if ill-equipped, army which moved into England led by Alexander Leslie, the earl of Leven, and men who, believing themselves to be the servants of God, imagined the results of their military labours might eventually change not only the British Isles but the whole of Christendom.[3] This proved to be very far from the case, as the unity of the Covenanters, already under very great strain, broke down completely.

For some time, Montrose had been disillusioned with the course taken by the extreme Covenanters and had joined the king in Oxford, where he pressed Charles to permit him to begin some kind of military action to prevent the army of the covenant from marching to the aid of English parliamentary forces. In February 1644, Charles appointed him commander in chief of the royalist forces in Scotland. In April, Montrose returned to Scotland at the head of a small number of mainly English troops, but found such limited support in the border regions that he had to withdraw again. His hopes for English royalist forces to help him in Scotland were ended when the king's army led by Charles's nephew, Prince Rupert, was soundly defeated at Marston Moor near York in July by the combined strength of the Covenanters and the English parliamentarians. Montrose, in spite of this defeat, returned to Scotland in August to meet up with a group of Irish Royalists raised by the Earl of Antrim. These men had crossed over to Scotland, and together with a number of Highlanders under the leadership of Montrose formed the basis of a very effective fighting force which quickly gained some important victories. In September, they defeated a covenanting army at Tippermuir and then moved north to take the city of Aberdeen. Argyll gathered an army to deal with this royalist threat, but Montrose was able to achieve one victory after another until when he was victorious at Kilsyth in August 1645. He entered Glasgow as ruler of Scotland and called a parliament.

The triumph of Montrose, however, was short lived. A covenanting army returned from England and defeated him at Philiphaugh in September. Following this battle, the Covenanters, remembering the atrocities the Irish and Highland troops had inflicted on their own people, imposed a merciless slaughter on royalist prisoners and civilians alike, although Montrose himself escaped. The royalist cause was effectively over. Charles and his troops had lost the battle of Naseby in June 1645 and had no hope of recouping their losses. Montrose tried unsuccessfully to raise another fighting force, but in May 1646, Charles surrendered to the Scottish army in England and quickly ordered the end of all resistance to the parliamentarians. The war was over and the jubilant Scots army moved to

3. Stevenson, *Scottish Revolution*, 198.

Newcastle with the king as their prize. Initially, it seemed as if the hopes and prayers of the Covenanters had all been granted. What they had to deal with after their victory turned out to be another set of problems.

The process of achieving uniformity in worship and government with the English church was not as easy as had been hoped by the Scots. While the civil war was being waged, an assembly was convened at Westminster Abbey, not under the authority of the church but that of the English Parliament. This began in July 1643, and its purpose was a revision of Anglican doctrinal statements, forms of worship, and government and the promotion of unity with the Scottish church. A group of Scottish commissioners comprising both ministers and elders attended the assembly with the authority of both the Scottish Church and Parliament. These men were not members of the assembly but advisors who had an enormous influence on the deliberations. The Solemn League and Covenant was accepted by all parties as a basis for political union, and the assembly produced a directory for public worship, the Westminster Confession of Faith, and the Larger and the Shorter Catechism. In spite of this measure of agreement, several problems remained. Delegates selected by the English Parliament included those who wanted to retain bishops and some who wanted the state to control the church. The biggest stumbling block to Scottish hopes, however, was the large body of Independents who were also very prominent in the English parliamentary forces. Indeed, as time went on, this army began to take on an identity of its own, distinct from that of Parliament for whose cause it was fighting, and it seemed as if Parliament was being controlled by the army and not vice versa. It was becoming clear that England was not going to adopt Scottish Presbyterianism as her own form of church government.

The other problem faced by the victorious Scots was what to do with the king himself. They did not want to take him back to Scotland where he might become the focal point for renewed royalist activity, and their hopes of persuading Charles to accept the Solemn League and Covenant were hardly realistic. The Covenanters were now in complete control of the Scottish state and church, and so the best solution to their problem seemed to be for the king to be enthroned again, but powerless, in England. The problem was still unsolved when, having received some measure of payment for their service in the English civil war, the Scots put Charles into the hands of the English Parliament and left Newcastle to go home in January 1647. The statements in both the National Covenant and the Solemn League about the commitment to "preserve and defend the King's Majesty person and authority" were not entirely empty words. No Scot wanted to be without a monarch, and the recent wars had not been undertaken to destroy the monarchy but to compel Charles to accept the authority of Parliament and church without interference. It was, therefore, with a measure of unease they saw the king forcibly taken into the hands of the English army in June 1647. Over the following months, Charles managed to gain an opportunity of freedom and made his way to Carisbrooke Castle on the Isle of Wight, where he thought he could find safety. Instead, what he thought was a shelter became in fact another prison. The only action he could take was to enter into secret communication with some of his Scottish subjects who now looked like his only hope.

Since the unity of the Scottish and English churches in a Presbyterian system was becoming more unlikely every day, and since England was now a nation whose Parliament was controlled by the army largely composed of Independents, it seemed to a number of the more moderate Covenanters that some kind of bargain with the king might be profitable. A group led by the Duke of Hamilton sent three commissioners to the Isle of Wight, where Charles was a prisoner, to work out some kind of agreement. In exchange for a promise to maintain a Presbyterian church in Scotland, and to have the same in England for a trial period of three years, the Scots promised military support for the king. This "engagement," as it came to be known, received a large measure of support in the Scottish Parliament but little among the ministers of the General Assembly. There were some Scots, specially in the southwest, who saw it as a betrayal. However, in spite of the opposition, Hamilton led an army into England in July 1648 to rescue the king. The hope was that it would be joined by whatever numbers survived among the English Royalists, and English Presbyterians concerned about the growth of independent churches. The Scottish invasion was a disaster. The best Scottish military tacticians were conspicuous by their absence, and by the end of August, the Scots were soundly defeated by an English army led by Oliver Cromwell at Preston. The attempt to rescue the king was over.

Those who had been most vehemently opposed to the Engagement saw the defeat of Hamilton as a God-given opportunity. In September 1648, an army gathered from the southwest of Scotland, and led by experienced military commanders like the Earl of Leven, marched on

Edinburgh. These "Whiggamores," as they became known, were successful enough against the forces of the Engagers to compel them to accept a
treaty. The committee of estates which had ruled Scotland between Parliaments left Edinburgh as a body. Politicians who were known to have
supported the engagement resigned. Nobles like Argyle, who was never
an Engager, and his fellow clansman the Earl of Loudoun, who had been
an Engager but then changed sides, became leaders in a new government,
but were only too well aware that their control of the whole country was
an impossible task. The answer to the problem was an astonishing new
Presbyterian alliance with the independent Cromwell, who arrived in
Edinburgh in October 1648. With the support of Cromwell's military
strength, Argyll and his allies became more confident.

One of the first actions by the new government was to pass the Act
of Classes in January 1649. This act brought about a purge from public
life and church offices of all who might hold Engager sympathies. Prominent Engagers and those who had fought with Montrose were banned
for life. Others who had shown sympathy for the engagement or even the
refusal to condemn it were subject to a sliding scale of exclusion from
public affairs. Others who were immoral or negligent in family worship
could be banned for a year. The lifting of the ban after the prescribed
period of exclusion took place when the offender had been examined by
the church, while ministers who refused to preach against the engagement were dismissed from their charges. Extreme Covenanters saw these
events as a blessed purifying of church and nation and were even confident that a smaller, purer army would, by the grace of God, be more
powerful than a larger but more corrupt force. Since it was the church
which decided whether men were fit for public office or not, the clergy
had never been in a stronger position than they were at that time. There
were great tensions in church and state, but on the immediate horizon
was an event which shocked every Scot, Engager, or otherwise. On 13
January 1649, the most aggressive group of the English Independents
brought about the execution of King Charles I. He was charged with being a tyrant, a traitor, a murderer, and a public enemy. Whatever measure
of truth there might have been in these accusations, the execution of a
king by his subjects sent shock waves throughout the three kingdoms and
across the continent of Europe. Within a matter of days, the indignant
Scots proclaimed his son Charles II as the new king.

By March, Scottish commissioners were at The Hague in the Netherlands negotiating with Charles II about the terms of his reign over the three kingdoms. The new king had hopes of some degree of support which might afford him room to negotiate with the extreme Covenanters. However, the possibility of royalist help from Ireland was ended by Cromwell's invasion of that country in August 1649. The following spring, in March 1650, the indefatigable Montrose, armed with a royal commission but not a lot else, landed in Orkney with a few hundred men. These were mainly foreign mercenaries. As he moved south, he was unable to gather many more to his cause and found that some he had expected to join him in fact supported the Covenanters. Whether Charles had any real hope of victory from Montrose's last campaign is doubtful, but it was useful as a factor in his negotiations with the covenanting Scots. Charles came to see fairly quickly that his hopes were slender and in fact sent word to Montrose to cease fighting and disband his army. Sadly for Montrose, this message could not reach him in time, and in April 1650 he was defeated at Carbisdale in Sutherland. Montrose himself escaped from the battlefield but was captured a few days later and executed in Edinburgh in May. Charles's latest negotiations were conducted at Breda in the Netherlands, and to ensure his acceptance with the Covenanters, who were strong enough to dictate the terms, he had no option but to accept the National Covenant and the Solemn League. These were signed onboard a ship anchored off the mouth of the river Spey on 23 June 1650.

These developments in Scotland could not be ignored by Cromwell, and so he brought his army north to face a Scottish covenanting force east of Edinburgh in July 1650. For the next month the Scots and English armies paraded back and forth, each attempting to manoeuvre the other into the worst position when battle commenced. On 3 September, the Scottish army, although outnumbering the English by about two to one, were soundly defeated near Dunbar. There were now no less than four separate "armies" north of the border.[4] One was English and three were Scots. Cromwell and his troops were still in the south of Scotland. The Scots he had defeated but who had survived had retreated to Edinburgh. There was still a small group of extremist Covenanters in the southwest and another small group of Royalists in the northeast. The Scots were humiliated and desperate, realising that a more pragmatic approach to their future was necessary. The king fled north to join the royalist forces in

4. Lynch, *Scotland*, 279.

the northeast. Argyll and a number of the more moderate Covenanters, still shocked by the execution of Charles I and mindful of the oath they had taken to "preserve and defend the King's Majesty's person," decided they must protect their present monarch, and so they allied themselves with the Royalists. The General Assembly was in two minds. Some felt they had been defeated by Cromwell because they had purged too many capable soldiers out of the army. Others believed the purges had not been severe enough and God had brought them to defeat because the army still contained too many ungodly men. Those who wanted a further purge composed a remonstrance to this effect in October 1650 and became known as the "Remonstrants." Those who were now convinced that the purging of the army had been foolishness passed in December a resolution to allow anyone who was not excommunicated or an obvious enemy to serve as a soldier. Those supporting this position were known as the "Resolutioners." The nation, the church, and the politicians were divided.

In December, the extremists in the southwest, by now hostile towards Charles, were thoroughly defeated by the English forces led by John Lambert, perhaps Cromwell's most brilliant general. In January 1651, Charles II was crowned by Argyll at Scone, and to provide the maximum protection for the monarch, the Act of Classes was cancelled in June to permit every available man to come to the defence of the king. The English forces in the summer of 1651 gained one victory after another over the Scots, and what remained of the Scottish army under the command of their king marched down into England hoping for help from English Royalists, but in vain. Cromwell's forces met and defeated them at Worcester in September 1651. Charles escaped to France, swearing that he would rather be hanged than go back to Scotland.[5] Any realistic hope of Scottish resistance to Cromwell was over.

The defeat of the Scottish forces and the flight of their king was a bad enough blow, but even worse was the capture of the Scottish committee of estates. Scotland was now a country without either monarch or army or government and about to be absorbed by its ancient adversary. England, having abolished the monarchy, had been a commonwealth since May 1649, and now in October 1651 the decision was taken that Scotland was to become part of that commonwealth under the authority of the English Parliament. The arrangement was called a union, but of course the Scots had no option but to submit. In October 1652, twenty-one Scottish

5. Ibid., 282.

commissioners went to London, where they found they were required to offer information, but took no part in the decision-making process.[6] The authority of the English Parliament was now required before any Scottish politicians could officially meet together, and that Parliament was virtually the political tool of Cromwell's army. The church in the new commonwealth, far from being uniform, was allowed to contain Presbyterians, but also Independents of every stripe.

The tensions in England between army and parliament meant that more than one parliament sat and dissolved before the Act of Union became law in April 1657, and the small body of Scots who were allowed to vote for it had to be nominated by their English overlords. A brief attempt at rebellion was made in August 1653, when William Cunningham, the earl of Glencairn, raised a modest force in the west Highlands, but with very limited success. The English occupying army was well able to keep firm control of Scotland. Courts were established and powers given to Highland chiefs to punish lawbreakers. There was a general reduction of crime and disturbances in both Highlands and Lowlands. The greatest problem in the life of Scottish society became the widespread poverty and the huge debts of some of the greater landowners.

In a defeated and weakened nation, the divisions in the church became more pronounced. The majority of ministers now supported the position taken by the more moderate Resolutioners, but the Remonstrants protested even more vehemently that the previous purges of army and church had not gone far enough, and their protests earned them the new name of "Protesters." One focus of their protest was the General Assemblies of 1651 and 1652, which they disowned. Some even formed their own Protester presbyteries, separate from those which they considered to be corrupted by Resolutioners. The quarrelling in the church must surely be considered as a factor in the general decline in spiritual life throughout the whole nation, and the commonwealth government gradually lost patience in their attempts to reach a settled condition. In 1653, the government dissolved the General Assembly. Approved ministers were forced on congregations against the will of worshippers. At first, it was assumed that the Protesters would be more cooperative with a commonwealth government because they were less royalist than their rivals, but it became clear in time that the Resolutioners, in spite of their greater sympathy for the king and their continued contact with him,

6. Donaldson, *Scotland*, 344.

were more flexible and cooperative. It was also the case that the Scots, in spite of the recent wars and subsequent occupation by the English army, were not in principle against union with England. There appeared to be solid advantages in political and commercial terms from such a union, provided it could be achieved without damaging Scottish interests. The events which most affected Scotland, however, were the changes to the commonwealth government in England.

19

Bring Back the King

We, therefore, the Lords and Commons now assembled in Parliament, together with the lord mayor, aldermen and commons of the city of London and other freemen of this kingdom now present, do, according to our duty and allegiance heartily, joyfully and unanimously acknowledge and proclaim that immediately upon the decease of our late Sovereign Lord King Charles the imperial crown of the realm of England, and of all the kingdoms, dominions and rights belonging to the same, did by inheritance, birthright and lawful and undoubted succession descend and come to his most excellent Majesty Charles the Second, as being lineally, justly and lawfully next heir of the blood royal of this realm, and that by the goodness and providence of Almighty God he is of England, Scotland, France and Ireland the most potent, mighty and undoubted king, Defender of the Faith, &c. And thereto we most humbly and faithfully do submit and oblige ourselves, our heirs and posterities for ever.[1]

A LL WAS NOT WELL in the commonwealth. In December 1648, all those members of the English Parliament who did not approve of the trial and execution of Charles I were dismissed, and those who remained became known as the "Rump." In 1649, the monarchy and the House of Lords were abolished. New governments, however, require funds, and the new system of taxation was far from popular. The great

1. Proclamation of both Houses of Parliament for proclaiming of his Majesty, King of England, Scotland, France and Ireland. Proclamation of allegiance to Charles II as legitimate heir to the throne, 8 May 1660.

need was to stabilize the nation and heal the wounds of the civil war, but many, including Cromwell himself, were not convinced that this work was progressing fast enough, and so in April 1653, Cromwell closed down Parliament, and it was replaced in July by a Nominated Assembly. Those who were to serve in this body were nominated by, among others, congregational churches. Cromwell used the title of Lord Protector, and when he died in September 1658, his son Richard succeeded him in this office.

Richard Cromwell was not his father. He had been a soldier but had never fought in a battle, and, more importantly, he did not have his father's drive and energy. He was not the man to deal with continuing tensions between Parliament and the army. When the first Parliament of his protectorate met in January 1659, it contained a complicated mixture of die-hard republicans, those who wanted to return to a monarchy, and moderates who were willing to cooperate with anyone who could come up with a working arrangement for the government of a country. A further complication was the creation of a second parliamentary house which looked suspiciously like the abolished House of Lords under another name. The impression grew among military leaders that the power and influence of the army was being deliberately undermined by Parliament. Their petitions to Parliament were ignored, and the military commanders played their last card. In April 1659, they demanded that the Protector should dissolve Parliament, and they reinforced this demand by a show of military force. Richard Cromwell crumbled. The current Parliament was dissolved. The Rump Parliament was reinstated and Richard resigned. "Tumble Down Dick," as he became known, quietly faded out of the political scene but lived for another fifty-three years in comparative obscurity. England looked like a nation under firm military control; however, within a matter of months the army was at war with itself.

In theory, at least, the army was under the authority of a seven-man government commission, but in October 1659, this commission was sacked, and in its place Charles Fleetwood was appointed as the commander in chief of all forces. Fleetwood had been a member of Parliament, but first and foremost he was a soldier with a great deal of military experience. He was also Oliver Cromwell's son-in-law and very much opposed to the rule of Richard Cromwell. When Richard was forced to resign, Fleetwood gave his support to another experienced soldier, John

Lambert, who had been one of the seven parliamentary commissioners in charge of the army before his dismissal. Lambert's response to the dismissal of the seven-man commission was to gather his troops, march on Parliament, and shut the members out of the house. In place of Parliament, a Committee of Safety, led by Lambert, now governed the nation, and while Fleetwood supported Lambert in this new step, there were other military commanders for whom this was one step too far.

The man in command of the commonwealth forces in Scotland was General George Monck. He was a soldier who had fought for both king and commonwealth. He had won decisive battles on land and sea. He had fought for the Dutch against the Spanish and for the English against the Dutch and the Scots. He had a reputation for being ruthless in warfare, but he was not a fanatic. Monck was not incapable of changing his mind, but he was not easily corrupted and generally considered to be trustworthy. At this point, he saw himself as a loyal servant of the English Parliament and was deeply disturbed by the use of military force to remove the government of a nation. Lambert, only too well aware of Monck's objections to a military state, moved a body of men north to confront Monck and his troops from Scotland. In the hope of avoiding open warfare between two sections of the commonwealth army, Monck contacted the Committee of Safety and tried to negotiate some kind of agreement about the future government of the commonwealth which could be obtained by peaceful means.

The urgency of finding some solution was increased by the attempts from the court of the exiled Charles II at Breda to persuade Monck to support the restoration of Charles to the throne. Monck was in a fairly strong position to confront Lambert either in battle or in negotiation. There were others besides Monck who believed that Lambert and his colleagues had taken upon themselves an authority they did not merit, and towards the end of 1659, Lambert's soldiers began to desert. In December of that year, Vice-Admiral John Lawson, in command of the English navy, threatened to blockade the port of London, and under this pressure, the Committee of Safety, realizing their days were numbered, was dissolved. The Rump Parliament was quickly reinstated. Monck and his army, stationed in Scotland, had been hovering on the border until the next steps could be assessed clearly, but now he marched south and demanded that those bodies of troops in the region of London should be scattered to other garrisons, to be replaced by his own forces. He reached and occupied London in February 1660. Lambert was no longer a threat. The members of Parliament who had been dismissed when the Rump was formed had now been recalled to take their rightful places. People everywhere looked for and expected a change in the political climate, and the way for the restoration of Charles II to the throne was wide open.

In March 1660, Monck, who was well and truly in the seat of power, was negotiating with Charles to arrange his return to England, and Charles, in consultation with his closest advisers, issued the Declaration of Breda, which dealt with the major factors affected by his return. The king had in fact been living not in Breda, but in the Spanish Netherlands. He was persuaded, however, that to issue the declaration from what was regarded as enemy territory would not be wise. He moved, therefore, to Breda in the United Netherlands in April, and the declaration, in official terms at least, bore that name. There was to be a general amnesty for those who had opposed the king in the commonwealth period. The wages owed to the army were to be paid in full. Crown and church lands acquired by other owners during the king's absence were to be renegotiated, and nonconformists were to be tolerated. Everyone appeared to gain something. It seemed also appropriate to remove the Parliament, which had for so long battled with the king, and so it voted itself out of office on 16 March, to be replaced by the Convention Parliament on 25 April. When the Declaration of Breda was presented to the new Parliament on 1 May, it was accepted as expressing legitimate grounds for the return of the monarch, and the parliamentary announcement on 8 May confirmed that "it can no way be doubted but that his Majesty's right and title to his crowns and kingdoms is and was completed by the death of his most royal father of glorious memory."[2]

The concessions given by Charles to his enthusiastic subjects were not as clear as they might have seemed, and the way they were interpreted in later days left many feeling they had been deceived, but the factor which was beyond doubt was that from now on the nation would be governed by the Monarch, the House of Lords, and the House of Commons. The Parliament to which Charles returned was certainly Royalist, but it was not inclined to go to extremes. It contained a number of moderate Presbyterians who were undoubtedly monarchists but wished to contain the king's power within reasonable boundaries. The changes which began to take place, however, almost immediately, radically altered church and

2. Ibid.

state. The king dissolved the Convention Parliament in December 1660, and what became known as the Cavalier Parliament took its place in April 1661. Charles himself, in the light of the Breda declaration, retained the hope of finding some kind of compromise between the Anglican and Nonconformist groups, but his new Parliament had no such intention. The first priority was to remove nonconformists from local government. The Solemn League and Covenant was jettisoned. Worship other than that of the Anglican church was proscribed, and the work of crushing the Puritans went on apace. In Scotland, politicians and ministers of the church looked at the restoration of their monarch with a mixture of anxiety and hope.

When the English Cavalier Parliament began its work, the Scottish church was as divided as ever. Both Protesters and Resolutioners saw the withdrawal of Moncks army and the restoration of the king as an opportunity to be grasped. Resolutioners hoped that because they were clearly in the majority, they could root out Protesters from parish churches and begin to negotiate a more moderate but advantageous settlement with the king. Protesters, on the other hand, remembering that Charles had signed both the National Covenant and the Solemn League and Covenant, insisted that these were still binding on the church and nation and that the king must recognise this.

The response of crown and Parliament to their insistence was quick and to the point. When a group of Protesters met in Edinburgh to formulate an appeal to the king lamenting the emerging episcopacy of the English church and reminding him that he also was a "Covenanter," they were arrested. Their leader, James Guthrie of Stirling, was bound and hanged in Edinburgh on 1 June 1660, and his severed head was fixed on the Netherbow gate. Before he died, he shouted out, "The Covenants! The Covenants shall yet be Scotland's reviving." Archibald Campbell, the covenanting marquis of Argyll, who throughout his life had a fair measure of success in choosing to support the winning side, finally lost his touch and was beheaded on 27 May 1661. Argyll had for many years been a powerful force in Scottish politics. It was Argyll's hands that had placed the crown on the head of Charles II at Scone in January 1651. When the king had needed his support, the promise was made that he would become a duke, and at one point, Argyll even entertained the hope that Charles might marry his daughter. All this changed at the restoration. Charles ordered his arrest. He was tried in Edinburgh and found guilty of treason because of his cooperation with the English commonwealth government. When he died, his severed head was placed on the same spike as had once held the head of his old rival, the Marquis of Montrose. The restored monarch, who had himself signed the National Covenant and promised to maintain the Presbyterian character of the Scottish church, was now determined to bring this system of church government to an end.

In 1662, an Episcopal church was restored in Scotland. The covenants were declared to be illegal. Churches again had lay patrons, and conventicles were outlawed. There was a measure of restraint and common sense exercised in the introduction of the new regime and liturgy in order to gain as large a measure of support as possible, but a little over a quarter of ministers in the church refused to conform and had to leave their parishes. The nobility generally were more at ease with a church where ministers had less authority, although there were exceptions like John Kennedy, earl of Cassillis, whose loyalties to the covenant were unmovable. Cassillis had been present at the Westminster Assembly. He had negotiated with Charles at Breda. He was a member of the Scottish privy council, but his sticking point was the Act of Supremacy which declared that "his majesty hath the supreme authority and supremacy over all persons, and in all causes ecclesiastical within this his kingdom." Cassillis refused to take the oath of supremacy, although he avoided any act of rebellion until his death in April 1668. It was people from a lower level of society who gave most support to the ministers who had been forced to leave their churches. These men were forbidden to live or preach within twenty miles of their former parishes, and their pulpits were filled by curates who seldom commanded the respect of their parishioners. Numbers grew of ministers who conducted illegal services and people who began to attend them until Parliament, in July 1663, began to punish those who refused to attend their own parish churches by the imposition of a heavy fine. The government used the army to collect the fines and break up illegal church services.

Among those loyal to the covenants, resentment of the government's policy continued to grow until, in November 1666, a body of government troops was captured by a group of rebels in the district of Dumfries. The rebels rapidly became an army of three thousand men, who set off for Edinburgh in the hope of putting some kind of pressure on the Scottish government. Lacking a united leadership, and discouraged by local people who resented government policy but were not willing to go to war over it,[3] the rebels pressed on until they reached Colinton. At Rullion Green, about eight miles south of Edinburgh, they confronted government forces and were soundly defeated. Some of the rebels were persuaded to take the oath of supremacy. Of those who refused, the leaders were hanged and others banished to the West Indies.

The responsibility for carrying out the king's policies in Scotland fell to John Maitland, earl of Lauderdale. He had been a moderate Covenanter whose loyalty to the monarchy cost him the loss of his estates, nine years in prison, and a period of exile with Charles II in the Netherlands. He was appointed secretary of state for Scotland when Charles returned to the throne, but his instinct for moderation and compromise meant that the execution and oppression of the more extreme Covenanters was not to his taste. As resistance to the king's authority over the church continued to grow, Lauderdale, attempting a carrot and stick policy, began to look for ways to woo covenanting ministers back into the national church and to keep their rebellious flocks in order. Rebels who would promise to keep the king's peace in future could be pardoned. Indulgences were granted to ministers who would accept a restricted form of Presbyterian ministry inside the Episcopal church, and a considerable number of the more moderate covenanting ministers took advantage of these indulgences, much to the outrage of those who refused. Those who remained outside of the law began to operate as a separate body, refusing to recognise the ordination, the sacraments, or the ministry of the official church. Conventicles began to multiply, and these provoked heavy fines for landowners who permitted the gatherings on their property. Ministers who conducted services without a license were also fined, together with their congregations, while those preaching at field conventicles were liable to execution. Parents were compelled to have their children baptised by an authorized minister, and those conducting unauthorised ordination could be imprisoned or banished to the colonies.

In an attempt to make landowners more responsible, they were required in 1667 to sign a bond guaranteeing the good behavior of their tenants, but in some areas of the country, particularly in the southwest, this was quite unrealistic. Since the conventicles were becoming larger and more militant, in 1678, Lauderdale reluctantly brought into the southwest region an army known as the "Highland Host" to be billeted in the homes of covenanting Presbyterians. These soldiers were mainly,

3. Donaldson, *Scotland*, 365.

although not exclusively, Highland Catholics, and while they were bitter-ly resented, their imposition on their unwilling hosts was not as violent as it might have been. Nevertheless, the opposition to the government continued to grow, and it became clear that a fragile peace could not last much longer. In May 1679, James Sharp, archbishop of St. Andrews, was murdered in Fife by a group of covenanting extremists. Sharp was heart-ily disliked as a traitor because he had been a moderate Covenanter who had been persuaded to accept episcopacy and had become one of the chief persecutors of the dissenting ministers. Those who murdered him fled the scene and met with a large body of likeminded men, who issued a document called the Rutherglen Declaration. This was mainly negative in tone, as it listed the legislation which the Covenanters felt obliged to reject. The document concluded, "We do this day, being 29 May 1679, publicly at the cross of Rutherglen, most justly burn the above mentioned acts, to evidence our dislike and testimony against the same, as they have unjustly, perfidiously, and presumptuously burned our sacred covenants." The temperature was rising.

One of the more energetic leaders of the government forces was John Graham of Claverhouse. He, like many other Scottish sons of the minor aristocracy, had learned his trade as a mercenary in France and Holland. He commanded a group of cavalry soldiers, and on 1 June 1679, he learned that a large number of Covenanters were holding a conven-ticle at Drumclog near Strathaven in Lanarkshire. When Claverhouse and his troops arrived to break up the gathering, they found that they were outnumbered by the Covenanters, and in the ensuing battle, the government troops were routed. The covenanting victory at Drum-clog attracted many more supporters, and the growing army of rebels marched north to Glasgow, where they quickly occupied the city. While they were unanimously in favour of the covenant, however, they were not unanimous about how it should be applied to national affairs. There were moderates who would have been satisfied if they had a monarch who would agree to relinquish control of Parliament and church. The more extreme Covenanters demanded a covenanted monarch and gov-ernment and would not recognise those who had taken advantage of the indulgencies. They seemed to spend as much time debating relations between church and state as they did in preparation for the impending battle which was inevitable. It took place at Bothwell Brig, a few miles east of Glasgow, on 22 June, and the government army, led by the Duke of Monmouth, an illegitimate son of Charles II, won an outright victory over the Covenanters.

Monmouth was not completely unsympathetic to his defeated enemies and in fact was responsible for gaining some degree of leniency in the judgement which followed their defeat. Those who promised to reject further warfare against the king were permitted to go home. Conventicles were to be tolerated, provided they were held within houses and not in the open field, and those who refused to comply were sentenced to banishment. Lauderdale's carrot and stick policy was making progress in controlling the majority of the Covenanters. There was, however, a small group who saw the conflict as a holy war between Christ and his enemies. For this group of extreme Covenanters, there could be no negotiation or compromise. The man in command of the king's forces they now had to face was, however, not Monmouth but James, the duke of York, brother to the king. For some time, Monmouth had been giving the impression that he wanted to succeed Charles as king, in spite of his illegitimacy, and Monmouth was not entirely hopeless in this ambition. It was clear that Charles II was never going to provide a legitimate child to succeed him, and his brother, the Duke of York, who was next in line to the throne, was a Roman Catholic. Many, in fact, would have preferred Monmouth to the Duke of York as Charles's successor. The threat Monmouth posed to the legitimate succession forced him to go into exile in the Netherlands in 1679, and so the man charged with the administration of Scotland and the crushing of the remaining Covenanters was James, duke of York, whose policy for dealing with the covenanting remnant was quite simple. They had to be eradicated.

On 22 June 1680, Richard Cameron, one of the remaining covenanting leaders, rode into the town square of Sanquhar accompanied by twenty armed men and read out what became known as the "Sanquhar Declaration." In this statement, Cameron identified his small group of supporters as the godly remnant representing "the true Presbyterian Kirk and covenanted nation of Scotland." The king and his government were "enemies to our Lord and his Crown," and were accused of perjury, tyranny, and usurpation in church matters. The small band of Covenanters declared themselves to be at war with the king, his magistrates, and all who supported them. The declaration ends with the promise that they will give their opponents the same treatment as they themselves have received, "as the Lord gives opportunity." There remained no room at all for negotiation. A month later, a group of government troops encountered a small band of Covenanters at Airds Moss, near the village of Lugar in Ayrshire. Cameron was killed. Hackston, another leader, was captured and executed, leaving the leadership to Donald Cargill. Cargill had been the minister of the Barony church in Glasgow until he was forced to leave. He was a veteran of the battle at Bothwell Brig and had spent some time in the Netherlands before returning to support the covenanting cause. After the death of Cameron, Cargill, at a gathering near Stirling in September 1680, issued a formal sentence of excommunication against Charles II, the duke of York, and most of the leading Scottish politicians. Some months later, with a price on his head, he was captured and executed in July 1681.

While the majority of Scots would not have allied themselves with the view the Covenanters held of the government, there was a considerable degree of discontent among the population generally. Government promises were made and broken. There was the perception that many of the politicians were corrupt. Malicious informers could report suspected Covenanters and profit from the fines imposed on them. The system of taxation was considered to be unfair, and public offices could be bought and sold, with Lauderdale himself seen as the chief culprit. Even the law courts were held in suspicion. Officers were appointed to posts solely at the king's pleasure, and Charles made it clear that he controlled the law and not vice versa. The result of this was an atmosphere in which Parliament felt inclined to oppose the policies of the king. There was also the perception that these policies were designed to benefit James, his brother, the duke of York. An act was passed to make sure that James would inherit the crown in spite of being a Roman Catholic, and in July 1681, the Act anent Religion and the Test became law. This act was a strange document which began by affirming that the king was the "vice-gerent of God" and calling upon his subjects to "preserve the true Protestant religion contained in the Confession of Faith recorded in the first parliament of King James the sixth." Parish ministers were required to provide annual lists of those who refused to attend worship, and sheriffs issued a list of the proceedings taken against those who avoided the parish church. The act ends with an oath acknowledging the king as supreme authority over all civil and church matters, the promise to reject covenants and assemblies, and the assurance that "there lyes no obligation on me from the National Covenant or the Solemn League and Covenant." There were contradictions within this legislation which made it hard to understand, and no Covenanter could swear to recognise the king's authority over the church. Even some of the parish ministers were ejected because they refused the oath. Circumstances for the Scots were to go from bad to worse.

Charles II died on 12 February 1685. On his deathbed he was received into the Roman Catholic Church, and his brother James II, another Roman Catholic, succeeded him. There was little realistic opposition to James's succession. The Duke of Monmouth, who had never abandoned his claim to the throne and had been forced to flee to the Netherlands, landed with three ships at Lyme Regis, declared himself to be the king, and was crowned by his supporters at Chard. His rebellion, however, was short lived. His forces were soundly defeated by the king's army. Monmouth himself was captured and executed on 15 July. A second ineffective rebellion was led by the Earl of Argyll, also in exile, who landed in Scotland with a small number of men. This force was likewise crushed fairly quickly. Argyll was taken prisoner and executed in Edinburgh on 13 June. King James II was very much in control of his realm. Measures against the remaining Covenanters grew even harsher. Commitment to the National Covenant was deemed to be treason and worshipping at field conventicles brought a death penalty. On the other hand, James brought a real degree of unease to his Parliament when he tried to have laws against Roman Catholics repealed. At the same time, a number of men in public office were removed and replaced by Roman Catholic supporters. A Roman Catholic chapel and a Jesuit school were established at Holyrood, while a new Roman Catholic printing press began to operate.

Freedom of worship for Roman Catholics was granted, first in private houses then in church buildings, and in June 1687, a similar freedom came to all the king's subjects. Moderate Presbyterians were not slow to take advantage of this concession. Some came home from exile and others began to gather in meeting houses as their numbers grew. The small group of Presbyterians who refused to conform to the new conditions were those Covenanters who still conducted illegal field meetings and conventicles. For this breach of the law the death penalty was still in force, and the most respected leader of the remaining outlawed Covenanters was a young man called James Renwick.

20

The Remnant Church

An Informatory vindication of a poor wasted misrepresented remnant of the suffering, anti-popish, anti-prelatic, anti-erastian, anti-sectarian, True Presbyterian Church of Christ in Scotland, united together in a general correspondence by way of reply to various accusations, in letters, informations &conferences given forth against them.[1]

WHEN THE COVENANTING LEADER Donald Cargill was executed at Edinburgh Cross on 27 July 1681, a young man called James Renwick was in the crowd which witnessed the event. The faith and constancy of Cargill, the confidence he had in Christ as he mounted the scaffold, and his words of encouragement to the onlookers had a profound effect on Renwick, who quickly identified himself with the covenanting cause. Those who had been followers of Cargill recognised in Renwick a gifted and earnest young man and sent him to the Netherlands for training and preparation for a ministry among the groups which met for worship and instruction. These were known as the "Societies," and Renwick became perhaps their most capable apologist. Called to minister to the Societies in October 1683, he began to preach at the forbidden conventicles wherever Covenanters could gather and to attract great crowds of supporters. His ministry could not be expected to escape the notice of the government, and although Renwick himself evaded capture for some time, several of his more prominent followers were imprisoned or executed. On

1. *Informatory Vindication.*

30 August 1684, he was formally summoned to appear before the privy
council, and in September, letters were issued against him describing him
as a seditious vagabond masquerading as a minister. The document, with
royal authority, read:

> We command and charge all and sundry our lieges and subjects
> that they nor none of them presume nor take upon hand to re-
> set, supply or intercommune with said Mr. James Renwick, rebel
> aforesaid, nor furnish him with meat, drink, house, harbour,
> victual nor no other thing useful or comfortable to him; or to
> have intelligence with him by word writ or message, or any other
> manner of way whatsoever, under the pain of being esteemed art
> and part with him in the crimes foresaid, and pursued therefore
> with all vigour to the terror of others. And we hereby require all
> our sheriffs and officers to apprehend and commit to prison the
> person of the said Mr James Renwick wherever they can find or
> apprehend him.[2]

An attack was also made on the doctrinal convictions of Renwick,
his Christian character, and his supposed intention to undermine the
Church of Scotland. It was in response to this that Renwick produced
his "Apologetical Declaration and Admonitory Vindication against Intel-
ligencers and Informers." In this statement he emphasised the commitment of the Societies to the Reformation and the Covenants and their
rejection of any "magistratical relation" between Charles Stewart and
themselves. Warning was given, not only against those who hunted and
persecuted the Covenanters but also against those who provided support and information for the persecutors to use. Renwick wrote, "Zeal for
Christ's reigning in our land, and suppressing of profanity will move us
not to let you pass unpunished . . . therefore expect to be dealt with as ye
deal with us, so far as our power can reach."[3] Renwick and his followers
were outraged by what they had to suffer, and he did not regard a meek,
passive acceptance of their tribulation as an option. They saw themselves
as warrior saints defending the sovereign rights of King Jesus and were
therefore ready and willing to scatter his enemies. On 8 November 1684,
copies of the Declaration were pinned on market crosses and church
doors as a public challenge to the government of Charles II. The response
of that government was to administer the Abjuration Oath to anyone

2. Carslaw, *Life and Letters of James Renwick*, 105.
3. Apologetical Declaration, 26 October 1684.

suspected of covenanting sympathies. Failure to swear the oath could result, in some cases, in execution on the spot. Suspects were required to swear,

> I doe hereby abhor, renounce and disoune, in presence of the Almighty God, the pretendit Declaratione of Warr lately affixed at severall paroch churches in so far as it declares a warr against his sacred Majestie and asserts that it is laufull to kill such as serve his Majestie in church, state, army or countrey, or such as act against the authors of the said pretended declarations now showne to me. And I doe hereby utterly renounce and disoune the villanous authors thereof who did (as they call it) statute and ordaine the same, and what is therein mentioned, and I swear I shall never assist the authors of the said pretended declarations or ther emissaries or adherents in any points of punishing, killing and making of warr any manner of way as I shall answear to God.[4]

Wives and families of offenders were also tested by the same oath and could lose home and property if they refused to comply. In spite, however, of a tightening net, Renwick remained at liberty. On 28 May 1685, he rode into Sanquhar at the head of two hundred men, and following the previous example of Richard Cameron, issued a "Protestation and Apologetical Admonmitory Declaration." In this, he protests against the reign of James II, Charles's successor, as a "profest Papist and excommunicate person." He calls the new king a murderer and accuses his supporters of "Confederacy with an Idolater." Renwick quotes from Acts of Parliament and the General Assembly to prove his case and argues that it is both sinful and irrational to entrust to an enemy the work and people of God. The declaration ends with the customary prayer, "Let King Jesus Reign and all his Enemies be scattered."

Although as time went by a number of moderate ministers took advantage of the increasing legal opportunities for worship in private houses and church buildings, Renwick and his followers continued to meet in illegal field conventicles, a practice which carried a death penalty. However, his days of liberty were coming to an end. In December 1687, while in the city of Edinburgh, he was recognised and arrested. The verdict at his trial was a foregone conclusion, and he died on the scaffold on 17 February 1688 at the age of twenty-six, not the last martyr, but the last of the covenanting ministers to die in this way.

4. Abjuration Oath, 25 November 1684.

After the death of Renwick, James II continued to increase Roman Catholic influence within his kingdom. Priests from the continent moved into Scotland. A number of children were sent abroad to be educated at Jesuit schools, and James is said to have boasted that "Edinburgh had the appearance of a Catholic city."[5] Of course some kind of reaction was inevitable, although organised opposition first began in England.

In both Scotland and England men involved in church and state were growing more and more uneasy, although some Scottish bishops continued to voice support for the monarch. In addition to the replacement of Protestants in prominent positions with Roman Catholic supporters of the king, there were specific issues which brought matters to a head. In 1687, James threatened the English church and Parliament by planning to repeal the Test Acts which had made it virtually impossible for anyone, except an Anglican, to hold civil or military office. The Test Act of 1673 required all holders of such positions to receive communion in an Anglican church within three months of taking office and to swear an oath which was revised in 1678 to read,

> I do solemnly and sincerely in the presence of God profess, testify and declare, that I do believe that in the Sacrament of the Lord's Supper there is not any Transubstantiation of the elements of bread and wine into the Body and Blood of Christ at or after the consecration thereof by any person whatsoever: and that the invocation or adoration of the Virgin Mary or any other Saint, and the Sacrifice of the Mass, as they are now used in the Church of Rome, are superstitious and idolatrous.[6]

Since these regulations were also used against English Nonconformists, James hoped that when he repealed them he might find support in the nonconformist ranks, but the factor which united Anglicans, Nonconformists, and Presbyterians alike was the fear of the king's determination to rule over a Roman Catholic kingdom. James's Declaration of Indulgence in April 1688 was able to woo some Scottish Presbyterians back into the Episcopal church, but in England, the Anglicans saw it as the beginning of the end. Seven English bishops who questioned its merits were put on trial for rebellion, although they were later acquitted. The only hope on the horizon was that the heir to the throne was the king's daughter Mary, a Protestant herself, who was married to her Protestant

5. McCrie, *Story of the Scottish Church*, 381.
6. Oath for the Test Act 1678.

cousin, Prince William of Orange. However, even these frail hopes were dashed when, on 10 June 1688, a new prince was born and James Francis Edward Stuart was baptised into the Roman Catholic Church. The same month, leading English politicians sent an appeal to William of Orange to come to their rescue.

William, who had been in touch with English Protestant leaders for some time, welcomed the chance to invade England. His greatest fear was a Catholic England united with France, which was becoming more and more of a danger to the Dutch state. In spite of threats of all-out war from Louis XIV, the French king, William's invasion forces landed at Brixham on 5 November and began to move towards London. The army which James mustered to meet the invasion was far from enthusiastic. Many of his officers were of doubtful loyalty, and anti-Catholic riots broke out in London. The writing was on the wall. Some measure of negotiation began between William and James, but for his own safety, James was allowed to escape with his family to France. On 22 January 1689, a Convention was held, and an elected body began to shape the future. Since only the king had the legal right to call a parliament, and William was not yet monarch, the term "parliament" was uncomfortable in many ears. Neither was there complete agreement about the role William should play in the realm. Some wanted Mary to be the only sovereign, but she refused to reign without her husband. The other problem was finding agreement in the matter of whose children would be next in line for the throne, those of William and Mary or those of Princess Anne.

The urgent need was for political unity. There was a firm intention to avoid the problems of the past and to safeguard a Protestant nation from the Stuart view of monarchy. A Bill of Rights was enacted by the English Parliament in February 1689. This document listed the ways in which James II had subverted the Protestant religion and had ignored the rights and liberties of his subjects. A Protestant succession was spelled out:

> Whereas it hath been found by experience that it is inconsistent with the safety and welfare of this Protestant kingdom to be governed by a popish prince or by any king or queen marrying a papist, the said lords spiritual and temporal, and commons, do further pray that it may be enacted that all and every person and persons that is, are or shall be reconciled to, or hold communion with, the see or Church of Rome, or shall profess the popish religion, or shall marry a papist, shall be excluded and forever

incapable to inherit, possess or enjoy the crown and government of this realm.[7]

When it came to the English coronation it was agreed that James had abdicated, and so when William and Mary were crowned king and queen on 11 April, they swore an oath to govern "according to the statutes in parliament, agreed on and the laws and customs of the same." This oath effectively transferred the authority to enact laws from the monarch to the elected Parliament. They further promised "to maintain the laws of God, the true profession of the gospel and the Protestant Reformed religion established by law."

In Ireland, William's accession to the throne was resisted with military force, and the exiled James II, in March 1689, invaded with an army of French soldiers who were joined by both Catholic and Protestant supporters. There were a number of inconclusive military engagements, and in June 1690, William himself landed at Carrickfergus with reinforcements. A discouraged James fled back to France to the disgust of his Irish troops, and the Treaty of Limerick in October 1691 brought the armed conflict to an end.

The reaction in Scotland to the new monarch was mixed. Although the invitation to William and Mary was an English initiative, nevertheless the majority of the Scottish privy council were quick to pledge allegiance. There was an attempt to raise an army to deal with any possible unrest, but it became clear to most of his subjects that the new king was there to stay. While William's relation to his Scottish subjects was broadly similar to that of England, his intentions towards the church were not so clear, simply because of the different groups competing for control of the Scottish church. Episcopalians, anxious to remain as the established church, tended to be loyal to James. Moderate Presbyterians who had accepted the limited freedom given to them by a number of indulgences did not want to risk what they had gained. Die-hard Covenanters saw an opportunity to return to the terms of the Covenants, while Roman Catholics, mainly in the Highlands, were ready for armed conflict. In some parts of the country there were local disturbances. An Edinburgh mob stormed into Holyrood, wrecked the royal chapel, and threw out the Jesuits. In the southwest, groups of Covenanters forced Episcopal ministers out of church and manse.

7. Declaration of Right, 1689.

Like the English, the Scots were determined to have their civil and ecclesiastical rights clearly understood by the new king. The English assertion that James had "abdicated" did not sit easily with the Scots. At a meeting of the Scottish Estates on 16 March 1689, an appeal for loyalty was received from both James and William, but James was held to have broken the contract he had with his people, and so while he was deemed to have resigned in England, he was effectively sacked by the Scots, and the crown offered to William in his place. In April, the Estates passed the Claim of Right Act and the Article of Grievances. The Claim of Right Act was amazingly broad and detailed. It dealt with constitutional issues like James II, who

> did assume the Regall power and acted as King without ever taking the oath required by law whereby the King at his access to the government is obliged to swear to maintain the protestant religion and did . . . invade the fundamental Constitution of this Kingdome And altered it from a legall limited monarchy to ane Arbitrary Despotick power.[8]

The same act also dealt with domestic matters like the cost and inconvenience of civilians who had to put up with soldiers billeted on them, and the protests of husbands who had been fined because their wives refused to go to the appropriate church. The Articles of Grievances dealt with a variety of legal matters and previous acts of Parliament which were now considered to be unacceptable. Control of church and Parliament by the crown was no longer possible, although not entirely eradicated. The church became Presbyterian, and legal issues were simplified. These were the conditions under which the crown was offered and accepted by the Prince of Orange, now to become King of Scots, although whether William and the Scottish Parliament shared exactly the same understanding of the conditions is doubtful. The new monarchy, however, was not without some degree of opposition, and John Graham, who had been created Vicount Dundee by James II, raised an army of Highlanders to support James's cause. The Highland army did win a victory over government troops at Killiecrankie on 27 July 1689, but Dundee himself was killed in the battle. The rebellion could not maintain its impetus, and at Dunkeld on 21 August a defeat of the Highland troops foretold the end of any effective opposition, which finally ended at Cromdale in May 1690.

8. Introduction to the *Claim of Right Act 1689* whereby the Scottish crown was offered to "William and Mary, king and queen of England, France and Ireland."

The first General Assembly of the Scottish church in thirty-seven years was held in November 1690. Government approval ensured the predominance of mainly moderate Presbyterians, who were warned by William of the need for caution in dealing with stubborn Episcopalians and Covenanters. Commissions were set up to rid the church of ministers who refused to accept the new situation, and a number of men were removed from parishes and universities. In the covenanting ranks, only three ministers remained: Alexander Shields, William Boyd, and Thomas Lining. These men reluctantly accepted the new settlement, although many of their followers disapproved strongly of their decision. This step left the covenanting societies virtually leaderless for the next sixteen years, although they continued to gather for worship and prayer.

In political terms, one of the greatest headaches was the remaining hostility of some of the Highland clans to the new monarchy and government. In some cases, an attempt was made to buy the support of the rebels who were considered to be loyal to James II. In other cases, military threat seemed to be more effective. The test of loyalty was an oath of allegiance to William which had to be taken by 1 January 1692, but to accept this, some of the Highlanders, already under oath to James II, sought the permission of their exiled monarch, and this was a process which took time to complete. The most notable victim of the exercise was MacIan of Glencoe. On the last day of 1691 he attempted to take the oath at Fort William but found no one qualified to accept it. He then set off for Inveraray, which he reached on 3 January 1692, but it was 6 January before he found an opportunity to formally pledge allegiance to King William. His failure to take the oath in time was a technicality, but John Dalrymple, master of Stair and Scottish secretary of state, was determined to demonstrate the penalty for disloyalty and issued orders, with the probable approval of the king, for the slaughter of MacIan and all under the age of seventy in Glencoe. The massacre sent a shiver of disgust throughout Scotland. An enquiry into the incident was held by the Scottish Parliament, and Dalrymple was removed from office for a time.

The years which followed the establishment of the Scottish Presbyterian Church did not bring about the settled unanimity in ecclesiastical affairs that might have been hoped for, and the praying societies of Covenanters became less and less influential in political matters. While the principles for which they had contested were not completely forgotten by any means, the opportunity to see them accepted and practiced by the national church was not offered to them. They watched from the sidelines as a church and nation they had hoped would be a single covenanted theocracy was moulded by political and commercial pressures.

The seemingly inevitable progress towards union with England continued and was underlined by the problem of William's successor. The heir to the throne was Anne, the younger sister of William's queen, Mary, who died in December 1694. Anne, in turn, would be followed by one of her children, but in fact after seventeen pregnancies, Anne had only one surviving child, William, duke of Gloucester. In July1700, the eleven-year-old William died, and in 1702, William the king also died, leaving Anne to be crowned Queen of England, Scotland, and Ireland on 8 March of that year. Clarification of Anne's successor was urgent, and to the immense annoyance of the Scots, the English Parliament had already, in 1701, without any consultation, passed the Act of Settlement, which would give the English crown, upon the death of Anne, to Princes Sophia, the Protestant electress of Hanover and the granddaughter of James I. The offended Scottish Parliament refused to take similar action. Sophia, however, never came to the throne because she died before Queen Anne, and when Anne herself died in 1714, Sophia's son became King George I.

Commercial interests also made the union of England and Scotland inevitable. In 1695, a Scottish trading company was formed to trade with America, Africa, and Asia. This venture initially attracted a large amount of English investment, which was withdrawn fairly quickly. The Scots, with insufficient backing, nevertheless attempted to establish a trading centre on the Isthmus of Darien. The scheme proved to be a failure mainly due to lack of support, for which the Scots largely blamed the English. William himself was noticeably lacking in sympathy for all the Scots had lost in the Darien venture, yet in spite of this, the advantages of free trade with England were too obvious to ignore.

In the Scottish church scene, the Toleration Act of 1712, which legalised existing conformist Episcopalians, did not go down well with the established Presbyterians, and the monarch's lack of respect for the General Assemblies further alienated the Kirk from the crown. When William died in 1702, and Anne came to the throne, the relations between England and Scotland were at such a pitch that the alternatives seemed to be either outright hostility or union. The English sought the assurance that Anne's Hanoverian successor would also be king in Scotland, and the Scots needed the opportunity to recover from the Darien fiasco and to trade with English colonies. This was reflected by the economic nature of the majority of the articles in the Union treaty. The Parliaments of England and Scotland were united on 1 May 1707 in an agreement that was far from unanimous.

In all these political and economic upheavals, the Scottish covenanting praying societies were disapproving bystanders. Their days of being a political or military force in Scotland were over. In spite of the 1707 Act of Union guaranteeing a Presbyterian church, they retained their suspicions of episcopacy and the recovery of the Stuart cause. In this they were not entirely unreasonable, since at the union of the parliaments there were over a hundred and fifty parishes in Scotland which were still occupied by Episcopalian ministers. They found at least one leader when, in 1706, a minister from the Church of Scotland, John McMillan, joined the covenanting remnant. McMillan had been ordained to the parish of Balmaghie in Galloway in September 1701 but seems from the start to have been at loggerheads with the presbytery which, in fact, deposed him in December 1703. McMillan and two others had brought a list of grievances before the Presbytery of Kirkcudbright addressing the issues which were of most concern to the Covenanters. He urged the need for Acts of General Assembly to assert the divine origin of Presbyterian government and the right of the church to call her own courts and make her own laws. He demanded the censure of those who opposed these views. He lamented the acceptance of so many curates into the church without any evidence of their repentance. He demanded that ministers who had accepted the previous indulgences should acknowledge their sin in doing so and condemned others for holding Arminian doctrines. It was clear that a minister like John McMillan could not function in the church of that day, and so after a period of negotiation with the praying societies, he was called to be their only minister in October 1706.

While a number of ministers in the established church were sympathetic to the convictions of the Covenanters, the continuation of the praying societies was a struggle marked by their growing alienation from other ecclesiastical bodies and their apparent conviction that they were the only true Christian church left in Scotland. In time, John McMillan was joined by a probationer minister called John McNeill, and on 24 July 1712, they led a group of followers to a renewal of the National Covenant and the Solemn League and Covenant at the hill of Auchensaugh, two miles south of the town of Douglas in Lanarkshire. This event, which in time became known as the "Auchensaugh Renovation," left behind a comprehensive written account of the proceedings. The account begins with a historical record and theological justification of the covenants. It continues by referring to the special relationship which the Covenanters believed to have existed between God and Scotland:

> Scotland by itself, as an independent nation, had in an eminent way and manner the honour above most nations in the world, to dedicate and surrender themselves to the Lord by a most voluntary free and deliberate choice, and to come under the bond of a most solemn oath, in a most religious manner, devoting their all to Christ, his interest and honour, the flourishing and thriving of his kingdom, the success of his gospel, and reformation of his churches.[9]

The authors of the renovation recognise that the National Covenant and the Solemn League and Covenant are not the same as the "covenant of grace" between God and believers, but they do see them as a "super-added and new obligation" and believe that God himself has led them as a "poor insignificant handful of people" to the step of covenant renewal.

Reasons for this are spelled out. The national covenants have been nationally broken and therefore need to be renewed. Many are blaming the covenants as the cause of recent warfare and bloodshed and this accusation must be vigorously denied. The point is also made that the "late sinful incorporating union" which joined Scotland to England is no substitute for the true and righteous bond of the covenants. The Covenanters also lament the growing practice of permitting people to come to the communion table without first having sworn and subscribed the covenant.

There is also at least one significant change from the original covenants in relation to the duty that was owed to king and Parliament. Where the first Covenanters had sworn to defend and preserve the king's majesty and government, those who now renewed the covenants could only accept such obligations towards "lawful sovereigns or supreme magistrates . . . when God shall be pleased to grant them to us." Plainly Queen Anne and the new government at Westminster did not come into this category. While the rejection of the existing political authority seemed dangerous, or even treasonable, the groups of covenanting praying

---

9. Introduction to Auchensaugh Renovation.

societies were hardly a threat to either church or state, and although small in number, they continued to function.

However, at the same period of time, the national church itself was not free from doctrinal controversy. There was a growing fear of a shallow, empty faith that did not lead to holiness of life, and the Kirk felt it necessary to form a "Committee for the Purity of Doctrine," which monitored publications which seemed to conflict with the Westminster Confession of Faith. Among these was the book by Edward Fisher entitled "The Marrow of Modern Divinity." Fisher had written this in two sections, in 1645 and 1649. The book was held by some of its readers to teach that Christ had actually died for the entire human race because it contained statements like, "Christ hath taken upon Him the sins of all men," or, "The Father hath made a deed of gift and grant unto all mankind," or, "Tell every man without exception that . . . Christ is dead for him."[10] It was feared that these words taught a universal redemption of all mankind and therefore was linked to the question of the nature of the terms in which men were called to come to Christ for salvation. Was repentance from sin necessary before sinners could come to Christ, or did coming to Christ produce the necessary repentance? If men could come to Christ without previous repentance, would they then continue in sin while relying on the grace of God? But if they required repentance as a condition of their coming to Christ did that not mean that a human work of repentance had to be added to God's grace in order to effect salvation? The problems were those which might seem to consume careful theologians rather than hungry sinners, but a minister in the Church of Scotland called Thomas Boston, from the parish of Ettrick, was convinced that "The Marrow of Modern Divinity" was very relevant to the ongoing debates and was sympathetic to its teachings. Boston was a commissioner at the General Assembly of 1717, which had to consider a "creed" composed by the Presbytery of Auchterarder. The creed required candidates for the ministry to agree that it was wrong to teach that men must forsake sins in order to come to Christ. When the question came before the General Assembly, the Auchterarder creed seemed to give the impression that it could be interpreted as an encouragement to rely on the grace of God and continue in sin. The assembly condemned it. Boston, however, was convinced that however badly the creed was worded, its intention, like Fisher's book, was to preserve a free and immediate offer of Christ to

10. *Marrow of Modern Divinity*, cited in *Standard Bearer*, vol 53, no. 19.

sinners, and his approval of the book contributed towards the decision to reprint it in 1718. The Committee for Purity of Doctrine condemned the book in May 1720 and warned ministers against its recommendation. However, at the General Assembly of 1721, Boston and eleven other men defended "The Marrow," claiming it was perfectly orthodox and had been misrepresented. This claim was soundly rejected by the Assembly, and Boston and his eleven colleagues were formally rebuked. While remaining in the Church of Scotland, the twelve "marrow men" were growing increasingly uneasy about the conditions under which they served and were concerned, among other matters, about the question of exactly who had the right to call ministers to their congregations. The alienation of this group of dissatisfied men continued to grow, and in December 1733, a number of them formed the Associate Presbytery. At first, the new presbytery deliberately refrained from acting like a church court, but fairly soon they decided to train and appoint their own ministers, and in 1740, the breach with the Church of Scotland was final. By 1745, the new church had more than forty congregations.

It might have appeared at first as if the secession offered a unique opportunity to increase the ranks of the Covenanters, but it was not to be, even though in 1743 the Associate Presbytery passed an act to renew the covenants. The willingness of the Seceders to recognise the current government and monarch as an appropriate civil authority was not acceptable to Covenanters, who demanded that those civil authorities submit to the covenants. In 1743, the Covenanters gained a second minister when Thomas Nairn left the Seceders and began to minister among the societies. On 1 August of the same year, those covenanting "societies" became the Reformed Presbytery of Scotland. As yet, this new presbytery did not call itself a church, but did begin to exercise ecclesiastical authority. On 11 April 1744, the presbytery licensed Alexander Marshall as a preacher of the gospel. Marshall and Nairn were sent to Ireland six months later to encourage and minister to a number of Irish societies, and shortly afterwards, Marshall was ordained as a minister of the Reformed Presbytery.

The measure in which the covenanting convictions were shared by other Presbyterians who had not been "Covenanters" in the strictest sense is seen in the growth of the Reformed Presbytery throughout the following century.[11] As numbers increased, men who had previously

---

11 Keddie, *Reformed Presbyterian Church*, in *Dictionary of Scottish Church History*, 698.

ministered to their whole community were able to be appointed to specific pastoral charges, and some found their way across the Atlantic to congregations in the American colonies. Continued growth of what was now the Reformed Presbyterian Church brought about, in the nineteenth century, a synod of six presbyteries having forty-seven congregations numbering more than six and a half thousand members. Missionaries were sent out to Canada, New Zealand, and the islands of the South Pacific, and a theological college was founded in Stirling. However, by far the most significant event for these children of the original Covenanters was the union with the Free Church of Scotland in 1876, when the majority united with the Free Church, leaving a few congregations to continue as the Reformed Presbyterian Church.

It was inevitable as the cultural, political, and social conditions in Scotland changed with the years that the pressure on the covenanted church to change also must increase. The core convictions, however, remained constant. These Christians believed themselves to be the only direct and faithful spiritual descendents of the Reformed and covenanted church of seventeenth-century Scotland. They refused to accept the terms of the Revolution Settlement of 1688 as they affected the church. They described the union between Scotland and England as "a sinful incorporating union."[12] They held that a covenant with God had been undertaken by the nations of England, Scotland, and Ireland which could not be set aside and was binding on future generations as much as on those of the past and present, therefore all the covenant obligations resting on the three kingdoms were still in force. To accept a monarch or a government which refused to recognise the covenant would be tantamount to a rejection of God himself. The need was felt to declare again the terms of the covenant from time to time and to testify against what Covenanters saw as the sinful backsliding of the established church and the failure of the civil powers to curb impiety and vice. The decision of the government to accept the reality of "popery, the Religion of Antichrist, with all its idolatries and blasphemies" in the Canadian province of Quebec brought forth the most strenuous objections and the accusation that the civil powers had violated the British constitution itself, since the coronation oath included the promise that "we shall be careful to root out all Heretics and Enemies to the true Worship of God, that shall be convicted by the true Kirk of God of the aforesaid crimes out of our Lands." The silence of the

---

12. *Act Declaration and Testimony 1761*, pt. 2.

Church of Scotland in the whole affair earned extremely harsh criticism from the Covenanters and the assertion that they had given up the right to be called a church but were more accurately described in the words of the prophet Jeremiah as "an assembly of treacherous men."

Over the years, the language in which deeply held covenanting convictions were expressed has mellowed to some degree, and those Christians who are most conscious of the gap between a covenanted people and an uncovenanted state have not always agreed about how to apply their church principles to secular issues. There have been differences of opinion about whether Covenanters should vote in the election of what they might see as a godless government, or whether their children should be educated in state schools, yet in spite of their differences to other church bodies, they have not only survived but exercised an influence out of proportion to the smallness of their numbers.

Christians in the Reformed Presbyterian Church would themselves admit to being a tiny group in twenty-first-century Scotland, although where Covenanters of former years settled outside of their homeland, their churches seemed to flourish. At the present time there are Reformed Presbyterian churches in Canada, the United States, Ireland, Australia, and Japan. Those in America, Ireland, and Japan have all established theological colleges and publishing bases, while teams of young people are engaged in missionary work on a regular basis. In a society where larger church bodies have lost confidence in their ability to survive without public approval and, as a result, are all too ready to follow popular opinion rather than mould it in line with the Christian Scriptures, it may be that there is more than a little to be learned from those in former times who were willing literally to shed their blood for what they called "the Crown Rights of King Jesus."

21

This Is My Covenant[1]

Now O Scotland, God be thanked, thy name is in the Bible.[2]

THE NINETEENTH-CENTURY ARTIST SIR George Harvey produced more than one painting to portray scenes from the life and times of the "Covenanters." His sympathy with his subjects is obvious, and they are usually shown as engaged in worship or warfare. A number of painters have shared the same theme, and the covenanting worshippers are typically displayed with eyes fixed on a preacher whose hands hold a copy of holy Scripture and whose eyes are raised heavenward as he preaches the word of God to the children of God. The worship is always outdoors and the little flock are surrounded by the bracken-covered hills and moors of their beloved homeland. One such work is entitled "Covenanters Worshipping on the Banks of the Whiteadder," and it perfectly captures the popular image of the covenanting community. In the picture's foreground the preacher is on his knees. There is an expression of holy earnestness on his upturned face so that we know that he is pleading with God for his faithful people. Those people are also kneeling around him, hands clasped in prayer. There are aged, white-haired saints, young men and women, little families huddled together, all of them with a humble, sincere faith in the living God and willing to risk everything for the sake of obedience to his word. But in the distant background of the painting, there are other figures, a group of mounted government troops gathering

1. Gen 17:10.
2. Samuel Rutherford, seventeenth-century Scottish Covenanter.

together on a little rise. Their leader has a drawn sword raised above his head. His troops are ready for the signal to swoop down on the praying Covenanters. Some of the worshippers will manage to flee to safety. Some will suffer wounds. Some will stain the lonely hillside with their life's blood. Their leaders may be captured and put to death on the scaffold. It is all there on the artist's canvas and it is also the image which comes to the mind of the great majority of Scots men and women when they hear that word "Covenanter."

There is nothing false about the picture, and it appeals to much that is best in Scottish Christians. The courage in facing overwhelming odds; the willingness to sacrifice even life itself for the principles of the faith; the priority of putting God before the highest human authority; the refusal to allow any national government to govern the church of Christ. All this can only call upon our respect and admiration. And yet if the covenants did not mean anything less than this, they surely meant a lot more which cannot command the same immediate approval. Most of us have the very human tendency to reduce a fairly complex situation to a straightforward "black or white" issue, because it takes less effort to understand it. The tyrannous and cruel government persecuted the faithful Christian Covenanters who were willing to die for what they believed to be the truth. That is the beginning and the end of it! There has been more than one Scottish clergyman who has expressed unbounded admiration for the Covenanters but seems to have forgotten, or even been unaware, that had the Covenanters remained in power, his own spiritual community would not have been permitted to worship at all. Whatever the Covenanters fought and died for, it was not the freedom for every Scot to have the right to worship as he saw fit. These were men and women who had entered into covenants with the Most High God on behalf of both church and nation, which in their eyes were two aspects of the same body, and human beings were simply not permitted to cancel the terms of a divine covenant. Not even governments had the right to modify the covenants to suit changed circumstances. They remained binding on men and nations no matter how they were despised or ignored or even unknown by future generations.

There is something about a cause which has produced martyrs that invests it with a special kind of authority. With the first shedding of blood, a disputed cause moves into a completely new category. The purpose of the struggle is no longer an argument to prove which side is right. It is rather a battle to decide which side will win, and the very intensity of the conflict forces many to simply choose a side and defend all it stands for. About five centuries before the Christian church was founded, the Greek dramatist Aeschylus wrote, "In war, truth is the first casualty." Sadly, even in the church, the comment is not irrelevant. To question the legitimacy of the covenants may seem like questioning the spiritual integrity of those godly worshippers kneeling in prayer on the river bank, but in truth they are two different things. A number of those principles dearest to covenanting hearts would be recognised by Christians in every age, and in this present day there are still parts of the world where Christ's followers find it necessary to be prepared to give up their lives as many of the seventeenth-century Scottish Christians had to do. However, the existence of the National Covenant in Scotland, and the apparent necessity of it, was the result of several factors and conditions produced by centuries of ecclesiastical development in the Christian church. The Covenanters could no more escape the influence and ideas of previous generations than any other Christian group caught up in the changing relationship between the church and the political community within which it must survive.

The National Covenant of 1638 and the Solemn League and Covenant of 1643 were far from the beginning of bonds or covenants in Scottish life. Before there was a strong central government in Scotland, it was necessary for social or economic groups to form mutually recognisable and enforceable arrangements to protect lives or property. These were not called covenants, but they did express the basic values of mutual support, benefit, and commitment. They frequently involved the idea of military service and the enforcement of law and order. As the strength of the monarchy grew and developed, the practice of forming bonds and alliances among the king's subjects was discouraged, although it could not be eradicated altogether. After the Reformation, since much of the political conflict had a religious basis to it, bonds formed to achieve a specific purpose in church affairs began to be called "covenants" and were increasingly expressed in biblical language. The Concordat of Leith 1572 dealt with church finances and royal authority, but it also considered the promotion of the gospel. Towards the end of the sixteenth century, the term "covenant" had acquired more and more of a theological flavor, and early in 1596, the General Assembly was calling for an agreement among ministers which was specifically termed a covenant.[3]

3. Burrell, "Covenant Idea," 340.

The covenant idea was certainly not limited to Scotland. It was found among other groups of Reformed Christians on the continent and even in the American colonies. Even on its own, it might have developed into a very effective expression of spiritual unity. In the seventeenth century there was a not wholly unrealistic fear that Scottish identity might be absorbed into that of its more powerful neighbour, and so the covenant gave shape to a Scottish determination not to become Anglicized. The concept of a nation bound together in covenant was, in itself, a powerful enough force, but when another explosive ingredient was added to the mix, it became social, political, and spiritual dynamite. The vital element was quite simply that the Scottish nation had been specially chosen by God for the fulfilment of his divine purpose.

Like any other national or spiritual movement, the covenant attracted all kinds of people who saw in it political opportunity, financial success, or personal advantage. Even the Marquis of Argyll, who became a great covenanting leader, was not overhasty in deciding to join the ranks. There was, however, at the heart of the movement, a sincere conviction that Scotland had a spiritual destiny, given by the Most High. On 6 April 1320, thirty-eight Scottish lords set their seals to the Declaration of Arbroath. This declaration of independence was addressed to Pope John XXII and claimed, among other things, that Christ himself had a special concern for the Scots who had migrated from a region northeast of Israel to their present homeland.

> The King of kings and Lord of lords, our Lord Jesus Christ, after his Passion and Resurrection, called them, even though settled in the uttermost parts of the earth, almost the first of His Apostles by calling, though second or third in rank, the most gentle Saint Andrew, first to his most holy faith. Nor would he have them confirmed in that faith by merely anyone but by the Blessed Peter's brother, and desired him to keep them under his protection as their patron forever.[4]

The claim of the Reformer John Knox that the Scottish Church was the purest in Christendom gained royal confirmation by King James VI when he addressed the General Assembly in Edinburgh in 1590: "I praise God that I was born in the time of the light of the gospel and in such a place as to be the king of the sincerest kirk in the world." These statements, in cold print, may raise a cynical smile on the face of a twenty-first-century

4. Declaration of Arbroath, 1320.

Scot, but when the covenanting theologian and preacher Samuel Rutherford, under the anointing of God's Holy Spirit, clothed these themes in living, powerful language and imagery, the effect was electrifying. When Rutherford proclaimed that "Christ and Scotland shall yet weep in one another's arms," he lit a fire in Scottish hearts. He expounded the forty-ninth chapter of Isaiah as "Scotland's Charter": "Listen O Israel, and hear O Scotland and England. Ye who lie far out in an isle of sea, listen unto Me and ye shall be my land and heritage. . . . Now O Scotland, God be thanked, thy name is in the Bible." In 1633, Rutherford wrote, "Scotland whom our Lord took off the dunghill and out of hell and made a fair bride to Himself. . . . He will embrace both us, the little young sister and the elder sister, the Church of the Jews."[5]

Lord Wariston, an Edinburgh lawyer and one of the Architects of the National Covenant described it as "that national oath of the whol land with our aeternal Lord, the God of Glory." The day it was signed was "the gloriousest day that ever Scotland sau since the Reformation." It was "the glorious mariage day of the Kingdome with God." He wrote in his diary, "The work is so wonderful in my eies that could scairse believe my auin eyes, bot was lyk a man in a dream. O glorious God, Haleluya, hosanna, al honor, prayse and glory be to the for ever and evermore."[6] Wariston continues to write about the Most High God: "He gave himselh to us, and then to the oath quhair we surrendred ourselves to him, quhilk was as solemn a day of marriage betuixt The Lord and us, hinc inde, in the greatest spiritual solemnities, as perhaps wil not fall out in ane aige againe."[7]

It is perhaps all too easy in twenty-first-century Scotland to dismiss all this as sheer patriotism wearing a theological cloak, and while nobody could deny that Knox, Rutherford, Wariston, and others were true patriots, their conviction of a God-given destiny for Scotland was absolutely genuine. There was the feeling that the Reformation was the beginning of the kingdom of God to be established over the whole earth and that God had made a covenant with Scotland as he had with Israel under a new dispensation.[8] When Alexander Leslie, the earl of Leven, led the army of the covenant across the Tweed, his men were gripped by a vi-

5. *Rutherford's Letters*, cited by Donaldson in *Scotland*, 316.
6. *Diary of Lord Wariston*, 322.
7. Ibid.
8. Burrell, "Apocalyptic Vision."

sion. They considered that they may indeed be the God-ordained weapon to drive Roman Catholics out of England, to sweep across Europe, and completely overthrow the Roman Antichrist.

It would have been too much to expect that Englishmen found the same degree of enthusiasm for the idea of Scotland's special destiny. Indeed, a similar sense of being specially favoured by God was not entirely absent from English thinking. In 1559, John Aylmer, a future bishop of London, wrote an address to counter John Knox's attack on female monarchs. This was a piece of writing in support of the reign of Elizabeth I of England. Aylmer portrayed England as the God-appointed refuge for Protestant Christians and Queen Elizabeth as a new Constantine.[9] There was also a distinct impression among many of the English commissioners to the Westminster Assembly that the Scots were arrogant and self-deceived about their role as the new Israel, and gradually the vision of the Covenanters became focused on Scotland itself rather than further afield. However, if the scope of the vision diminished, the intensity of it did not. The smaller the numbers grew in the covenanting ranks, the more they were harassed and persecuted by the government, the greater grew their conviction that they represented the only faithful Christians left in the United Kingdom who could uphold the sacred covenant between God and their nation. Foundational, however, to all their thinking were two ideas which were never fully examined because they were never ever questioned.

9. See Wormald, "Union of 1603," in Mason, *Scots and Britons*, 17–40.

22

The Visible Church

> The visible church, which is also catholick or universal under the gospel, (not confined to one nation, as before under the law), consists of all these throughout the world that profess the true religion, together with their children; and is the kingdom of the Lord Jesus Christ, the house and family of God, out of which there is no ordinary possibility of salvation.)[1]

THE CONCEPT OF A nation or empire which was also a church was not original to the Covenanters of the seventeenth century. In the pre-Christian pagan world, the Roman empire was also a religious community in which every citizen was required to engage in the appropriate acts of worship. Political and military activity had religious significance and were believed to reflect the relationship between Rome and the gods. As the Roman Empire grew in size and influence, localised religion became increasingly state controlled. The focus of worship moved to the Roman state and, eventually, to the emperor himself. It was the custom to deify emperors after their death, but in time, living emperors were also considered to be gods. Although the Roman state was fairly tolerant of other religions, the cult of emperor worship was not an empty formality. It was a real expression of loyalty to Rome and a privilege of Roman citizenship.[2] It was actively promoted and practised. It required places

1. *Westminster Confession of Faith*, ch. 25, para. 2.
2. Bailey et al., *History of Christianity*, 35.

of worship and an army of priests of whom the emperor was "pontifex maximus."

Although the belief in one true God was a growing conviction in Roman society even before the conversion of the emperor Constantine, it was his adoption of the Christian faith which changed the church for ever. State funding poured into church coffers. Magnificent centres of worship were built at imperial expense. Bishops exercised many of the functions of government officials, and although Constantine himself stopped short of establishing the Christian church as the official religion of the empire, his successors were less restrained. The clear distinction between the government of the state and the government of the church was lost. Yet for Christ and his apostles, a state church would have seemed like a spiritual monster. In a final encounter with Pontius Pilate just before his crucifixion, Christ points out that while he might well have called on his followers to take up arms to prevent his arrest by the Jewish authorities, he did not do so because his kingly right to rule was not of any human origin but came from God. The survival, expansion, protection, development, or control of Christ's church was never to be entrusted to any political authority. Nevertheless, Constantine saw himself as the God-appointed agent for the expansion of the church throughout the known world, and his role as head of the church was unquestioned. It was the emperor who called church councils and who presided over them. It was Constantine who ruled not only in matters of administration and government but also in the formation of doctrine.

Opinions of Constantine have varied from the perception of him as a genuine convert to Christ with almost apostolic stature to that of a far-sighted politician who could see which way the wind was blowing. The two conditions need not be completely mutually exclusive, but it is hard to avoid the impression that no matter how sincere the emperor may have been, he still saw God through pagan Roman eyes. The gods of Rome had to be acknowledged and obeyed because they could give or withhold abundant harvests, victory on the battlefield, and political stability to the empire. This was the basis of the divine-human relationship in the Roman empire and church. When the emperor and his subjects turned from Roman gods to transfer their allegiance to the God and Father of the Lord Jesus Christ that basis seems to have been unchanged. The welfare and continuation of the empire depended on it. Constantine was not a simple believer, convicted of his sin and driven to Christ to seek for personal salvation. He was the head of a state facing what he was convinced was spiritual reality, and for the good of the empire he must bow the knee to Christ. Even though he knew that the Christian faith could not be forced on men, and therefore did not turn his empire into a theocracy, he nevertheless merged church and state together in such a way that they could not again be disentangled completely, not even by the Covenanters.

In AD 380, less than half a century after Constantine, the emperor Theodosius made the Christian faith binding on all his subjects, and as rivalry grew between the eastern and western empires, the churches in each of these regions mirrored the same struggle. Popes and patriarchs were established by state power and sometimes maintained by military strength. When the old Roman empire in the west began to crumble, it was the papacy which emerged as a unifying force among the new nation-states. The growth of papal power, however, stimulated a fierce conflict between state and church in Europe. Pope and monarch wrestled for supreme control of their world, and theological justification was produced to support the power struggle. The Holy Roman Empire established in the tenth century simply prolonged the battle between ecclesiastical and political authorities, and the influence of the church became overwhelming. Popes organised crusades against Islam and established or excommunicated kings. Pope Innocent III, who was a political giant as well as head of the Western church, in 1198 issued his famous decree "Sicut universitatis conditor," claiming divine authority of the church, over the state and everything else. Even throughout the upheaval of the Reformation, when so many changes took place in the Western church, this tension between state and church did not disappear but continued in new shapes and colours to become one of the key issues for the Covenanters of Scotland.

The great achievement of the Covenanters was to break the power of the Stewart kings over the church and their royal claim that they were rulers by divine right. Nevertheless, in spite of the ecclesiastical revolution in seventeenth-century Scotland, there was one concept which remained intact. The church and the state were still bound together and had mutual obligations since they were not to be seen as two completely separate groups of people but rather as two aspects of the same body. The English Theologian Richard Hooker, dealing with the same subject in an English context, wrote, "We hold that seeing there is not any man of the Church of England, but the same man is also a member of the commonwealth; nor any man a member of the commonwealth, which is not also of the Church of England; therefore as in a figure triangular, the base doth differ from the sides thereof, and yet one and the selfsame line is both a base and also a side."[3] Scots were clear enough that the civil government could not rule the church, but the civil rulers were part of that same ecclesiastical body. They were her "nursing fathers." Their purpose was to maintain the true religion in the nation-church. Not only was it acceptable for Christians to be civil rulers, but those rulers were responsible for the peace and purity of the church, for its discipline and worship, and to fulfill that responsibility the civil ruler had the authority to call church synods and to ensure that their decisions were in line with God's will.[4] Not everyone would be happy with the term "theocracy" to describe this kind of society in Scotland, but this was surely the ambition if not the achievement of the Covenanters. Linked to the conviction that Scotland had a special place as a nation-church in the plan of God, the covenant, whatever may have been its failings, held the hearts and minds of men in an iron-like grip. It is no accident that it came into being in an age when Scotland had an absentee king. Although the uniting of the two nations under a single monarch was hailed as a blessed union, and poets wrote ecstatic verse about the benefits which should be expected to begin with the reign of James I of Great Britain,[5] the reality was that the Scots were seen very much as the poor relations tacked on to England. Godfrey Goodman, bishop of Gloucester and chaplain to Queen Anne, the wife of James I, fiercely criticised the Scots at court as a "number of Hang-bies" claiming that they put the English courtiers in fear of infection and dangerous diseases. They wore dirty linen, and "as poor people flock to a common, so did they flock only for diet." Goodman claimed that it was hatred and detestation of the Scots which bolstered the failing reputation of Queen Elizabeth at the end of her reign.[6] Even before James I came to the English throne, one English politician prepared an oath to be taken by James recognising Elizabeth as "the Noble and Superior Lady of the kingdome of Scotland." James himself assured his English government in 1616 that he intended to bring Scottish law into conformity with English

---

3. Hooker, *Of the Laws of Ecclesiastical Polity*, bk. 8, ch. 1.2.

4. *Westminster Confession of Faith*, ch. 23, para. 3.

5. Wormald, *Union of 1603*, in *Scots and Britons*, 18.

6. Wormald, cited in *Scots and Britons*, 21.

law, not vice versa. He further assured them that union meant joining Scotland to England and not England to Scotland.[7]

There was a desperate need for Scots to assert not only their independence and appropriate status in the seventeenth century, but also to build it on a theological foundation. When the General Assembly of the Church of Scotland, on 19 August 1643, sent its eight commissioners down to the Westminster Assembly in London, they may have been commissioned by their church, but they advised and consulted on behalf of the whole nation. The National Covenant was not enacted between God and the Scottish church but between the Most High and the nation of Scotland. Screeds were written, sermons were preached, and arguments were used over the years to justify Scotland as a covenanted nation, and a great deal of it was based on the text of Scripture. Parish ministers were rebuked if they were not enthusiastic enough in "preaching up the Covenant." But where was the biblical warrant for Scotland's covenant to be found? Not in the teaching or ministry of Christ and his apostles but in God's ancient covenant with his people Israel. Scotland was the new Israel. She was Israel's little younger sister. She was one of the only two nations ever covenanted to the Lord. This was more than carefully considered theology. There was a great deal of hot-blooded patriotism and national resentment against the old enemy folded into the mix. There was also one great theological error which seemed to be invisible in the flames and smoke of a fiery age. The Covenanters did not seem to understand that there could never be a "second Israel" in the purposes of God for his church. Not even the modern state of Israel founded in May 1948 could ever be "a second Israel" in the biblical sense of the term because the church-state of Israel was a unique component in the development of the church of God, which was unrepeatable in any form. Scotland was a nation which wanted to be a church, whereas Israel had been a church which, contrary to God's best purposes, wanted to be a nation.

When Israel entered the land of Canaan, they were not a nation like the seventeenth-century Scots, although the English word "nation" may have been used to translate the biblical term for the redeemed community. John Bright writes, "Early Israel seems in fact to have existed as a sacral league of tribes founded in covenant with Yahweh. Although this is contested and doubtless will continue to be, one feels strongly that no

7. Ibid., 40.

satisfying alternative explanation of early Israel has yet been advanced."[8] The biblical record indeed presents a people redeemed from the slavery of Egypt by the miraculous events of Passover night and the opening of the pathway through the sea. The occupation of Canaan was certainly part of the covenant promise which God made to his holy people, but for almost the first three centuries of Israel's life in Canaan there was no king, no central government, no civil service or taxation system, and no national army. The factors which bound the tribes of Israel together were their shared historical roots, their common experience of a miraculous redemptive act of God, and their dependence on the Lord God of Israel who had created the theocratic community when he first called Abraham to leave Ur of the Chaldees and set out for the land God would give to him and his seed.

The church which began with Abraham and his immediate household was never meant to be a community fixed within unmoveable boundaries. It was a living, growing, developing spiritual body. It had already outgrown its initial form when Jacob went down to Egypt to escape the famine, and over the following four centuries, the church of the patriarchs had become the tribal federation which found its identity in a common worship of the Lord and a life lived in obedience to his revealed laws. The children of Israel were a spiritual brotherhood related to one another because they were related to the Lord, and their leaders were not monarchs but priests and prophets. It was a military problem that turned the church into a nation in the modern sense. The church of Israel could never forget that they were surrounded by enemies. They were compelled to engage in warfare simply to survive, and the book of Judges portrays a people whose loyalty to the Lord was anything but constant. It was their failure to understand the uniqueness of their identity as a church which made them worship the gods of Canaan and seek their favour. The story in the book of Judges is one of idolatry, discipline, and repentance, over and over again, as the Lord delivered Israel out of one crisis after another, but it was the failure of the priesthood in the last days of Samuel which led to the demand for a king. We read that the sons of Eli, the chief priest at the central shrine of Shiloh, were morally corrupt and turned the worship of God into an empty formality which they treated with contempt. In spite of the excellent spiritual leadership given by Samuel, his own sons, who would succeed him in the priesthood and served at Beersheba,

8. Bright, *History of Israel*, 163.

were not much better. It was this state of affairs which made the insecure Israelites decide that a king was the answer to their needs.

This request for a human monarch was in itself a further evidence of spiritual failure. The church of Israel already had a king. He was God the Lord. It was this which made Israel different from other tribes around them, yet a desire to be like the pagan inhabitants of Canaan was precisely the reason given to Samuel by the Israelite leaders to justify their demands. They said to the ageing prophet, "We want a king over us. Then we will be like all the other nations with a king to lead us and to go out before us and to fight our battles."[9] Approximately three centuries before, when the Israelites were about to launch at attack on the walled city of Jericho, Joshua their military leader encountered "a man standing in front of him with a drawn sword in his hand. Joshua went up to him and asked, 'Are you for us or for our enemies?' He replied, 'Neither, but I have come as commander of the army of the Lord.'"[10] Here was the fundamental lesson which should never have been forgotten. Victory, whether military or spiritual, would be won by obedience of the church to their divine commander and under no other conditions. The king the Israelite leaders demanded of Samuel was already theirs, by covenant, and far superior to any fallible human monarch. What they were asking for was a human imitation of the divine reality, and God made it clear that the demand was in opposition to his perfect will. He told Samuel, "It is not you they have rejected as their king, but me."[11] It was this rejection of the divine monarch that brought Israel under judgement and discipline, and of all the means by which God judged the sin within his church, this was the most severe. He gave them what they wanted!

In vain did Samuel spell out the danger of the church becoming a monarchy. He warned them of a system that would demand a crown-controlled military service, a manufacturing industry, and compulsory taxation. He warned them that monarchy would become a burden they would pray to be removed, but that their prayers would not be answered.[12] Of Israel's kings, the first became a deranged tyrant who committed suicide. The second was an adulterer who tried to hide his sin by arranging the murder of the faithful soldier he had betrayed. The third indulged in

9. 1 Sam 8:19.
10. Josh 5:13.
11. 1 Sam 8:7.
12. 1 Sam 8:18.

forbidden marriages to pagan wives and ended his life in the construction of pagan temples for the worship of idols, and the fourth brought about the division of the church-nation into the northern and southern kingdoms with the eventual loss of the northern kingdom altogether. There were indeed some godly kings in Israel who gave inspired spiritual leadership to their subjects and even brought revival to the church, but on the whole the monarchy was not a success. How could it be, when it was never anything more than God's second best? In reading of these events, the modern Christian would certainly fail to be impressed by the faithfulness of the church but might well bow in worship before a gracious God, who in spite of the failings of his people, continues to develop and preserve his church through the worst of circumstances. While in one sense the exile of the church to Babylon in the sixth century BC was a disaster and a mark of God's judgement, in another sense it was a further stage in the preparation of the church for the coming of Christ. The worshipping community, now shrunken to the southern kingdom of Judah, lost the temple and all that depended on it. The sacrificial system was disturbed. The priestly families were broken up, but the exiles carried with them the greatest gift God ever gave to his unfaithful people. They still possessed the written word of God. The end of the Jewish form of the church-nation was still some centuries away, but God was already preparing for the greatest change that would ever take place in the church's history. The ministry of the study and communication of the Scriptures was developed in the years of exile. The scattering of the Jewish church into other lands did not cease when a remnant returned to Jerusalem after seventy years. Over the following centuries, the church had to face many more crises. There was the Hellenisation of Israel and the Maccabean revolt it provoked. There was the absorption of Israel into the Roman Empire, and in spite of the temple being rebuilt by the returning exiles and later again by Herod shortly before the coming of Christ, the era of the Jewish church was inevitably drawing to a close. God was counting down the days until the Jewish church would fulfil its greatest calling to bring the light of the gospel to the whole world.

When Christ looked out over the holy city, he said, "O Jerusalem, Jerusalem, you who kill the prophets and stone those sent to you, how often I have longed to gather your children together, as a hen gathers her chicks under her wings, but you were not willing. Look! Your house is left to you desolate." By this statement, the Lord declared that the church in the form of a Jewish nation was at an end. After Calvary and Pente-cost, the church became international, and the Gentiles could enter it immediately, through faith in Christ, without first becoming Jews. The new covenant replaced the old. The time had come for the gospel to go to the ends of the earth, and the church could no more return to a national form that it could return to a patriarchal form. The outward shape God gave to his church was appropriate to the age and culture in which it functioned and ministered, and nothing could be gained by an attempt to model the church within any European nation on the church-nation of pre-Christian Israel.

If Scottish Covenanters had simply tried to base church life on the faith of Israel at its best, they might indeed have chosen a good example to follow. One of the great blessings of the Reformation, particularly in Scotland, was the re-emphasis on the "Jewishness" of the Christian church. It would be hard to find a single idea in New Testament rev-elation which is not rooted in the Old Testament. The very concept and word "church" is Jewish. The title by which God's son is identified is sim-ply a Greek translation of the Jewish term. Nothing but commendation could be offered to the church within any nation who saw themselves as a chosen people on spiritual pilgrimage to the heavenly Canaan. The ability to see the church within Scotland in Jewish terms represented a healthy aversion to the horrific medieval view of the Jews as the "Christ killers." The massacre of Jews that had taken place in Cliffords Tower in the city of York in 1190 would have been unthinkable to Scottish Presbyterians. They knew too clearly the teaching of the Apostle Paul that Gentile be-lievers were the wild branches grafted into the cultivated Jewish olive tree and not vice versa, so that there were no people on earth more "naturally Christian" than the Jews.

Had it simply been a matter of the church following a good example, the history of seventeenth-century Scottish Christians might have been much different. The Reformation, however, and its developments were sealed by acts of Parliament, not by church councils, and it was these circumstances wedded to the exciting and fascinating but dangerous idea that the Scottish nation was now the new Israel which led to untold conflict and misery. The vision of the new Israel had to be based on a mis-understanding of the old Israel which was never indissolubly linked to monarchy and nationhood. The children of Abraham were "Israel" before there ever was a monarch or a kingdom, and the covenant promises of

God to his people were made to a church, not to a nation. The life of the Old Testament church was as indestructible as the throne of God. That of the monarchy and the nation was not. There is no nation on earth which could ever stand in relation to God as the church-nation of Israel once did, and even in that situation the relationship was there because Israel was a church, not because it was a nation.

If at any time a recognisable body of people from a Christian culture is facing political or military threat, or are even in a situation of conflict where they are confident of victory, there is the enormous and perfectly understandable temptation to believe that the special favour of God must rest on their endeavours. This conviction can easily grow beyond a straightforward plea for divine aid or a trust in the providential government of God. It may slip seamlessly into the conviction that they are chosen by God for the task they hope to accomplish, and since there are no examples of Christian political parties or armies in the New Testament they must inevitably turn to the model of pre-Christian Israel. There were all kinds of political, cultural, and economic reasons for the nineteenth-century Afrikaners setting out northwards on the Great Trek. These were, however, not the factors which sustained them and drove them on. The extra ingredient was their conviction that they were the "New Israelites." What else could have given less than five hundred Voortrekkers, on 16 December 1836, the confidence to hold out and defeat a force of thousands of Zulu warriors. Before the battle of Blood River began, they entered into a covenant with God:

> Here we stand before the Holy God of heaven and earth, to make a vow to Him that if He will protect us and give our enemy into our hand, we shall keep this day and date every year as a day of thanksgiving like a Sabbath and that we shall erect a house to His honour wherever it should please Him, and that we also will tell our children that they should share in that with us in memory for future generations. For the honour of His name will be glorified by giving Him the fame and honour for the victory.[13]

These were not just Boer farmers moving into new territory. They were Israelites moving into Canaan to defeat the heathen tribes in order to

13. From the speech of Sarel Cilliers, deputy commander of the Voortrekker 464 commando before the battle of Blood River, 16 December 1838. Reported in a biography of Cilliers by Gerdener in 1919, but this is a reconstruction, not a verbatim account.

establish a Christian nation. This, they believed, was their God-given destiny which must be fulfilled.

The clear conviction that God must be on "our" side continues to the present day. There are still faded and scarred old photographs of the famous Christmas Day ceasefire during the First World War where German and British soldiers argued about why each side fought against the other which surely had the blessing of God on its own righteous cause. The Falklands War in the 1980s saw prime minister Margaret Thatcher critical of Robert Runcie, the archbishop of Canterbury who had himself been a decorated British soldier, but as a Christian, insisted on praying for the Argentinian forces as well as British troops. The Prime Minister's mindset would not have been out of place in pagan Rome, and the element of simple patriotism in theological dress, while not the complete explanation of the Covenanters views, certainly makes up a large part of the picture.

The major and unquestioned conviction in the covenanting cause was the right of Scottish Christians to function and worship in conformity with the will of God as they saw it, free from the control of crown or parliament. This right and the Reformed theology behind the National Covenant would have been perfectly acceptable to thousands of Christians in future days had it been simply the theological foundation of a church. The theology, however, was not separated by the Covenanters from the national and political concerns of the day. They were bound together in the same covenant. The architects of the covenant wrote, "The quietness and stability of our religion and Kirk doth depend upon the safety and good behaviour of the King's Majesty." There are in the Covenant references to sixty specific Acts of Parliament, as well as more general references to parliamentary authority. It had to be subscribed by people of every rank, because the true worship of God and the king's authority were "so straitly joined as that they had the same friends and common enemies." This was intended to bind not only those who swore and subscribed the covenant in the mid-seventeenth century but Scottish citizens for all time to come. It simply could not last, because it ignored the profound change in the church from its national form to its international form. There is nothing in the New Testament to give Christians grounds to believe that God would enter a covenantal relationship with the people of any nation as distinct from those of any other nation. The only covenant in force after the events surrounding the cross is the covenant God made, in Christ, with his entire church, worldwide, and that cannot be on a national basis.

There is indeed a consistent strand of teaching by the Lord and his apostles in the New Testament that Christians, whether considered individually or in national or local groups, should be good citizens. There is no encouragement to be rebellious or ignore legitimate civil authorities, while there is every reason to believe that God will call some Christians to take a prominent part in political affairs. The Roman state in apostolic times was hostile to the church, and yet the Apostles Peter and Paul instructed their people to recognise the legitimate authority of the government because it was part of the process by which God ruled over the affairs of men. Nothing, however, in the apostolic writings could ever support the idea that God would enter a covenant with a nation as he did with Israel. No matter how powerful the idea of a national covenant might be and how much it might grip the minds of men and set their hearts on fire, its origin was not divine but very much human.

23

The Legacy of the Covenant

My Lords, I cannot cease in the name of Christ Jesus to require of you that the matter may come in examination; and that you the estates of the realm, by your authority, compel such as will be called bishops, not only to desist from their cruel murdering of such as do study to promote God's glory in detecting and disclosing the damnable impiety of that man of sin, (the Roman Antichrist) but also that you compel them to answer to such crimes as shall be laid to their charge for not righteously instructing the flock committed to their cares.[1]

JOHN KNOX'S UNDERSTANDING OF the part which the nobility, as the natural political leaders of Scotland, ought to play in the Reformation was not set in stone. R. A. Mason writes, "Formulated in terms of a new Mosaic covenant, the avoidance of idolatry was transformed from a simple scriptural precept into a clause in a formal 'contract' drawn up between God and the elect. . . . Knox had thrust the covenant firmly into the political arena but did not see forcible resistance as one of its terms."[2] The period of time to which these words refer is the early 1550s. At that point, Knox was focused on the biblical command to submit to governing authorities, and being therefore wary of offending God, his advice to Reformed English Christians was to leave God to deal with their persecuting rulers. In less than a decade, however, his views had developed

1. Knox, *Appellation from the Sentence.*
2. Mason, introduction to Knox, *On Rebellion*, xii.

and he was urging the Reformed Scottish nobility to be responsible not only for the punishment of those who had been persecutors but also those who are pastorally incompetent. By 1558, Knox held that the civil sword was supreme and could discipline the clergy.[3]

The National Covenant, resting on the foundation of Reformation principles, was heavily dependent on the political leaders of the nation for its strength and effectiveness. These leaders were men from long-established families with histories of service to the crown, and the spiritual leaders of the church saw their support as essential. Fifty-four years before the National Covenant, a group of ministers had tried unsuccessfully to challenge the king's control of the church, but it took the political weight of a covenanting nobility to gain such a victory. Since the nobles and lairds were the first to subscribe to the covenant in 1638, it was known for some time as the "Noblemen's Covenant."[4] The identification of the National Covenant with Scottish political leadership may have seemed like an advantage in the seventeenth century, and the reasons for it were not entirely without theological justification, but the history of the church is not short of examples where an accepted theology was formed not by biblical revelation but by perceived political necessity. The idea of a covenant between God and a nation, powerful as it was and advantageous as it seemed to be, contained the seeds of its own destruction simply because it cannot be justified from the biblical revelation God has given to his church. The covenant which seemed so politically appropriate in 1638 could not be forced to fit the changed political conditions of later years, and therefore became a fascinating subject for church historians, but not a genuine vehicle for the expression of spiritual life.

When William of Orange accepted the Scottish crown, an Act of Parliament was passed on 17 June 1690 making the Church of Scotland once again Presbyterian. The National Covenant was not part of the settlement, but the concept of the nation-church was far from dead. Although over the following centuries disputes, divisions, and theological and political controversies disturbed the peace of the Kirk, the identification of the Church of Scotland with the nation of Scotland remained unbroken. By the Church of Scotland Act 1921, the Articles Declaratory of the Constitution of the Church of Scotland were given legal effect, and in the third of those articles it was stated,

3. Ibid.
4. Lynch, *Scotland*, 249.

This Church is in historical continuity with the Church of Scotland which was reformed in 1560, whose liberties were ratified in 1592 and for whose security, provision was made in the Treaty of Union of 1707. The continuity and identity of the Church of Scotland are not prejudiced by the adoption of these Articles. As a national Church, representative of the Christian faith of the Scottish people it acknowledges its distinctive call and duty to bring the ordinances of religion to the people in every parish of Scotland through a territorial ministry.[5]

The vision of the church expressed in this third Article is not identical with that of those who framed the National Covenant, but neither is it completely unrelated. The Church of Scotland is said to represent not simply the faith of Scottish Christians but of "the Scottish people," which even in 1921 was not entirely true, since a considerable body of Scottish Christians were not Presbyterian, and a great number of Scots were not Christian in any real sense at all. However, while no one in the twenty-first century would see Scotland as a theocratic community, there is still very much evidence to support the vague idea that in some sense, at least, the Christian culture which shaped the thinking of past generations means that they can still look on every Scot as having the right to what are called "the ordinances of religion." Parish ministers who would firmly reject universalism in the strict theological sense find themselves nevertheless treating Scottish believers and unbelievers alike, as if they were all regenerate children of God.

Most Scottish funeral services still take place in a parish church, but there is, in the church, no separate funeral service for the majority of Scots who today have firmly and openly excluded the worship of God from their lives. Although ministers conducting such a service may walk a tightrope in a very sincere attempt both to emphasise the universal offer of God's grace in the gospel and, at the same time, to carefully avoid any statement declaring that the deceased is one of God's elect, the general perception of the community is that we are all God's children and will all reach heaven in the end.

Parish ministers face a similar problem when marriage services are requested. In spite of the growing number of secular weddings and the fashion of prospective brides and grooms to invent their own wedding

5. Article III of "Articles Declaratory of the Constitution of the Church of Scotland," declared lawful by an Act of the British Parliament, the Church of Scotland Act 1921.

vows, there are still countless occasions where a very specific Christian form of the marriage service is the only one on offer. The service is very obviously designed for a Christian man and woman who are about to become a family unit and to enter a completely new social, sexual, and spiritual relationship under the lordship of Christ. However, the number of couples who fit this category becomes fewer and fewer as time goes on. Even where the minister has attempted to prepare the couple by holding marriage preparation classes, in perhaps the majority of cases, where there is no existing relationship to Christ, the participation of the bride and groom will be legally correct but of little spiritual value. Ministerial consciences suffering twinges of guilt will be soothed to some extent by the thought that "marriage is a creation ordinance" or that they are helping to make a morally bad situation better, but he would be a battle-hardened clergyman indeed whose conscience was perfectly at peace in these circumstances.

In the case of parents requesting the baptism of their children, the ideal condition is where at least one of the parents was a baptised communicant member of the church; however, since there is a variety of other options, in practice it would be very unusual for a minister to refuse to baptise children living in his parish. Where the church's obligation to provide a ministry is related not simply to the faith of men and women but to the "territory" in which they live, the temptation to provide the ordinances of religion for all who request them, no matter what their spiritual condition might be, is hard to resist, and yet the enormous changes in the religious, political, and social composition of Scotland which have taken place since the seventeenth century mean that the claim to be the church of the Scottish nation becomes increasingly difficult to sustain with any kind of integrity.

Even in these circumstances, it can hardly be surprising that the national status of any church will not be surrendered easily. To be recognised by crown and parliament emphasises the important position the church has occupied in society in past centuries. Office bearers in the national church are given international recognition. Committees of the church provide input to local and national government. The church's ministers are still appointed to school and hospital chaplaincies. Church officials would be less than human if there was not some element of personal prestige linked to the historic status of the church. As an expression of this, a new ecclesiastical creature has appeared in recent decades. Its name is "the central church," and reference to it is found in magazines and several kinds of correspondence. Those who use such an inappropriate expression are usually referring to the General Assembly and its councils and committees, and while no one would deny that these cogs in the administrative machine are used by the Holy Spirit for the welfare and blessing of God's people, there can hardly be a less accurate term to describe them than "the central church." It is precisely because the vision of the Christian church in Scotland has become so clouded and hardly distinguishable from secular society that the name of "church" is being levered away from the worshipping community and attached to the administrative body which is constructed to serve it.

Perhaps the most obvious attempt to cling on to the appearance of healthier times can be seen in the inflated statistics produced year after year. It is very common to find in parish churches of Scotland that the number of actual worshippers in a congregation might be between 10 and 20 percent of the reported communicant membership. The condition of general decline in the twenty-first century, in terms of numbers, funds, and candidates for the ministry, has led to, or perhaps been caused by, a devastating lack of confidence in God himself. No longer is there the assurance that Christ is the builder of the church against which the gates of hell cannot prevail. Church leaders still issue confident statements, but the reality is that the focus of the local congregation's energies is, in many cases, inwards rather than outwards. Mission is seen too often in terms of a need to sustain the church by finding new members to replace those who have passed on. In many a parish church, the need for office bearers to keep the wheels turning leads to a position where the recognition of a divine calling to spiritual leadership is hardly even considered. Men and women are "recruited" and pressed into ordination as elders, occasionally reluctantly. Church law demands that they must indicate their acceptance of the Scriptures of the Old and New Testaments as the "supreme rule of faith and life" and the recognition of the Westminster Confession of Faith as the church's subordinate standard, when a large proportion of those making such a promise have never read the confession and a small number do not know what it is. The promise is underlined when new elders "sign the formula," but the procedure is often the recognition of a historic custom rather than an act of personal faith.

Nominalism is a problem for every church on earth, and church history is littered with the ecclesiastical corpses of groups of Christians who were forever searching to find the perfect church and dying themselves in the process. The authors of the Westminster Confession wrote, "The purest churches under heaven are subject both to mixture and error and some have so degenerated as to become no churches of Christ."[6] Even if the Church of Scotland today is still a long way from such a sorry condition, it cannot afford to cling on to a form which, in spite of the modifications at the time of the Reformation, has its long distant source in a pre-Christian view of church and nation. In the seventeenth century, the Covenanters had the vision of the covenant between God and Scotland as Israel's "little young sister." This return to a view of the church as it was before the coming of Christ brought with it the conviction that the terms of a covenant with God must be enforced on every citizen in the covenanted nation. The resulting nominalism on an unprecedented scale was unavoidable. Robert Leighton, bishop of Dunblane in the 1660s, wrote, "There is unquestionably, among those who profess themselves the people of God, a select number who are indeed his children, and bear his image both in their hearts and in their lives . . . but with the most, a name and a form of godliness are all they have for religion."

This was his fairly accurate view of Scotland in the seventeenth century. It never could have been otherwise and the problem would always be there no matter what shape the church took, but the identification of the church with the nation did not help to solve the problem but rather encouraged it. Over the years, the church which once exploded into the Mediterranean world of the pagan Roman Empire to offer eternal life to lost sinners has become, in Scotland, to a large extent, a weakened and hesitant religious body desperately anxious to avoid collapse by courting public opinion. Secular society demands changes in spiritual or moral standards. The church rushes to obey, and new theological insights are discovered to justify the changes.

There is no lack, at the moment, of prophets predicting the complete demise of the church in Scotland in a fairly short time. Certainly if present statistical trends were to continue, death would be inevitable. This view of the future is, however, about as realistic as that which claims that all is well and the church is in good heart. It would be more accurate to recognise that while some sections of the church jettison more and more of their biblical principles in order to win the approval of a society in rebellion against God, others are being prepared for a renewal of genuine

6. *Confession of Faith*, ch. 25, sec. 5.

spiritual life. A church which hopes to survive by giving a corrupt society what it demands is committing spiritual suicide. Its days are numbered. There are, however, even in Scotland, signs of a hunger for spiritual reality. While there is an obvious decline in the Christian church there is no decline in pop-religion, including popular atheism. Although television soap operas and tarot cards provide a view of the supernatural that men and women once sought for in the Christian Scriptures, these popular substitutes for divine revelation simply do not meet the real needs of a society that has become alienated from the Creator. It is this growing sense of need that provides an opportunity for a revitalised church, and there is no group of Christians in Scotland in a better position to take advantage of such an opportunity than the Church of Scotland. When the Kirk has abandoned the flawed notion of representing a nation and parish churches give up the fiction of being the spiritual centre of the community, only then can local congregations become what they should be, a weapon in the hands of the Holy Spirit to save sinners and build them into family of God. In emphasising the eternal difference between those who are in Christ and those who are not, the impact on nation and community, far from being diminished, will be greatly increased.

The covenanting vision of an entire nation in a real covenant with God had to fail for two reasons. It was not a realistic idea and resulted in large numbers taking and subscribing the covenant under duress. Even King Charles II was a Covenanter in this sense. But it had to fail also because it was a contradiction of the international and non-national nature of the New Testament church. It was an attempt to reproduce a stage in the development of the church which was unique to the nation of Israel. Yet in spite of this flawed vision, the spiritual qualities of the later Covenanters are the very qualities needed to rebuild a church in Scotland, where every congregation is not the church which represents the community, but the church which represents Christ, calling the community to be saved from sin. For all their faults, the Covenanters were concerned about the personal glory of the Son of God and were opposed to whatever they perceived as a rival to that priority. It was Christ himself and not his church that was at the centre of their worship, their praying, and their spiritual endeavours. Whatever their flawed understanding of the relationship between the church and the nation, their hearts and actions were focussed on glorifying and uplifting the Son of God before their fellow men so that they might be drawn not to the church but to

Christ himself. The nineteenth-century hymn writer Anne Ross Cousin, in her famous hymn "The Sands of Time Are Sinking," set in verse what were believed to be some of the last writings of the great covenanting preacher and theologian Samuel Rutherford. One of her verses has the lines, "The bride eyes not her garment but her dear bridegroom's face. I will not gaze at glory but at the king of grace." This, however, is exactly what today's church could not honestly say. Enormous efforts are made to make the bride's garments as glamorous as possible. The bridegroom is most certainly not the centre of attention. Indeed, the customary theological justification is offered to suggest that if condemned men and women spend enough time with the bride, they may come to meet the bridegroom eventually. Misguided people are encouraged to believe that they are welcome to enjoy the wedding reception and subsequent married life in the hope that a marriage may take place sometime in the future. The energy, the funding, the thinking, and the genuine hard work that goes into trying to attract men, women, and especially young people into the ranks of the church rather than to Christ himself would have mystified the first apostles. Whatever flaws there might have been in the notion of a covenant with a nation, the Covenanters themselves had the Lord of glory right at the centre of their agenda.

In the twenty-first century, the idea of martyrdom is not quite as inspirational for Christians as it once was. The association of the concept with religions other than Christianity and its frequent link to violence means that we are not so quick to admire those who are ready to sacrifice their lives for religious convictions. Even in the case of the Covenanters of the seventeenth century, not every instance of martyrdom would meet with unqualified approval. What is undeniable, however, is that those men and women who defied the government of the day, risking their lives in doing so, believed that obedience to God was unconditional and without limits. Where loyalty is to the church and service is for the church, limits can be reached fairly quickly. Our obligations to the church are to other flawed human beings like ourselves. They have the right to expect so much but no more. The church might reasonably expect us to go so far, but no further. We may be urged to give a proportion of our time and goods to church causes, and we will be congratulated on our generosity if that giving is better than average, but rarely will people think of themselves as stewards of what is God's property, including their own lives, and moreover stewards who must give account at some time to the real owner. Whatever the faults of the Covenanters, they clearly regarded their entire lives as belonging to God and were willing to hand them over when required to do so. Of course martyrdom is not for every Christian and requires a special grace from the Holy Spirit for its acceptance, and not every Covenanter had to surrender his life to the cause, but who could deny that men and women with a limitless and unconditional commitment to Christ and his gospel could, in the will of God, bring about a spiritual revolution in modern Scotland. For so many members of the church in the present day, loyalty, service, and goods are given to the church, and they are carefully measured out with all the other commitments life brings. For the Covenanters it was an "all or nothing" business, and while their adherence to a national covenant might be questionable, their commitment to what they believed to be the will of God was such that it gave them a strength and influence out of all proportion to their limited numbers. There are sufficient examples in society today of how small a group is necessary to be able to change a whole nation. What could not be accomplished by even a relatively small group of Christians fired by the enthusiasm and determination of the Covenanters and controlled and guided by the Holy Spirit?

Some time ago, the minister of a large and prosperous congregation was giving a lecture to a group of ministerial colleagues about how he had achieved such a successful ministry. He described the kind of church services that would attract and make an impact on the surrounding community. One uneasy listener asked him why the worship of God should be designed to attract unconverted men and women. The speaker looked surprised at first, as if a question with such an obvious answer were an indication of lack of intelligence. He then decided, charitably, that the questioner meant to ask, not *why* the services should be made attractive but *how* it could be done. He went on to further explain that Sunday services which appealed to the taste of modern men and women would soon prove to be as successful as his own. Sadly, in many congregations in Scotland today, his advice would be received as if it had an authority equal to that of the gospel itself.

While the covenanting struggle was taking place in Scotland, there was a clerical politician in France who exercised enormous influence in French affairs. He was Jules Mazarin, an Italian who had plotted and intrigued his way into the highest levels of French political and religious life. Educated at the Jesuit college and the University in Rome, he was made a cardinal in 1641 and became the joint ruler of France alongside the regent Anne while King Louis XIV was still a child. A ruthless politician who delighted in the power he exercised, Mazarin fought against the weakness of advancing years and ill health. As his life force ebbed away, greater and greater efforts were made to make him appear as young and vigorous as ever. On 4 March 1661, his servants carefully shaved his beard and curled his moustache. They applied rouge to his cheeks and lips. He was propped up by cushions in a sedan chair and carried outside his house to be viewed by the community. The props and cosmetics were meant to give the impression of continued youth and vigour but succeeded only in displaying his weakness. Five days later, he died.

The idea of creating a form of worship and church life which appeals to popular demand but has little concern as to whether or not it is pleasing to God is a sign of a dying church. In spite of an appearance of brief popularity, nothing can halt its eventual death. All the propping up and cosmetics in the world cannot hide its real condition from Christians with any degree of spiritual perception. The difference, however, between Cardinal Mazarin and the Scottish church today is one that is absolute. The approach of death for the French cardinal could not be delayed or prevented. The church, on the other hand, is ruled by a Lord who stands at the tomb of Lazarus and utters one single command. A dead man emerges from darkness and death, pulling off the grave clothes, stretching stiff limbs and blinking in the sunlight. Time after time in the history of God's dealings with his people he has rent the heavens and come down. The days ahead are days of new opportunity for the people of God if there is faith enough to respond to it. The result would certainly not be another Israel, neither Israel the church nor Israel the nation. In that ambition, the Covenanters were mistaken. It could, however, very well be a renewed church whose life and worship could be exercised within a renewed Scotland.

Bibliography

Abjuration Oath, November 1684. Issued by the Scottish Privy Council. Legally binding oath offered to suspects to demonstrate their rejection of Covenanter James Renwick's Apologetical Declaration of his intention to punish oppressors.

Act anent Religion and the Test, July 1681. Passed by the Scottish Parliament. Required, among other things, an oath rejecting the Covenants.

Act anent the Supremacy, November 1669. Act giving the king authority over all church decisions.

Act, Declaration, and Testimony, June 1761. Issued by the Reformed Presbytery in four parts at Ploughlandhead, Scotland. Called Scottish Christians back to original Covenanting principles.

Admonitio generalis. Issued AD 789 by Charlemagne. Legislation concerning educational and ecclesiastical reform.

Airy, Osmund, ed. *The Lauderdale Papers.* Vol. 2. London: Camden Society, 1885.

Apologetical Declaration, October 1684. Issued by Covenanting leader James Renwick, promising punishment of persecutors and informers.

Auchensaugh Renovation, July 1712. Renewal of the Covenants by Reformed Presbyterians near the village of Douglas in Scotland.

Bailey, Cyril, et al. *The History of Christianity in the Light of Modern Knowledge: A Collective Work.* New York: Harcourt, Brace, 1929.

Baillie, Robert. *Letters and Journals: Containing an impartial account of public transactions, civil, ecclesiastical, and military, in England and Scotland. . . .* Vol. 1. Edinburgh: Gray, 1775.

Baynes, Norman Hepburn. *Constantine the Great and the Christian Church.* London: Milford, 1931.

Bettenson, Henry S., ed. *Documents of the Christian Church.* London: Oxford University Press, 1963.

————. *Early Christian Fathers: A Selection from the Writings of the Fathers from St. Clement of Rome to Athanasius.* London: Oxford University Press, 1956.

Boardman, Stephen I. *The Early Stewart Kings: Robert II and Robert III, 1371–1406.* East Linton, Scotland: Tuckwell, 1996.

Bright, John. *A History of Israel.* London: SCM, 1960.

Brown, Michael. *The Wars of Scotland, 1214–1371.* Edinburgh: Edinburgh University Press, 2004.

Bruce, F. F. *The Spreading Flame: The Rise and Progress of Christianity from Its First Beginnings to the Conversion of the English.* London: Paternoster, 1958.

Bryce, James B. *The Holy Roman Empire.* London: Macmillan, 1873.

Burckhardt, Jacob. *The Age of Constantine the Great*. London: Routledge & Paul, 1949.

Burrell, Sidney A. "The Apocalyptic Vision of the Early Covenanters." *Scottish Historical Review* 43 (1964) 1–24.

———. "The Covenant Idea as a Revolutionary Symbol: Scotland 1596–1637." *Church History* 27 (1958) 338–50.

Bury, John B. *History of the Later Roman Empire*. New York: Dover, 1958.

Cameron, Nigel M. de S., ed. *Dictionary of Scottish Church History and Theology*. Edinburgh, T. & T. Clark, 1993.

Carslaw, W. H. *Life and Letters of James Renwick*. Edinburgh: Oliphant, Anderson & Ferrier, 1893.

Chadwick, Henry. *The Church in Ancient Society: From Galilee to Gregory the Great*. Oxford: Oxford University Press, 2001.

Cheney, Christopher R., and William H. Semple, eds. *Selected Letters of Pope Innocent III: Concerning England (1198–1216)*. London: Nelson, 1953.

Coleman, Christopher B., trans. *The Treatise of Lorenzo Valla on the Donation of Constantine*. Newhaven: Yale University Press, 1922.

Council of Basel. Session 11, 27 April 1433. Called by Pope Martin V a few weeks before his death to determine whether supreme authority in the church lay with the pope or with a general council.

Cowan, Ian B. *The Scottish Covenanters*. London: Gollancz, 1976.

Danielou, Jean, and Henri Marrou. *The Christian Centuries: A New History of the Catholic Church*. Vol. 1. London: Darton, Longman & Todd, 1964.

Dawson, Jane A. E. *The Politics of Religion in the Age of Mary, Queen of Scots: The Earl of Argyll and the Struggle for Britain and Ireland*. Cambridge: Cambridge University Press, 2002.

———. *Scotland Re-formed: 1488–1587*. Edinburgh: Edinburgh University Press, 2007.

Declaration of Arbroath, 1320. An open letter from the Scots nobility to Pope John XXII affirming Scotland as an independent nation.

Declaration of Right, 1689. Act of the English Parliament to prevent the crown passing to a Roman Catholic or an heir married to a Roman Catholic.

Digeser, Elizabeth DePalma. *The Making of a Christian Empire: Lactantius and Rome*. Ithaca, NY: Cornell University Press, 1999.

Donaldson, Gordon. *Scotland: James V–James VII*. Edinburgh: Mercat Press, 1965.

Douglas, J. D., ed. *The New Bible Dictionary*. London: Inter-Varsity, 1962.

Drake, H. A. *Constantine and the Bishops: The Politics of Intolerance*. Baltimore: John Hopkins University Press, 2000.

Eusebius. *Eusebius: Church History; Life of Constantine the Great; and Oration in Praise of Constantine*. Translated by Arthur C. McGiffert and Ernest C. Richardson. Eerdmans, Grand Rapids, 1952.

———. *Eusebius: The History of the Church from Christ to Constantine*. Translated by G. A. Williamson. London: Penguin, 1965.

Fisher, Edward. *The Marrow of Modern Divinity*. Tain, Scotland: Christian Focus, 2009.

Fleming, David H., ed. *Diary of Lord Wariston*. Edinburgh: Scottish History Society, 1919.

Harries, Jill, and Ian N. Wood, eds. *The Theodosian Code*. Ithica, NY: Cornell University Press, 1993.

Henderson, G. D. "The Aberdeen Doctors." *Aberdeen University Review* 26 (1938–1939) 10.

Hooker, Richard. *Of the Laws of Ecclesiastical Polity*. Edited by John Keble et al. Oxford: Clarendon, 1888.

Hughes, Philip. *The History of the Church*. London: Sheed & Ward, 1979.

Huttman, Maude A. *The Establishment of Christianity and the Proscription of Paganism*. New York: Columbia University, 1914.

Keresztes, Paul. *Constantine: A Great Christian Monarch and Apostle*. Amsterdam: Gieben, 1981.

Knox, John. *Appellation from the Sentence pronounced by the Bishops and Clergy*. Edinburgh: Stevenson, 1855.

———. *Knox: On Rebellion*. Edited by Roger A. Mason. Cambridge: Cambridge University Press, 1994.

———. *The Reformation in Scotland*. Edited by John Guthrie. Edinburgh: Banner of Truth, 1982.

Lactantius. *The Epitome of the Divine Institutes*. Whitefish, MT: Kessinger, 2004.

Latourette, Kenneth S. *A History of Christianity*. London: Eyre & Spottiswoode, 1953.

Lumsden, John. *The Covenants of Scotland*. Paisley, Scotland: Gardner, 1914.

Lynch, Michael. *Scotland: A New History*. London: Century, 1991.

Macdougall, Norman. *James IV*. East Linton, Scotland: Tuckwell, 1997.

Mackie, Robert L. *A Short History of Scotland*. London: Oxford University Press, 1929.

Mason, Roger A., ed. *Scots and Britons: Scottish Political Thought and the Union of 1603*. Cambridge: Cambridge University Press, 1994.

M'Crie, Thomas. *The Story of the Scottish Church: From the Reformation to the Disruption*. Edinburgh: Blackie, 1875.

National Covenant; or, The Confession of Faith, of the Kirk of Scotland . . . 1638. Edinburgh: General Assembly of the Free Church of Scotland, 1973.

Oath for the Test Act 1678. Oath required by Act of English Parliament to ensure that civil or military office was held only by Anglicans.

Pharr, Clyde, trans. *Theodosian Code and Novels, and the Sirmondian Constitutions*. Princeton: Princeton University Press, 1952.

Pragmatic Sanction of Bourges, 1438. Decree of a Synod called by King Charles VIII of France to limit papal power.

Pullan, Leighton. *From Justinian to Luther: A.D. 518–1517*. Oxford: Clarendon, 1930.

Rait, Robert S. *The Making of Scotland*. London: Black, 1929.

Rees, Roger. *Diocletian and the Tetrarchy*. Edinburgh: Edinburgh University Press, 2004.

Renwick, James, and Alexander Shields. *An Informatory Vindication of a Poor, Wasted, Misrepresented Remnant. . . .* Edinburgh: Gray, 1744.

Rutherford, Samuel. *Letters of the Rev. Samuel Rutherford*. Edited by Thomas Smith. A. Edinburgh: Oliphant, Anderson & Ferrier, 1899.

Schaff, Philip. *The Creeds of Christendom*. Vol. 3. Grand Rapids: Baker, 1984.

———. *Nicene and Post-Nicene Fathers*. Grand Rapids: Eerdmans, 1952.

Solemn League and Covenant. Established September 1643 between English Parliamentarians and Scottish Covenanters to oppose Charles I and Royalist supporters.

Sordi, Marta. *Christians and the Roman Empire*. Translated by Annabel Bedini. London: Croom Helm, 1983.

Stevenson, David. *The Scottish Revolution 1637–44: The Triumph of the Covenanters*. Edinburgh: Donald, 2003.

Tertullian. *The Apology of Tertullian*. Translated by William Reeve. London: Griffith Farran, 1889.

Bibliography

Thomson, Thomas, and Cosmo Innes, eds. *The Acts of the Parliament of Scotland*. Vol. 5. Edinburgh: Printed by authority of the Lords Commissioners of Her Majesty's Treasury, 1870.

Ullmann, Walter. *Medieval Papalism: The Political Theories of the Medieval Canonists*. London: Methuen, 1949.

Westbury-Jones, John. *Roman and Christian Imperialism*. London: Macmillan, 1939.

Westminster Confession of Faith. Composed by an Assembly of ministers of English churches, called by the English Parliament in June 1643. Scottish parliamentary commissioners attended, not as members but as advisors.

Williams, Stephen, and Gerard Friell. *Theodosius: The Empire at Bay*. London: Routledge, 1998.

Wynkfielde R. "The Execution of Mary Queen of Scots." In *Eyewitness to History*, edited by John Carey, 136–37. Cambridge: Harvard University Press, 1987.

Lightning Source UK Ltd.
Milton Keynes UK
UKOW05f0850070414

229516UK00001B/7/P